ANCIENT
ROME

For Mum and Dad, who took me to castles, forts and museums and waited patiently for me to come out.

And for Tiddles, Bunty, Whisky, Lady Cat, Socks, Bobby, Wendy, Tibby, Trajan, Tiger, Cleo, Tiddy, Felix, Stripy Kitten, and Slasher.

ANCIENT ROME

The Empire 30BC - AD476

PATRICIA SOUTHERN

AMBERLEY

This edition first published 2011

Amberley Publishing
The Hill, Stroud,
Gloucestershire, GL5 4ER

www.amberleybooks.com

ISBN 978 1 4456 0428 2

Typesetting and Origination by Amberley Publishing Plc
Printed in Great Britain

Contents

About the Author

Patricia Southern has written and researched on Roman history for over thirty years. She has written ten books on Roman history including *Antony & Cleopatra: The Doomed Love Affair That United Ancient Rome & Egypt*, *The Roman Empire from Severus to Constantine*, *The Roman Army* and seven classical biographies; *Mark Antony, Augustus, Cleopatra, Julius Caesar, Pompey the Great, Domitian: Tragic Tyrant* and *Empress Zenobia: Palmyra's Rebel Queen*. She lives in Northumberland.

Preface & Acknowledgements

Judging by the number of new books that have appeared and the frequent programmes on television, there has been an upsurge in the popularity of ancient Rome in the past decade or so, which provides an excuse, if an excuse is required, for writing another one. This book attempts to tell the story of the Empire from its establishment by Octavian – Augustus from the beginning to the fifth century, to provide the background for all the particular aspects that have achieved popular coverage, and many that haven't. As far as possible it is arranged chronologically, but when things were happening simultaneously in different parts of the Roman world, the linear treatment is not always feasible. One advantage of a chronological approach is that it can be seen how Rome evolved, adapting to circumstances by amending political and military procedures. The Romans continually developed the system of government that had been intended for one relatively small Italian city so that it could fulfil the demands of a growing empire. They assimilated the provincials and bestowed citizenship on selected individuals or whole communities, Romanizing them and admitting them into their government. The longevity of the Roman Empire makes it impossible to cover all events and all aspects in a book of this length, so inevitably some details have to be selected and others left out. Another point to note is that history is about people, whose mind-set we cannot totally penetrate, but the Romans were not too different from ourselves, and we know a great deal about some of the many personalities who shaped Rome. This book describes who they were and what they did, and sometimes why they did it. It is intended for the non-specialist audience, who might want to find out more from the selection of books listed in the bibliography.

My thanks are due as always to a number of people who have helped in the production of the book. Jonathan Reeve of Amberley Publishing was always willing to discuss details and answer questions, Jacqui Taylor, Jim Eden and Graeme Stobbs let me raid their photos and use their maps.

Patricia Southern
Northumberland
2011

A Note About Dates

The starting point and end point for the Romans is problematic. The traditional dates of 31 BC for the foundation of the Empire, and AD 476 for the fall of the western Empire, are convenient but artificial. The transition from Republic to Empire was stealthy and veiled, and though late fifth century Rome became part of a Germanic kingdom, life went on after AD 476. History does not start and stop, nor does it change as abruptly as the choice of dates for turning points would suggest.

In the study of ancient Rome, modern scholars have typically utilized historical divisions largely based on significant events – significant, that is, according to our modern views, retrospectively applied. Such divisions are necessarily artificial, and may not have been so obvious to contemporaries who lived through these significant events, nor even to the ancient historians who examined the events at a later date. Turning points are not always recognized as such until comparison can be made, with the benefit of hindsight, between what went before and what came afterwards.

The great advantage of the use of artificial historical divisions, utilized throughout this book, is that such a scheme facilitates the study of the subject by creating manageable chunks, with a starting point and an end point before the next epoch begins. The dates of these starting points and end points always demand the addition of the qualifying symbol 'circa' because they are not absolute. The inhabitants of early Rome did not keep records of their activities, or if they did, such records have not survived, so it was left to their descendants to work out the age of their city and the probable time slots when military and political developments took place, or the most likely dates of the achievements of important men. Ancient historians were sincere in their attempts to write their accounts using ascertainable facts, but there is considerable discrepancy in their opinions, just as there is still debate among modern scholars about the many controversial issues in Roman history. There are lots of questions and not enough foolproof answers, but this engenders debate and contemplation, and that's what makes Roman history enjoyable.

1

Octavian Augustus: The Republic Becomes an Empire 30 BC–AD 14

There is no firm agreement about the date when the Republic ended and the Empire began, so the choice of 30 BC as the date when the Republican government became Imperial rule is somewhat arbitrary. Various events have been suggested as the turning point: the battle of Actium in 31, the fall of Alexandria in 30, January 27 in Rome when Octavian offered to return the government to the Senate, and the developments of 23 when Octavian-Augustus was ill and forced to think very seriously about the succession. But in reality there was no sharply defined moment of history when everything changed, because it was an evolutionary process rather than a sudden change of tack. What went on before the Empire was formed was similar to what came after, with small adjustments made over a period of time while Octavian consolidated his position.

After the fall of Alexandria in 30, Octavian was the wealthiest, most influential and most important man in the Roman world, and Rome controlled a large extent of territory that included Sicily, Sardinia, Corsica, Spain, Gaul, Illyricum, Macedonia, Achaea, Asia, Bithynia, Syria, Cyrenaica, Crete, Cyprus, Africa and latterly Egypt. This last province provided a large part of Octavian's wealth and from the very beginning it was treated differently from the other provinces. The first governor was

Cornelius Gallus, an equestrian, responsible to Octavian, and when the world was more settled and Octavian's position was ratified, that was how it remained, throughout the Empire. The Prefect of Egypt was always an equestrian appointed by the Emperor. No senator was even allowed to set foot in Egypt without Imperial sanction, much less become the governor of such an important province.

The wealth of Egypt enabled Octavian to pay his troops and arrange for the settlement of veterans. Before he marched to Alexandria he had already discharged some veterans and either paid them off or purchased land for them, settling the bill out of his own pocket. He recouped the expense once he gained control of Egypt. It is estimated that at the end of the civil war he commanded sixty legions, having acquired all of Antony's soldiers as well as his own. This was far too many to keep under arms, so he established colonies for veterans in Italy, Gaul and Spain, finally reducing the number of legions to about twenty-eight.

Octavian needed the army to shore up his power, but he could not afford to make a great display of military support. He required legal backing, freely bestowed and not coerced, if he was to remain at the head of state. At the time of his victories over Antony and Cleopatra, he had saved Rome and brought peace, so for the time being he was a hero and was as secure as it was possible to be. Numerous honours were voted to him throughout his career, but as he pointed out in the *Res Gestae*, the memoir that he left recording his achievements, he did not accept all of them, especially if he deemed them inappropriate for his age or experience. These honours formed an important part of his supremacy but did not provide him with the long-term legal basis that he required. He was unassailable in 29, because he was consul for the fifth time. On 1 January of that year all his acts were confirmed by the Senate. As consul, Octavian remained in the east attending to the organization of the provinces, the frontiers and the relationship with the territories that bordered on Roman territory. It was not necessary to undertake a thorough revision of Antony's arrangements for the east, but during the civil war, some cities and kingdoms had supported him, while others had sided with Octavian. Rewards and punishments were decided upon, outstanding debts were collected, or reparations made for those communities which had suffered. An understanding was reached with Parthia, Rome's most powerful neighbour.

Later in the year Octavian returned to Rome and celebrated three triumphs on three separate days, from 13 to 15 August, over Illyricum (where he had waged war largely to keep an army together and rival Antony); over Cleopatra; and for the victories at Actium and Alexandria. There was no overt mention of Antony in the triumphs, but his memory was damned, monuments bearing his name obliterated, and his birthday, 14 January, was declared *nefastus*, when no public business could be transacted. For the following year, 28, Octavian entered his sixth consulship with his friend and general Marcus Vipsanius Agrippa. The two men were granted the powers of the censors, and undertook the first census of citizens for twenty-eight years. They also revised the list of senators, rejecting some but also promoting men who were deemed worthy of inclusion. If they lacked the necessary wealth, Octavian provided it. As for himself he was made the leader of the Senate, *princeps senatus*.

All this was very prestigious but not permanent. The consulship was still an annual office and, although he was to be consul for the seventh time for 27, there would surely come a time when he would either have to relinquish the consulship and rely on his moral supremacy, and the tribunician sacrosanctity that had been voted to him, or incur the suspicion that he intended to keep a hold on consular power for ever, and suffer the possible consequences. He had already been offered and had refused the Dictatorship, and now it was no longer appropriate because there was no state of emergency which would justify the appointment. Although he had enjoyed what he called spontaneous universal support when all Italy took the oath to him at the start of the civil war with Antony, there were some dissidents. He could not afford to provide them with any cause to challenge him, and if he continued to rely on the consulship to put forward his ideas for government of Rome and the Empire, his potential enemies would have a greater opportunity to build up a case. It has been suggested that throughout his life opposition to him was minimal, but it may have been a different story if he had not been sensitive to the way in which the Romans conceived of and abhorred the domination of one man.

Embarking on his consulship in 27, Octavian made a speech on 13 January, offering to hand back power to the Senate and people, thereby restoring the Republic. The Senate promptly handed it back. A compromise was arranged. Octavian would govern the provinces of Gaul, Spain, Syria, Cilicia and Cyprus, and Egypt. These provinces were either close to foreign powers and therefore potentially threatened from time to time, or they were areas where internal strife might at some time break out. In either case, they would all require the presence of an army, and Octavian would be the commander of those armies. Government would be carried out via legates personally chosen by Octavian, which gave him the opportunity to appoint men whom he trusted and who would owe their advancement to him. According to the size and importance of the province these governors differed in rank, those with two or more legions being entrusted to ex-consuls, less important provinces to ex-praetors. Whatever their rank, all these legates were titled *legati Augusti propraetore*, expressed on inscriptions in abbreviated form as *leg. Aug. pp.* In the fully evolved system, smaller Imperial provinces with no legion but housing auxiliary troops, would be governed by equestrian prefects, including Egypt. For Octavian, this was power even greater than Pompey had received when he was put in charge of the war against the pirates, but it was not yet permanent, since a prudent time limit of ten years was set on Octavian's command.

The remaining provinces were to be governed by the Senate. All governors of senatorial provinces would be called proconsuls, whether or not they were of praetorian or consular rank, and some of them would command armies. There is some evidence, not without dispute, that Octavian could issue commands to the proconsular governors of senatorial provinces, but the technicalities of how this was done are not established. He may have held legally based consular or proconsular power, or he may simply have maintained an influence over the whole Empire that gave him the moral if not the legal right to interfere in non-Imperial provinces. This summary by no means reflects the amount of scholarly debate that surrounds this topic.

The day after this seminal speech of 13 January was Antony's birthday, which was *nefastus*, precluding the transaction of any public business, and on the day after that there was a religious festival, so it was not until 16 January that the Senate could deliver its vote of thanks. Munatius Plancus suggested that Octavian should now be addressed as Augustus, the name by which he is known to posterity, and which was adopted as a title by succeeding emperors. The name had no connotations of magisterial office or political power, but it was a tremendous honour, connected to *auctoritas*, the full meaning of which is nowhere near properly conveyed by the English translation 'authority'. It suggested power, but was distinct from *potestas*, which contained a more arbitrary element.

Many more honours were voted to Augustus, signifying his supremely elevated position in the Roman world. He accepted them gracefully and took them seriously, including the *corona civica*, or civic crown awarded for saving the lives of citizens. His previous history of eliminating the lives of citizens was tactfully avoided. The honours were important but not guaranteed to preserve power, a point which Augustus was in any case anxious to avoid. He chose to represent himself as first among equals, and eventually adopted the title *Princeps*, for which there was an established precedent when Pompey took the title. Augustus was already *princeps senatus*, or first senator, but *Princeps* was distinct from that, denoting much more.

The first challenge to Augustus's supremacy came in summer 27, when Marcus Licinius Crassus, the grandson of Crassus who was killed in Parthia, claimed the title of *Imperator*, and a triumph for his military success in Moesia. He had personally killed the enemy leader in battle, and also claimed the honour of *spolia opima*, that of dedicating the dead man's weapons and armour to Jupiter. Augustus objected, though on what legal grounds is suspect, and though Crassus held his triumph he was denied the other honours. From then onwards the old Republican tradition of successful generals holding a triumph in Rome was limited to members of Augustus's family, and the adoption of the title *Imperator* by commanders outside the Imperial family, and even sometimes within it, was regarded with suspicion, if not an attempt at usurpation.

The next challenge came in 23. Augustus had left Rome for the provinces in 27 and stayed away for nearly three years. In 24 he arranged the marriage of his daughter Julia with his nephew Marcus Claudius Marcellus, the son of his sister Octavia and her husband Gaius Claudius Marcellus. It was the first attempt to found a dynasty. Then in 23 Augustus fell seriously ill. Never in the best of health, this time it was thought that he might not recover. He gave his signet ring to his trusted friend Marcus Vipsanius Agrippa. Significantly, Agrippa was the only one of Augustus's circle who came near to sharing his power, indicating the high regard that Augustus held for him. He would have been the only man besides Augustus himself who could have commanded the armies and earned the respect of the Senate, but if Augustus had died at this point, even he may not have been able to establish himself as ruler of the state. Marcellus, Augustus's son-in-law and being obviously groomed for succession, was considered too young and inexperienced, and certainly not yet ready to take on the task.

By the summer of 23, Augustus had recovered, but from that time onwards he relinquished the consulship. This may have come about because he was physically unfit, and because he realized that by this time he did not need the office, or as some of his contemporaries suspected, a conspiracy was discovered. The details are obscure, and no one knows what the so-called conspirators hoped to gain. The main suspects were executed and everything was smoothed over.

The nature of Augustus's power is the subject of debate. In return for the consulship, which he never held again save for those years when he wanted to introduce his grandsons to the business of ruling, he was awarded *imperium proconsulare*, the powers of a proconsul. The disputed factor is whether this *imperium* was equal to all other provincial governors, or whether it exceeded that of the proconsuls and propraetors. In the end the argument is largely academic, since Augustus clearly wielded much more influence than other officials, and was entitled to command all the armies. He would not have wished to advertise this so blatantly, nor would he have wished to use his military power to force through what he wanted to achieve. As a military commander, he could not legally cross the *pomerium*, the city boundary, without laying down his powers, so a special law was passed to exempt him from this inconvenience. At the same time it tacitly proclaimed to all other commanders that the privilege did not extend to them and they had to obey the old law.

Tribunician Power

The mainstay of Augustus's rule, and that of all succeeding emperors, was tribunician power. He had already been granted the sacrosanctity that went with the office, but he may not have achieved the full panoply of tribunician power until later, perhaps in separate stages, or perhaps all at once in 23. Since he was not of plebeian origin, he could not hold the actual post of tribune, but the power and the office were separated so that he could wield the power without being tribune. He bestowed this power on no one else except Agrippa, and later in his reign he granted it to Tiberius. *Tribunicia potestas*, abbreviated on inscriptions to *trib. pot.*, gave him the right to veto any proposals from whatever source, but with the important exception that Augustus was not subject to the veto of other tribunes. He did not use his veto, but the possibility that he could do so if he wished perhaps served to keep the senators compliant, and at the same time reassured the populace that the senators could not oppress them without meeting opposition from Augustus. It was a neat solution to retaining power after he had relinquished the consulship, and it did not require frighteningly novel ideas. Augustus established the basis of Imperial rule, but he did it by embedding it in Republican tradition.

Augustus's Reforms

Once he was assured of supreme, unchallenged, and above all legally established powers, Augustus could attend to the government and administration of the Empire, and the well being of the various classes of people who made up the Empire. Everything about the state required attention: the city of Rome, the provinces and the frontiers, the army, the senators and the equestrian order, the people and religious matters. This is not to imply that Augustus had achieved nothing in these areas since the fall of Alexandria, but he could now make long-term plans, even though he avoided the notion of permanence and still subscribed to annual or periodic renewal of his powers.

In any brief overview of Augustus's achievements from 23 until his death in AD 14, it is easy to convey the impression that from the very beginning he had a fully developed plan for the formation of Imperial government, which he was merely waiting for an opportunity to put into place. He may well have been aware of the broad outlines of what he wanted to do, but there was no unimpeded direct line to the finished product. There were military conquests, taking Roman control up to the Danube area, and there were diplomatic successes, such as the carefully negotiated return of the captured standards of Crassus's army from Parthia in 20, an event which is depicted on the breastplate of the famous statue of Augustus from Prima

Porta. But there were setbacks and near disasters as well, and Augustus could not achieve all that he wanted to do without loyal allies. Agrippa worked tirelessly on Augustus's behalf, turning his hand from everything from military conquests in Gaul to beautifying the city of Rome and attending to its water supply and sewage system. Livia's sons, Drusus and Tiberius, spent many years campaigning on the Rhine and Danube, and Tiberius fought long and hard putting down the Pannonian revolt and tidying up after the German revolt of AD 9.

Augustus came to power at a relatively young age and despite his constant ill-health, he lived until his late seventies. The long life that Augustus enjoyed or endured was his greatest asset in reforming the state, because he was allowed the time to work slowly and persuasively rather than hurriedly and arbitrarily imposing his will on a reluctant Senate. Like Julius Caesar, he could discern what was wrong and in need of reform, and could suggest the remedies, but he did not resort to Caesar's dubious methods of forcing ideas through by issuing laws and appending signatures of senators who had not even been present at discussions. After the turmoil of the civil wars, Augustus was careful to keep well within the law, avoiding the concept of permanent or limitless power in the hands of one man, even if it meant that he had to backtrack now and again. *Festina lente*, hurry slowly, was one of Augustus's maxims.

The Senate, the Equestrians & the Roman People

In his dealings with the Senate, Augustus realized that it was necessary for senators to feel that they had some stake in government, otherwise they would either sink into apathy, or erupt in revolt. Gradually, he laid the foundations of a more structured career path for senators, which his successors could develop and refine. Julius Caesar had increased the size of the Senate to 900 members, but Augustus reduced it to a much more manageable figure of 600. Sulla had made the quaestorship an automatic entry to the Senate, and this rule was preserved, but Augustus raised the property qualification for senators from

400,000 sesterces to 1 million sesterces, so only the wealthiest young men, theoretically immune from corrupt practices to gain the office, could hope to become quaestors. Senators were distinguished by the broad purple stripe on their togas, and their sons, who belonged to the equestrian order until they too entered the Senate, were allowed to wear a narrow purple stripe on their togas. Before the age of twenty-five, the sons of senators could seek various junior appointments, which were not rationalized until several decades after Augustus's death. Then they would probably serve as quaestors, then aediles, then praetors, with a gap of some years between posts, so that no one could reach the consulship until he was about thirty-three. This was an improvement on the old Republican system, where men did not normally become consuls until the age of about forty-two. There were various posts for ex-praetors, some of them in the gift of Augustus himself, such as legionary legate, or *legatus Augusti propraetore* or governor of a praetorian Imperial province. There were also posts as governors of the praetorian senatorial provinces, though these carried the title of proconsul. Ex-consuls could look forward to governing an important senatorial province such as Asia or Africa, or an Imperial province. In most cases each man would have to be known to, and trusted by, Augustus.

For the equestrians too, there were opportunities for promotion, especially in Egypt, where Augustus and succeeding Emperors excluded all senators. The legionary commanders in Egypt, and the governors, called prefects, were always equestrians. Augustus also created three more prefectures for equestrians. In 2 BC he transformed his personal bodyguard into the Praetorian Guard, and appointed the first two Praetorian Prefects, who shared the command. Towards the end of his reign he appointed other prefects, of the *annona* or food supply probably in AD 8, and the *vigiles*, the combined police force and fire service, which was formed in AD 6.

For the people of Rome, a secure and constant food supply was one of the most important considerations. The somewhat piecemeal attention that had been given to it in the past was only successful in overcoming short-term problems. There was no continuous policy or relevant personnel dedicated to the food supply. Augustus created a permanent system for its administration, supervised by the equestrian *Praefecti Annonae*, who organized the storage of food from Italy and the provinces and supervised its distribution. Gaius Gracchus had instituted the monthly allocation of grain to the people of Rome at a price below the market value, and the tribune Clodius had removed the charge so that grain could be distributed free to the poor who qualified for the dole. Julius Caesar reduced the number of recipients, and Augustus finally settled on a figure of 200,000.

The phrase 'bread and circuses' has entered modern terminology in connection with conciliating the populace, and Augustus was no exception to the rule. Lavish entertainments had always been laid on by many prominent Romans but, according to Suetonius in his biographies of the first emperors, they were all completely outdone by Augustus, who paid assiduous attention to games and shows, including gladiatorial combats, athletics and sports festivals, and theatrical performances. Like their modern counterparts, the ancient Romans would have loved football, television and opera. These festivals and celebrations served several purposes, not just as entertainment and diversion, but also in fostering unity, and a sense of a brilliant past and a brilliant destiny. Sometimes festivals were of a religious nature, such as the Secular Games in 17 BC, hailed as the beginning of a new era. The shadow of the civil wars of the last few decades was obliterated by the promise of peace and prosperity.

The Propaganda Machine & the Imperial Cult

Outward display, literature and art were all commandeered in Augustus's scheme, not just in Rome, but all over the Empire. The representation of Augustus himself as ruler has been thoroughly investigated by more than one modern author. Coin portraits and sculptures were widely distributed throughout the Roman world as part of the positive propaganda concerned with Augustus as saviour. It was an integral part of this propaganda that he was always presented as a youthful figure, despite the fact that he lived to a ripe old age. If he had allowed himself to be portrayed as an older man his credibility may have been destroyed, so even on coins issued late in his reign he appeared as he had always done. In the ancient Roman world there was nothing like the glaring searchlight of newspaper and television media attention, where he could not have avoided the visible evidence that he was ageing.

Augustus controlled his own publicity department via the visual imagery that was produced, and also in literature. Leading Republican Romans often gathered around them literary circles and some like Pompey the Great became the patrons of various writers and artists. Through his equestrian friend Maecenas, who likewise gathered around him poets and literary men, Augustus utilized the system for the benefit of himself and Rome, employing several writers, among them poets such as Horace (Quintus Horatius Flaccus) and Virgil (Publius Vergilius Maro) to celebrate Rome and its past. Both these men were Italians rather than native Romans, demonstrating the social mobility that had begun in the later Republic and which Caesar and Augustus promoted. Publius Vergilius Maro, more commonly called in modern times Virgil with an 'i' instead of an 'e', was a native of Mantua, and was the elder of these two poets, born in 70 BC. His *Eclogues* and *Georgics* venerate the rustic life, and his great work, the *Aeneid*, celebrates the greatness of Rome, linking the city with ancient Troy. Aeneas and his son Anchises escape the fall of Troy and make their way to Italy, encountering various obstacles on the way, like the Greek hero Odysseus in Homer's *Iliad*. Although the work looks back towards a historical perspective, it is not an accurate portrayal of the foundation of Rome, but refers to the new Augustan age. In the sixth book, Aeneas visits the realm of the dead, where the future of Rome is told to him.

Horace was born in 65 BC in Venusia (modern Venosa) in Apulia, the son of a freedman who had amassed a fortune sufficient to provide Horace with a typical upper class Roman education in Rome and Athens. Horace was on the wrong side in the civil war between the forces of Brutus and Cassius and those of Antony and Octavian, but escaped unscathed, and was recruited by Maecenas before Octavian and Antony went to war with each other. Horace celebrates the rule of Augustus bringing peace and well-being, but not with the customary sickening flamboyancy of overt panegyrics.

The Imperial cult of emperor worship had several different roots that Augustus joined together to produce a system which demonstrated certain unifying elements, but varied in practice and method in different parts of the Empire. There were precedents when Pompey was treated as a living god in the east, and Julius Caesar was deified after his death. As Caesar's heir Octavian-Augustus presented himself as the son of a god. In Rome and the west, the worship of a living person was not the norm, but in the east it was customary. Soon after the battle of Actium, Octavian-Augustus allowed the Greeks to worship himself and the goddess Roma, but Roman citizens who may have been uncomfortable with this worshipped instead the deified Caesar and Rome. In the west, the Imperial cult was established some time later. It started in Spain where altars to Augustus were set up from about the year 25 BC. The cult spread to Gaul, then to Germany, appearing in Italy after the dedication of the temple to Mars Ultor, Mars the Avenger, in 2 BC. The cult was not imposed on any community, but its development relied on local initiatives that were then endorsed and encouraged. Sacred altars were established at Lyons for the Three Gauls, and another for the tribe of the Ubii on the Rhine, at a place which was called literally the altar of the Ubii, *Ara Ubiorum*. Later a colony was founded there by the Emperor Claudius, and the place was renamed *Colonia Claudia Ara Agrippinensium*. The modern name for the city simply commemorates the first element of the title, *Colonia*, as the city of Cologne. There were no temples at Lyons and Cologne, only the altars, where priests called *sacerdotes* officiated at the ceremonies dedicated to Augustus and Rome. The Imperial cult provided another unifying influence, but since it took some time to become embedded in provincial life and administration it was probably of more benefit to the successors of Augustus than to Augustus himself.

The Army & the Frontiers

Although there had been several armies in the field on a more or less permanent basis during the period of the civil wars, there was no standing army before the reign of Augustus. After the battle of Actium and the fall of Alexandria, the major task facing Octavian-Augustus was to reduce the numerous armies to a manageable size, which entailed the discharge of time served soldiers and settling veterans on the land or pensioning them off. When this process was complete there were about twenty-eight legions still in existence.

There was a need for legions and auxiliary troops to keep the peace in the provinces, and to protect the frontiers where Rome met tribes and communities not yet absorbed into the Empire. A more pressing requirement for troops, but not one which was overtly proclaimed, was to provide support for Octavian's regime, and for all succeeding Emperors. When Octavian made the gesture to return the government of Rome and the Empire to the Senate in 27 BC he emerged as governor of most of the provinces which contained armies, with only a few areas where senatorial governors could command troops. Since the appointment of the legates of legions and the commanders of the auxiliary units remained within the gift of Augustus, and since he could also intervene in senatorial provinces, the loyalty of all troops was directed to him. It became the norm to swear an oath of allegiance to the Emperor on enlistment, and to renew it annually at a parade on the reigning Emperor's birthday.

Once Augustus was secure as supreme commander, he could begin to rationalize the organization of the army. This process was extended over a number of years and did not spring fully fledged from a couple of all-embracing decrees passed in any particular year, so what is described here is the evolved form of the army, developed from the foundation created by Augustus. Each legion was given a number and a name, but some of them already possessed such forms of identity, for instance *V Macedonica* had been formed during the latter days of the Republic, and *V Alaudae*, 'the Larks', was one of Caesar's legions, and neither of them wished to give up their numbers and names. There was therefore some duplication of numbers, with the result that although there were twenty-eight Augustan legions they were not labelled from I through to XXVIII.

Pay and length of service was eventually standardized, in stages from 13 BC onwards. The Republican soldiers were eligible for service for a period of sixteen years or sixteen campaigns, so Augustus used the same principle to set the terms of service for the legionaries of the standing, professional Roman army, who were under arms for twenty years, that is for sixteen years and then as veterans in reserve for another four years. They were paid 225 denarii per annum, in three instalments, with deductions for food, clothing, the burial club and savings. At the end of their service, they were given pensions instead of lands, from a military treasury (*aerarium militare*) that was set up by Augustus in AD 6, financed initially by 170 million sesterces from his own funds and thereafter from taxation, in this case a 1 per cent tax on sales at auctions, and 5 per cent on inheritances. From AD 14 when Augustus died there was finally an end to the redistribution of lands on which to settle discharged veterans, which had plagued the Republic every time a victorious general returned home. Provided with their pensions, some of the veterans set up businesses, or bought farms on their own initiative. The scheme was designed to prevent crowds of penniless and aimless veterans from wandering around the countryside and endangering the public in Italy and the provinces.

The command structure was adapted to the needs of a permanent army, stationed sometimes far from Rome. The legionary legates of Caesar's day were commanders appointed by him on a more or less temporary basis according to the current location and the nature of the campaign. Augustus appointed legionary legates, usually senators who had served as praetors in Rome, and who would be over thirty years old. They would stay in their posts for a few years and then move on. Next in rank was the *tribunus laticlavius*, literally the broad stripe tribune, another man of senatorial rank, but younger and less experienced than the legate. Continuity was provided by the next most senior officer, the *praefectus castrorum*, or the prefect of the camp, who would be a professional soldier and would have served in the legions for a long time. Prior to this post he had usually been promoted to senior centurion, the *primus pilus*, literally 'the first spear'. Ranking above the senior centurion were the five equestrian officers serving as tribunes, distinct from the senatorial tribune, and designated *tribuni angusticlavii*, or narrow stripe tribunes. Commonly described as the backbone of the army were the sixty centurions commanding the sixty centuries, containing not one hundred men as the title suggests, but eighty men. These were grouped together into ten cohorts, six centuries in each, but there is no evidence that there was ever a cohort commander in the legions, so the centurions were the men upon whom the senior officers depended.

The legionaries were all Roman citizens, but at this period this did not mean that they all came from Rome itself. As time went on citizenship was extended to individuals and communities throughout the Empire, and until the third century at least there seems to have been no lack of them to fill the gaps in the legions, which were filled mostly by volunteers, although in especially stressful times the Romans had to resort to conscription.

The auxiliary troops of the Imperial army were not Roman citizens. Their organization was based on the Republican system of recruiting soldiers from among Rome's allies. If campaigns were fought in foreign countries, the same principle was applied, and troops were provided by rulers or states who were attached to Rome. These men would fight under their own officers, and would go home when the wars ended. At Augustus's death in AD 14 the *auxilia* was not fully established, so it was left to his successors to complete what he had begun. In the evolved system, the auxiliary troops consisted of cavalry units called *alae*, and infantry units called cohorts, each 500 or 1,000 strong, and mixed units combining some mounted men and some foot soldiers, called *cohortes equitatae*. The commanders of these units would follow a prescribed career path, beginning with about three years as an infantry cohort commander and working up to the command of a cavalry unit of 500 men. There were only a few 1,000 strong cavalry units and no province had more than one; the commander of these units was an important officer who could expect to go on to further military commands and civilian posts.

The auxiliaries may have been paid at the same rate as the legionaries, though this is very much discussed by modern scholars. They served for 25 years, and on discharge they received pensions and Roman citizenship, which at first was extended to their children, even though they were not supposed to marry while serving in the army. Later on, these privileges were reduced.

The legions and the auxiliary troops were stationed in the provinces where internal policing was necessary, or where the frontiers required vigilance and sometimes armed combat. In the Augustan period, the camps and forts where the armies were housed were not of a permanent nature and had not yet attained the regular layouts of the later Imperial era. When wars broke out troops could be moved to the war zone, and extra troops could be recruited, for instance in AD 6 when the Pannonian revolt began on the Danube, conscription was applied in Italy, and the future Emperor Tiberius gathered a large army, including legions brought in from the east, to put the rebellion down.

Though the Roman world had boundaries in Republican times and in Augustus's day, there was no concept of frontiers in the form of running barriers dividing Roman controlled territory from other lands ruled by client kings allied to Rome, or where Rome perhaps influenced but did not direct affairs. That came later under the Emperor Hadrian. In the first days of the Empire the Romans subscribed to the theory of constant expansion, *imperium sine fine* or power without end, in both the territorial and the temporal sense. Towards the end of his reign Augustus abandoned this idea. In AD 9 the German tribes beyond the Rhine, seemingly pacified and ready for Roman settlement and consolidation, suddenly erupted under their leader Arminius, who had served in the Roman army and therefore understood the way in which the military men functioned. He trapped and annihilated three Roman legions, and the Romans pulled back to the Rhine. Augustus advised his successor Tiberius not to try to expand the Empire beyond its current boundaries. Later emperors ignored the advice and added territories here and there, sometimes for reasons of defence, or for economic gain, or both.

The Succession

There was a continuous problem about the succession and what would happen to the Empire after Augustus's death. As sole ruler of the state, Augustus did not accept power on a permanent basis. Instead it was renewed in five or ten year batches, neatly avoiding the hated concept of kingship or the domination of one man. In 13 BC his powers were bestowed on him once again for another term of five years, expiring in 8 BC, when he would be fifty-five years old. He was the only man in the Roman world with the relevant political and military experience to govern, and above all he was the man who had earned the faith and support of the Roman people. He tried to ensure that his chosen heirs also earned the same support, demonstrating that they were worthy of the power to govern.

The major problem that he had to overcome was that the hereditary principle had not yet been applied to the government of Rome. Possessions, legal status and even personal influence could be passed down to heirs, but not political power. It was therefore a matter of introducing a successor and ensuring that the Senate and people of Rome, and above all the army, accepted the chosen heir. Augustus's dilemma was that all his designated heirs died young, giving rise to the suspicion expressed in some ancient sources, and utilized to great effect by Robert Graves in *I, Claudius*, that Livia had poisoned or otherwise despatched them all in favour of her own son Tiberius. A contributory factor to the demise of Augustus's heirs, with or without interference from Livia, is that in a country with a hot summer climate, no refrigerators, but a lot of mosquitoes, death at a relatively young age was not uncommon in Roman families. Despite the fact that Graeco-Roman medical science was relatively advanced, doctors could not always combat food poisoning, malaria, contagious diseases, or accidents, none of which have ever been known to respect youth.

Augustus's first choice of heir, his nephew Marcellus, died late in 23, leaving Augustus's daughter Julia a widow. She was then married off to Marcus Vipsanius Agrippa, and together they produced three daughters and two sons, Gaius and Lucius, who were adopted by Augustus and groomed for succession. They were introduced at an early age into public life, under his supervision. Augustus had not held the consulship for some time but he entered on his twelfth term of office when Gaius was consul in 5 BC. Three years later in 2 BC he took up his thirteenth consulship with Lucius as colleague. The boys were gradually given more responsibilities, and were accorded certain honours, but nothing too much or unsuitable for their abilities or experience.

Unfortunately Lucius, the younger of the two boys, died in AD 2, and Gaius died two years later. In AD 4, Tiberius, who was back in Rome after his self-imposed exile in Rhodes, but without any particular office, was brought back into the government, receiving tribunician power for ten years. In the summer of that year, Augustus adopted as his own sons Tiberius and Agrippa Postumus, the son of Marcus Vipsanius Agrippa and Augustus's daughter Julia. Agrippa Postumus was so named because he had been born after the death of his father in 12 BC, and he was almost alone in the world, since his mother Julia had been banished in 2 BC after a notorious sexual scandal.

In his turn Tiberius adopted his nephew Germanicus, the son of his brother Drusus, who had died in Germany in 9 BC. There were now potentially four successors to Augustus: Tiberius and Agrippa Postumus in the first rank, and Germanicus and Tiberius's own son Drusus, in the second rank. Of them all Tiberius was the man who was most experienced, and Germanicus was the man who was the most popular. Once again the succession did not go according to plan. Agrippa Postumus was allegedly involved in a plot and banished in AD 7.

On his way to Capri in AD 14, Augustus fell ill. He reached Nola, where he owned property, and prepared for the end, gathering his friends around his bed to ask if they had enjoyed the performance. On 19 August the greatest showman and most astute psychologist of the Roman world died, to take his place among the gods of the Roman world shortly afterwards when he was deified. His adopted son Tiberius reluctantly inherited the government of the Empire.

2

Julio-Claudians:
Tiberius to Nero AD 14–68

The Emperor Tiberius AD 14–37

Tiberius was an outsider, being of purely Claudian stock, while Augustus, Caligula, Claudius and Nero could trace their ancestry through both Claudian and Julian bloodlines. Although Tiberius had been associated with Augustus since childhood, and eventually marked out for the succession after all the other candidates had died, he was very reluctant to take on the task. He was in his mid fifties, not experienced in politics or the social life of Rome, but he knew enough of the world to realize that governing the Empire was going to be difficult. He had no precedents to fall back on, since hereditary succession had not yet been fully established, and though Augustus had reigned for such a long time that the Republic was all but forgotten, it lived on as an ideal in the minds of some men.

Tiberius's reluctance to take on the government of the Empire was variously interpreted, as were most of his actions. It seemed that he was simply being coy about it so that the Senate would implore him to take command, or that he was trying to imitate Augustus in 27 BC. There may have been no subterfuge at all. Tiberius could never dissemble as Augustus did, nor hide his true feelings. His sense of responsibility ensured that he did become Emperor, but he did not accept with a good grace and smiling countenance, and thereby crystallized his reputation for churlishness. It did not help that one of the first actions of his reign was the execution of Agrippa Postumus, banished some years before by Augustus. It may have been Augustus himself who ordered Postumus's death, but the bad odour attached itself to Tiberius.

For many years Tiberius had been absent from Rome, usually with the army. He was in Armenia in 20 BC when the Parthians ousted the Roman candidate for the throne, and from 15 until 6 BC he was almost continually on campaign, in Raetia and Noricum north of the Alps, in Illyricum and Germany. When these campaigns ended he took himself to Rhodes, allegedly because he felt overshadowed by the promotion of Gaius and Lucius Caesar. He was also unhappy in his marriage, which had been forced on him by Augustus. When Marcus Vipsanius Agrippa died, his widow Julia, Augustus's daughter, was thus eligible to marry again. She and Tiberius were treated as pawns in Augustus's scheme to provide for the succession, so they were thrown together in a marriage that neither of them desired or enjoyed. If they had liked each other, the dynastic problems might have been overcome, but they most definitely did not like each other, and the only offspring born of the ill-fated marriage did not survive. What made it worse for Tiberius was his enforced estrangement from his beloved wife Vipsania, the daughter of Agrippa. This marriage had been very happy and at the time of the divorce Tiberius's son Drusus was still an infant. If Tiberius was as embittered as the ancient historians said he was, this was one of the reasons.

Modern historians have reinstated Tiberius by concentrating less on his sensational idiosyncracies and more on the political and military history of his reign. When Augustus died, the Roman world was leaderless, potentially ripe for another power struggle and civil war. The historian Velleius Paterculus comments on the narrow margin between the preservation of stability and the possible descent into chaos. But there was no war, no chaos and no opposition from the Senate, the Praetorian Guard or the people. Everyone kept their heads, in both the figurative and physical senses.

Tiberius, a soldier and commander, had a firm grasp of the realities of power. Immediately after the death of Augustus, Tiberius made sure of the Praetorians by paying them a donative, and secured the loyalty of the armies in the provinces by administering the oath that had been established by Augustus. He adopted the name Augustus but refused the title *Imperator* and *Pater Patriae*. These were highly honorific titles but they gave him no real political power. That was provided by his proconsular *imperium* and his tribunician power, which he eventually accepted for life. In this he departed from Augustan precedent, by not choosing to set a temporal limit on these powers. Perhaps he considered that after only a five or ten year term he would not be given a second chance.

Although Tiberius did not cultivate the populace by putting on frequent shows and games, or even attending them when they were organized, there was no serious discontent with the new emperor among the people of Rome or the provinces. It was a different case with the soldiers. They took the oath of loyalty, but they thought less about political matters than they did about their conditions of service and their pay, and the armies on the Rhine and in Pannonia seized the opportunity to make their grievances known. Their actions have been termed as revolts, but setting up a usurper was not the prime concern of the armies. They wanted a pay rise, and proper dismissal when they had served their full terms. Tiberius despatched his son Drusus to the troops in Pannonia, and his adopted son Germanicus to Germany. Drusus, aided by Lucius Aelius Sejanus took a firm hand and quelled Pannonian troops. But Germanicus adopted a softer approach and promised to meet most of the soldiers' demands. He was probably genuinely sympathetic. The story goes that one soldier grabbed Germanicus's hand and thrust it into his mouth, to demonstrate that he was old and toothless and ready for demobilization.

Some suspicion attached to Germanicus's actions, because he could so easily have exploited the unrest among the soldiers and turned it into a bid for supreme power. Instead he gave the soldiers something to do by mounting a campaign across the Rhine, which achieved little but incidentally discovered the remains of the legions which had been annihilated by Arminius in AD 9.

In his dealings with the Senate, Tiberius was conciliatory. The election of the chief magistrates was taken from the people and given to the Senate, so there was some semblance of choice rather than mere confirmation of Imperial wishes. Tiberius tried to foster true debate and individual thought, but it was probably too late for that. With Augustus, senators knew the rules and where they stood, but with Tiberius they were uncertain. He took part in senatorial proceedings but only succeeded in making the senators ill at ease, as he did when he sat in on court hearings. In encouraging senatorial participation in government, Tiberius did not wish to dominate, even to the point of accepting opinions contrary to his own, but since he did not always make his wishes clear, and worse still was sometimes inconsistent, the senators lost confidence and became either apathetic or far too familiar with the Emperor who insisted that he was only the first among equals. Augustus had managed to play the part while still making it clear where the boundaries lay, but Tiberius seemed to give out contradictory messages, treat me as one of yourselves, he seemed to be saying, and then, if anyone did so, he disliked the closeness. The relationship between the senators and the Emperor gradually soured, irretrievably. Trials for treason, *maiestas*, increased in number, informers multiplied, and freedom of action became more and more constrained, because there were no hard and fast rules as to what constituted treason.

As his reign progressed Tiberius himself became more embittered. He had always tried to avoid public life and the Imperial court, and all his successes had been achieved far from Rome, on the frontiers and with the army. His military and administrative skills were never fully appreciated, and he had not promoted himself in Rome among the senatorial class or the people. He had not been first choice of successor to

Augustus and, when he finally became emperor, he was almost at the age when he should have been able to look forward to retirement, but was then thrust into another job for which he had neither aptitude nor experience. For nearly ten years his rule was balanced and fair. The provinces benefited from his rule because he recognized efficient and honest governors and left them in their posts for several years. The continuity enabled the provincials to flourish under governors who did not use extortion to make themselves wealthy, but in the longer term the policy stultified the careers of equestrians and senators alike, since the normal tour of duty consisted of only one or two years in a province followed by appointments to military commands or civil posts in Rome. In this way many men gained a varied experience of government and a coterie of available manpower was built up.

There were few signs of unrest in Rome or Italy, save for the discovery of a conspiracy hatched by Scribonius Libo in 16, and two rebellions in the provinces, in Africa under Tacfarinas, and in Gaul under Florus and Sacrovir. These were all suppressed without calamity. More troublesome were the actions of Tiberius's nephew and adopted son Germanicus, who campaigned in Germany in 15 and 16, without achieving very much except for instigating an inordinate loyal following among the soldiers. His popularity made Tiberius suspicious of his possible designs on the Empire, a situation which Germanicus did nothing to remedy when he was sent to the east, where Parthian interests in Armenia were escalating. Germanicus succeeded in coming to an agreement with the Parthian king, Artabanus, but then he exceeded his brief by travelling to Egypt, where he behaved as if he were Emperor, commendably sorting out various problems. The problem was that Germanicus had not asked permission to go to Egypt, and it was in direct contravention of Augustus's ruling that no senator should enter the province without Imperial permission. Germanicus was a little too arrogant for Tiberius's taste, so when he died suddenly in Syria, in 19, it was rumoured that the Emperor had arranged for his removal. There was further scandal attached to the case, since Tiberius had appointed as governor of Syria an experienced and trusted colleague, Gnaeus Calpurnius Piso, perhaps to watch over Germanicus, possibly to report on his actions. Piso had quarrelled with Germanicus, and tried to stir up the troops against him. Germanicus ordered him to leave Syria. Piso said that he left of his own accord but, before he had departed from the east, unwelcome news reached him that Germanicus was dead. Not only that but, before he died, Germanicus said that Piso had poisoned him. Piso rushed back to Syria and attempted to take over the province again without checking first with the Emperor. It looked suspiciously like a military coup, and Piso also made the mistake of allowing Agrippina, the widow of Germanicus, to return to Rome with her family and friends, where they built up a case against him.

The unfortunate Piso was put on trial when he was recalled to Rome. He was cleared of the poisoning charge, but it was certain that he would be condemned for interfering with the loyalty of the army and forcing his way back as governor of Syria. He killed himself before a verdict was given. It was not this charge that interested most people. Scandalmongers said that Tiberius had used Piso to get rid of Germanicus, and had then abandoned him to the courts. The rumours went on to insist that all this was done to promote Tiberius's own son Drusus. Modern scholars discount this theory, but in Tiberius's own lifetime the scandal persisted. Four years later, Drusus also died. The death of his son marked a turning point in Tiberius's life. He did not recruit or actively promote a successor for over a decade.

Drusus's death also marked the rise to prominence of Lucius Aelius Sejanus. He was the son of Lucius Seius Strabo, who had been Praetorian Prefect under Augustus. On his accession in 14, Tiberius promoted Sejanus as his father's colleague as Praetorian Prefect, and in 17 he made Seius Strabo Prefect of Egypt. He did not bring in a colleague for Sejanus, who was now sole commander of the guard. The Praetorians were stationed in different parts of Italy at the time, but Sejanus soon made plans to concentrate them in a camp just on the outskirts of Rome. Tiberius's son Drusus had foreseen the immense accretion of power that Sejanus would enjoy if the guardsmen were brought to Rome, and had not been in favour of the idea, but after his death, Tiberius presumably acquiesced and the Praetorian Camp was built near the Porta Viminalis.

Sejanus harboured ambitions of his own, aiming for connections with the Imperial family. He sought permission to marry Drusus's widow Livilla, but Tiberius refused him. Undeterred, Sejanus started a campaign to eliminate Agrippina, the widow of Germanicus. She was openly inimical to Tiberius and rather free with her opinions, doing herself no favours in the long run. Concentrating at first on Agrippina's supporters, Sejanus used the loose definitions of treason to bring various people to trial. He was patient, and it took him a few years to bring about the banishment of Agrippina and her elder son Nero in 29, and the imprisonment of her younger son Drusus the following year. Only Gaius, the youngest son of Germanicus and Agrippina, was left unmolested.

By this time Tiberius had removed himself from Rome and gone to live on the island of Capri. He had promoted Sejanus and still trusted him, all the more so because Sejanus had saved his life by throwing himself across the Emperor to protect him from a fall of rocks. So for a while the Praetorian Prefect had an almost free hand in Rome. Tiberius had not relinquished control altogether. He attended to government and administration from Capri, but he was perhaps not kept fully informed of the growing power of Sejanus, who was elected consul for the year 31, with Tiberius as colleague, and was to have proconsular power bestowed on him. At this point, it is said that Tiberius was alerted to Sejanus's ambitions by his sister-in-law Antonia, the widow of his brother Drusus, and the mother of Germanicus. She does not seem to have been personally threatened by Sejanus, but she suspected that he was about to remove Gaius, and possibly Tiberius's grandson Gemellus, until only Tiberius himself barred his path to supreme power. It is not certain whether Sejanus really plotted against Tiberius, but he was certainly aiming for shared power. History may have been different if Sejanus had been allowed to eliminate Gaius, who became the notorious Emperor Caligula, but he was stopped in his tracks when Tiberius appointed Naevius Sutorius Macro as Praetorian Prefect, with instructions to replace Sejanus. It was almost comic in the way in which it was done. Macro handed Sejanus a letter from the Emperor, and since he was expecting to be granted proconsular power, Sejanus had no reason to believe that half way through the letter would suddenly turn into an accusation and denouncement. His fall from power was immediate. Everyone melted away, and he was executed that same day. His followers and his young children were also despatched.

Tiberius now knew that he could trust nobody. One unfortunate result of his isolation was that he began to fear that his governors and military commanders might turn against him and use the armies to raise rebellion, a feature of Roman government that was to come to prominence in the next three decades. Wearily but conscientiously Tiberius continued to administer the Empire after the suppression of Sejanus. He was not out of touch with current affairs, and in 33 when there was a financial crisis, he gave 100 million sesterces to the state treasury, at 0 per cent interest, to improve monetary circulation. People of the early twenty-first century will recognize a distant echo.

In 35, he decided to name his heirs. There were only two possibilities from the Julio-Claudian house, his grandson Tiberius Gemellus and Gaius Caligula, the son of Germanicus. Despite the nomination of successors, Tiberius did not promote Gaius, the elder of the two boys, perhaps recognizing his unsuitability for holding office. He may have promoted Gemellus if he had been older. Unfortunately, he was not granted the time to train either of his heirs. He fell ill in 37 and decided to go back to Rome, but he died at Misenum. He was seventy-eight years old and had led an arduous life. There was probably no need for Gaius, who was with him, to smother him, as rumour would have it. Two days later, supported by the Praetorian Prefect Macro, Gaius became emperor. Tiberius, unlike his adopted father, was not deified after his death.

Gaius, or Caligula AD 37–41

Gaius's father Germanicus usually took his family with him when he was with the army, and had a miniature uniform made for his youngest son, complete with a pair of boots (*caligae*) like the soldiers wore, so Gaius was soon called Little Boots, Caligula, and the name stuck. On his accession, which was seemingly unopposed, Gaius was the darling of the people and the army. He started well, abolishing the notorious treason trials and conciliating the nobility, allowing the Senate to make decisions, and entertaining the populace via a series of games and shows.

Aged twenty-five when he succeeded Tiberius, Gaius had not held any important offices and had little experience of government. He had been quaestor in 33, a junior post which would not have afforded much training as Emperor. His whole life up to now had been bizarre. His father Germanicus died when Gaius was only a child, and his domineering and outspoken mother Agrippina was not exactly well-disposed to the Emperor Tiberius, who was suspected of some subterfuge in arranging for Germanicus's death. The followers of the family and then the family members themselves were persecuted by Sejanus, who removed Agrippina and her eldest son by having them banished, and shortly afterwards he imprisoned her younger son Drusus. Since it seemed at the time that Tiberius probably condoned these acts, the teenaged Gaius would hardly feel secure. Clearly he was next in the firing line, but before Sejanus could act, Tiberius engineered his downfall and replaced him with the new Praetorian Prefect, Macro. Then Gaius was invited to Capri, where the septuagenarian Tiberius made him and his cousin Gemellus his joint heirs. It was an unsettling beginning, but at first Gaius seemed to have emerged unscathed.

Turning to the Julio-Claudian family, Gaius adopted Gemellus, marking him out as his intended successor, and bestowed the consulship on his uncle Claudius, who had played little part in public life, ignored by the Imperial household because of his physical infirmities, his stammer, his lameness and his alleged tendency to drool. To strengthen the alliance, Claudius married his third wife, Messalina, whose paternal and maternal ancestor was Augustus himself. There was no sign as yet of the despotic, megalomaniac, absolutist emperor that Gaius would become.

After a serious illness in 37, not properly documented, the monster of the ancient sources emerged. Excuses have been made for Gaius's increasingly absurd behaviour on account of this unexplained illness. It has been claimed that Gaius had a nervous breakdown, or that he had suffered brain fever. The debate is insoluble, and hostile portraits in the ancient sources partly obscure the reasons for his subsequent actions. He quickly executed Gemellus and the Praetorian Prefect Macro, reinstated the treason trials, and reduced the Senate to a nonentity by taking total control of the government. His policies, as described in the sources, are not consistent. He annexed Mauretania and deposed the client king, Ptolemy, and he mounted a military expedition to the Rhine, where the Germanic tribes were engaged in raiding. The campaign may have been in response to a plot hatched by Aemilius Lepidus, who had married Gaius's sister Drusilla, and after her death had started an affair with Agrippina, Gaius's other sister. If Lepidus managed to stir up the Rhine legions and get the commanders on his side, he could launch a coup against the Emperor, but the plot was suppressed, with the help of two competent military men, the future emperors Sulpicius Galba and Flavius Vespasianus. It was said that Gaius also planned an invasion of Britain but it never took place. Allegedly he reached the coast of Gaul and made his soldiers collect seashells. Various explanations have been advanced for this strange tale. It is possible that the soldiers refused to embark, as they did later when Claudius mounted the invasion of Britain. Gaius may have suddenly become alarmed about leaving Italy where more plots could be formed against him, and the story about the seashells may have arisen from confusion over terminology. The word *musculi* denotes shells, but it is also the term used for military siege equipment, which would have to be carted back to the legionary bases.

In the east, Gaius managed to undo Augustus's carefully strengthened borders with Parthia, by interfering with the provinces and client kingdoms. As a result the Parthians gained a preponderant influence in Armenia, always a bone of contention between the two empires. In Judaea, Gaius favoured his friend Herod Agrippa by placing him in control of the territories ruled by his relatives, and he caused further resentment by making it clear that he intended to have a statue of himself as a living god placed in all synagogues, including the temple at Jerusalem. Before the order could be put into effect, the Praetorians assassinated the living god.

By the end of his reign, the darling of the people had upset virtually everyone from all walks of life. He had tried to keep the Praetorians well-disposed by a cash payment on his accession and by various favours thereafter, but in the end even the guardsmen lost patience with him, possibly forming an alliance with some senators who wished to be rid of Gaius. The men who killed the Emperor were Praetorians, and it was also a group of Praetorians who found Claudius hiding behind a curtain in the Imperial palace, and dragged him out, not to assassinate him, but to declare him emperor.

Claudius AD 41–54

On his accession Claudius was fifty-one years old, and had always been considered the least likely candidate for Imperial rule, because of his physical infirmities and his supposed weakness of intellect. But Claudius was nobody's fool. He devoted himself to academic study, kept a low profile, and survived intact through the reigns of Augustus, Tiberius and Gaius Caligula. His father was Tiberius's brother, Drusus, and his mother was Antonia, the younger daughter of Mark Antony and Octavia, Augustus's sister. Claudius had witnessed the death of all his close relatives. His father died after an accident in Germany when Claudius was less than one year old. His brother Germanicus died under suspicious circumstances in Syria. Germanicus's wife Agrippina, from then on hostile to Tiberius, paid for her attitude when Sejanus banished her. Claudius's sister Livia Julia, or Livilla, was accused of having an affair with Sejanus, and of arranging the death of her husband, Drusus, the son of Tiberius. She was executed and her memory was damned. Antonia, Claudius's mother, was instrumental in the downfall of Sejanus, since she was respected by her brother-in-law Tiberius, who listened to her when she came to warn him of the rising ambition of the Praetorian Prefect, who had asked permission to marry Livilla and been refused in 25. When Gaius Caligula became emperor, he first bestowed various honours on Antonia, who had brought him up after the death of Germanicus, but only a few weeks into his reign he tired of her and drove her to suicide. From 37 onwards Claudius trod very carefully. He was made consul with Gaius as colleague, but this would not guarantee his future security. Tiberius had intended that Gaius and his own grandson Tiberius Gemellus should be his co-heirs, but Gemellus was soon murdered, leaving Claudius no doubt very wary.

When Gaius was assassinated, Claudius could not be certain whether the plotters had decided to despatch him as well. As a member of the Julio-Claudian house, which had provided two emperors of dubious character, he may have been tarred with the same brush. The senators were ready to reinstate the Republic, but could only acquiesce when the Praetorians declared Claudius emperor. All the emperors depended on the armed forces to gain and retain power, but Claudius was the first who was so blatantly indebted to the Praetorians, and to keep them well-disposed he paid huge donatives to each man, setting a dangerous precedent for the future. He took the name Caesar, which was eventually transformed into a title, to connect himself with the Julian family. He courted the favour of the Senate, treating all senators respectfully, trying to encourage them to take a more active part in government, asking their advice and sometimes following it. He was not altogether successful in reviving the Senate. Two reigns had begun well and ended badly, and at this stage there was no reason to believe that Claudius would be any different. He put an end to the treason trials, abolished some of the taxes that Gaius had established to fill his depleted coffers, and provided the people with games and shows. Tiberius had started out with liberal views, but had ended by reintroducing treason trials and becoming more estranged from the Senate and people. Gaius had displayed a very short-lived leniency, and had become unpredictable and vindictive. Claudius's benevolent attitude was not wholly trusted, and eventually there were executions, about thirty-five senators and many more equites who were perhaps their clients or supporters. There was an attempt at rebellion, led by Furius Camillus Scribonianus, the commander of the army in Dalmatia, but fortunately the soldiers were not interested in fighting and dying for him, being happy to accept Claudius, who attended to their needs and gave them things to do.

Since he was not a military man, Claudius relied upon his generals. When rebellion broke out in Mauretania, he sent Suetonius Paullinus and Hosidius Geta to suppress it. The country had been annexed by Gaius, after he had deposed King Ptolemy. It was not unusual for the inhabitants of new provinces to try to shake off Roman rule, but the country was quickly pacified and Claudius created two provinces, Mauretania Tingitana and Mauretania Caesariensis. Romanization in the two provinces never proceeded rapidly, but the Mauri, or Moors, provided excellent cavalry for the Roman army.

For the first time since Augustus had advised against extending the Empire, Claudius embarked on just such a policy. He reversed Gaius's policy and converted Judaea into a province as it had once been, annexed Lycia together with Pamphylia, and annexed Thrace. His most famous achievement was the conquest of Britain. Julius Caesar had invaded the island in 55 and 54 BC, but had not attempted to conquer and annexe it. Augustus had refused to contemplate such a task even when approached by a British king seeking Roman assistance in regaining his throne. Gaius had started the project, using the same excuse that one of the tribal rulers needed help, but never finished it. In 43, Claudius authorized the invasion.

The British tribes knew all about the Romans and had been trading with them for years. British rulers often squabbled with each other, and deposed kings knew where to go for help. The King of the Atrebates, Verica, had been expelled by the brothers Caratacus and Togodumnus, and his kingdom had been absorbed into theirs as part of their aggressive expansion policies. Verica fled to Rome and the two brothers demanded his return. The Romans of the Republic had been in this position before, several times, and the intervention usually resulted in annexation. Claudius decided to take up the challenge. Besides, Britain was a stronghold of the Druids, and Claudius was determined to suppress the cult. He assembled four legions, three from the Rhine and one from Pannonia, and placed Aulus Plautius Silvanus in command. The Romans made steady progress, until it was considered safe for the Emperor himself to visit the new province, bringing with him some war elephants to impress the natives. The conquest was by no means complete when Claudius died, but despite various reversals, successive emperors tenaciously held onto Britain, until Honorius withdrew the troops in 410.

The annexation of new territories greatly enhanced Claudius's reputation, earning him the respect of the Senate and the people, and several acclamations as *Imperator* from the army, assiduously numbered by the emperors and utilized on inscriptions as part of their titles. Claudius achieved twenty-seven acclamations in all, and was proud of his military reputation, even though it was achieved via his generals. The work of Aulus Plautius in Britain was continued by Publius Ostorius Scapula and Aulus Didius Gallus, and on the Rhine, Domitius Corbulo strengthened the Rhine frontier.

After annexation, Claudius did not simply exploit the new provinces. He took great care of the whole Empire, fostering Romanization where there was a willing population, extending Roman citizenship and Latin rights to various communities, founding Roman colonies (*coloniae*) and building roads. He admitted some of the enfranchised Gallic nobility to the Senate, not without some disapproval from existing senators, among whom a joke circulated that they would refuse to show the new Gallic senators the way to the Senate House. Such snobbery persisted, but Claudius laid the foundations of a more cosmopolitan senatorial order, in which the provincials gradually played a greater part, without obliterating the Roman and Italian senatorial class.

With an energy and enthusiasm that belied his age and his semi-obscure background, Claudius launched into every detail of administration. He centralized and expanded the administrative machinery, by dividing its functions into groups and placing a secretary over each. These were mostly freedmen, though some equestrians were given posts in the central administration. Finances were looked after by Pallas, the freedman secretary *a rationibus*, correspondence by the *ab epistulis*, a post held by Narcissus. The library and archives were supervised by *a studiis*, legal matters and petitions by *a cognitionibus* and *a libellis*. This is the product of an analytical mind anxious to bring everything under control, and Claudius's system endured. The Emperor also improved the water supply for the city of Rome, extended the boundary (*pomerium*) and improved communications in Italy by building roads to the coast and to the Alps. He built a new harbour at Ostia, the port of Rome, and tried to increase trade and to improve agriculture.

In his personal life Claudius was less successful. His marriage to Messalina ended in scandal and her execution, and his subsequent choice of spouse led to his own death. He married the younger Agrippina, daughter of Germanicus and Agrippina the elder, hence Claudius's niece. It was not a love match, but might have secured the succession if only Agrippina's ambition and the character of her son Lucius had been more moderate. Lucius was Agrippina's son by her first husband, Gnaeus Domitius Ahenobarbus, and on his adoption he took the name Nero Claudius Caesar. He was quickly betrothed to Claudius's daughter Octavia, and rapidly began to eclipse Claudius's son Britannicus who was much younger than Nero. Agrippina, inordinately ambitious for power, was instrumental in the rise of her son, through whom she hoped to rule the whole Roman world.

Claudius promoted Nero as Augustus would have done, designating him consul for the year 58, by which time he would perhaps have been considered mature enough, and appointing him as city prefect. In 53 he married Octavia, and in the following year, when Nero was sixteen and his acceptance as heir to the throne was secured, Claudius died. He was probably poisoned by Agrippina, who could not afford to wait for her husband to expire naturally, in case that took a long time, allowing Nero to extricate himself from her control. Without protest from the Praetorians, the Senate, the people or the army, Nero became emperor on 13 October, 54.

Nero AD 54–68

The three most important individuals who guided the young Emperor were his mother Agrippina, the Praetorian Prefect Sextus Afranius Burrus, and Lucius Annaeus Seneca, who had been brought back to Rome from exile by Claudius to be tutor to Nero and Britannicus. Agrippina's power was greater than any of the Imperial women had so far enjoyed. Coins were issued with her head on the obverse, whereas Imperial women were normally depicted on the reverse, subordinate to the emperor.

The first task was to ensure the loyalty of the Praetorians by distributing cash to each man. The people would be similarly tamed via cash payments, and kept entertained with the usual games and shows. But first Nero must be made secure closer to home. There were some immediate changes of personnel. Claudius's freedman secretary Narcissus was executed, and Pallas was removed from his post, even though he was favourable to Agrippina, and perhaps had been her lover when she was making her way into Imperial power. Britannicus, Claudius's son, was poisoned in 55, and some years later in 62, Nero's wife Octavia was also killed. No one rose up to avenge Claudius's children. With all potential rivals removed in the first years of Nero's reign, Agrippina tried to control her son, but was eventually removed from the palace in 56, leaving Nero in the hands of Burrus and Seneca, whose influence was effective, sound and beneficial for the Empire until 62. They allowed Nero to imagine that all the ideas for government sprang from him, while he pursued his interests in art and literature.

Inevitably, as he grew older Nero began to demand greater independence. The most important obstacle to achieving it was his mother, so he planned to have her permanently removed by scuttling the boat in which she was to make a journey, but although it sank she managed to reach the shore at Baiae. If she thought that she had been the victim of an accident she was quickly made aware of the truth. On Nero's orders, the Prefect of the Fleet at Misenum sent some sailors to kill her. Nero lay low for a while, but when he realized that there was to be no retribution, save for a dent in his popularity, he also realized that he could do as he wished.

In 62 the Praetorian Prefect Burrus died, thus removing one of the better influences on Nero's behaviour. He chose two new Praetorian Prefects, promoting the Prefect of the *Vigiles*, Ofonius Tigellinus, and the Prefect of the Annona, Faenius Rufus. These men were no friends of Seneca, and he chose to recede out of the limelight and pursue his private studies.

Nero then turned on his wife. He divorced and then murdered Octavia, which highly displeased the populace. But once again, only Nero's image suffered. There was nothing anyone could do about his actions. Autocratic rule began again in Rome.

Distant relatives of the Imperial family were singled out and removed. In 62 Nero murdered a grandson of Tiberius called Rubellius Plautus, and the son-in-law of Claudius, Cornelius Sulla. In 64, Didius Junius Silanus was driven to suicide because he was descended from Augustus. Just as previous emperors had done, Nero revived the treason laws. On the whole Nero ignored and despised the Senate, but he clearly did not ignore individuals. Senators began to fear wider persecutions. Having alienated the senatorial class, Nero also succeeded in alienating the populace in Rome. The fire that destroyed much of the city in 64 did nothing to enhance his reputation, since it was rumoured that he had started it deliberately, even though he was not in the city at the time, and made strenuous efforts to bring the fire under control, and he also relieved the people who had lost their homes and livelihoods. If his actions had ended there he may have been able to raise his reputation by several notches, but he blamed the Christians for starting the fire and embarked on religious persecution, possibly confined to the city and not spreading all over the Empire. In this the people were mostly supportive, since the Christians were not popular. Then it was made clear that Nero was not going to rebuild housing and restore the city, but he was going to flatten several acres of what was left and build an unimaginably large palace complex, the famous *Domus Aurea*, so that he could be properly housed at last.

In the provinces, Nero relied upon his generals as Claudius had done, but did not treat them so well. The British rebellion of Boudicca in 60 cost many lives and was only put down after tremendous destruction of the three main cities that had been founded at Colchester (Camulodunum), where a colony had been established for veterans of the Twentieth legion, and St Albans (Verulamium) and London (Londinium). The general

Suetonius Paullinus, diverted from his attack on the Druid stronghold in Anglesey, hurried to London, but then abandoned the south and withdrew to assemble his troops somewhere in the Midlands to meet Boudicca head-on. He won the battle but re-establishing control of the province and pacifying it took much longer. Suetonius was recalled because he treated the natives too harshly, and more lenient governors were sent out, whose background was not military but administrative and legal. This is probably the work of Seneca and Burrus, who were still able to influence the young Emperor at the time.

At the very beginning of Nero's reign the Parthians had overrun Armenia. Gnaeus Domitius Corbulo, who had successfully pacified the Rhine frontier under Claudius, was sent out to drive the Parthians back. He did so, campaigning in the difficult terrain of Armenia for several years. He was made governor of Syria in 60 and for the next few years he kept the eastern part of the Roman world secure. He commanded a large territory and large armies, until Nero realized that such a powerful general represented a threat, and drove him to suicide in 67. In the previous year, the Jewish revolt had begun in Judaea, necessitating Roman intervention. Nero appointed Gaius Licinius Mucianus as governor of Syria, and gave the command in Judaea to Titus Flavius Vespasianus, allegedly as punishment for dozing off while the Emperor recited poetry on his tour of Greece. But Vespasian was a tried and tested soldier who had commanded a legion in the invasion of Britain, and had served as governor of Africa. The world was soon to hear more of Mucianus and Vespasian.

Towards the end of his reign, Nero had offended and frightened most of the classes of Roman society. Like Gaius Caligula he had emptied the treasury and began to have wealthy men murdered so that he could take over their property. A plot was formed to remove him in 65, and replace him with a senator called Gaius Calpurnius Piso, but it was discovered and the ringleaders were executed. The Praetorian Prefect Tigellinus set up a secret service to watch people, and another reign of terror began. It was aimed principally at the nobility, but in reality no one was safe. Meanwhile, Nero proclaimed himself a living god, and toured Greece where he entered literary and artistic competitions and was awarded all the prizes, some of which he received without having even entered the competition. It could not continue in this vein.

The protest began in spring 68 with a short-lived revolt in Gaul led by Gaius Julius Vindex, the governor of a Gallic province, but it is not certain which one. The governor of Upper Germany, Lucius Verginius Rufus, quelled the rebellion, but made it clear that he did not want to be emperor himself, and declared his loyalty to the Senate, not to Nero. At the same time in Spain, Servius Sulpicius Galba at first supported Vindex, then struck out on his own with the intention of replacing Nero. One of his supporters in Rome, Nymphidius Sabinus, acting on Galba's behalf, offered 30,000 sesterces to each Praetorian guardsman. It was now too late for Nero to act, even if he had possessed the means to do anything. He had alienated everyone and had not cultivated the soldiers. On 9 June 68 he committed suicide, with a little help from his friends, and Galba found that he had bought the Empire.

During the years from the fall of Alexandria to the death of Nero, the administrative systems of the Empire, and the organization of the army, were gradually adapted and developed. The Imperial government did not spring fully fledged from Augustus's head, nor did he start out in 30 BC with a master plan that he intended to put into effect. He felt his way slowly to avoid controversy, adapted to circumstances, and sometimes had to backtrack and start again. When he died, the machinery of government was not finalized. Tiberius and Claudius were the men who refined and shaped the system, and their successors adapted it as circumstances changed.

Ruling the Roman world without the benefit of modern communications defies the imagination. Many different lands and peoples made up the Roman Empire. Economically and administratively the various nationalities were part of a unified whole but they were not entirely subsumed by Romanization, which was not actively enforced but encouraged where the provincials expressed an interest. The administration of such a large and diverse territory was tidied up by Claudius, whose system survived, with adjustments, until the fourth century.

As the Empire grew, one factor that provided a measure of cohesion was the Imperial cult. The Romans subscribed readily enough to the concept of deification of prominent men after their deaths, but the evolved form of the Imperial cult included worship of the deceased members of the Imperial families, and the spirit (*numen* or *genius*) of living ones. This bestowed on the emperors a sacrosanctity that was to play a large part in Imperial rule in the third century.

Under Augustus, a limited social mobility had begun, cutting across the snobbery of the Roman upper classes by allowing men from humble backgrounds to become senators, with access to the higher offices of state. The composition of the Senate changed as successive emperors allowed Italian equestrians, then provincials to enter its ranks. The process continued throughout the history of the Empire, but although the elevation of provincials was an honour, the power of the Senate declined because even the most conciliatory emperors could not allow the Senate to direct policy. All the Julio-Claudians began by establishing good relations with the senators, and then to varying degrees soured the relationship by either ignoring them, or actively persecuting them.

In the provinces there was a gradual extension of citizenship or Latin rights, a policy that had been in existence since Augustus's day, but was usually limited to deserving individuals or members of local government. Claudius extended citizenship to whole peoples, providing a pattern for future emperors to follow. The Republican attitude towards the provinces as territories to be exploited was replaced by integration. Tiberius was concerned to alleviate tax burdens, because he realized that squeezing the provincials dry was not conducive to long-term, steady profits.

Behind all the innovation and growth of the Empire was the army. It was the soldiers and their commanders who conquered new territory, protected it and helped to administer it. The vast extent of the provinces and the need to protect their boundaries required a large standing army, with regular recruitment, adequate pay, and provision for retirement. Augustus provided all this, and successive emperors refined the system. The legions were well established by the end of Nero's reign, but the auxiliary troops were still under development. Some units fought like their predecessors during the Republic, under their own native commanders, and they often served near their homes. The regular infantry and cavalry units of the later first century, with specified terms of service and tangible rewards on retirement, were still to be established. Wise emperors attended to the troops, and to their commanders, since they all knew that it was the soldiers who could create and dismiss emperors, over and above the wishes of the Senate or the people of Rome. This was to be made painfully apparent in the year following the death of Nero.

3

Expanding Empire:
Pushing the Boundaries
AD 69–117

Galba AD 68–69 & Otho AD 69

Servius Sulpicius Galba was in his seventies when he was declared emperor, a member of the senatorial aristocracy, but not related in any way to the Julio-Claudian family. He adopted the name Caesar in order to engender loyalty among the armies, since the soldiers were loyal to the Julian house, and the name, which eventually became a title, established Galba as the successor of Nero. The adoption of the name pacified the armies for a while, and Galba's pretence that he was acting on behalf of the Senate served to mollify the senators, who recognized him as emperor and conferred Imperial powers upon him. He arrived in Rome in the autumn of 68 with his supporters. One of these was Marcus Salvius Otho, who had been governor of Lusitania for the last ten years. Nero had sent him there in order to steal his wife Poppaea, whom he married as soon as she was divorced, and it seemed that the lady herself was not unwilling.

Galba made several mistakes. He encountered feeble opposition from Clodius Macer in Africa, but with only one legion Macer had no real chance of prevailing against the troops of Galba, who easily arranged his assassination. He also persuaded Fabius Valens, a legionary commander, to murder the governor of Lower Germany, Fonteius Capito. Galba replaced him with one of his supporters, Aulus Vitellius, an appointment that was to contribute to the chaos of the year 69, called the 'Year of Four Emperors'.

Galba eradicated Nero's soldiers and supporters in Rome, instead of trying to win them over or to buy them, but his stern principles would not allow him to pay money for loyalty. This was perhaps the biggest mistake of all, because he also reneged on his offer of 30,000 sesterces for each of the Praetorians, who never received anything from him, and therefore conceived of him as untrustworthy. Perhaps it would not have been so irritating if he had not rewarded his supporters from Gaul, but he was so obviously partisan, conferring appointments on his own followers, that he alienated many men who might otherwise have helped him.

At the beginning of 69, news arrived of the discontent of the armies, in particular the legions of Upper Germany, who refused to take the oath of loyalty to the Emperor. Then the troops of Lower Germany declared for the new governor Vitellius. He accepted their proclamation and made plans to march on Rome. Fabius Valens and Aulus Caecina Alienus, recently appointed legionary legate in Upper Germany, joined with Vitellius.

In Rome, Galba tried to strengthen his regime by adopting an heir, choosing Lucius Calpurnius Piso, who had little claim to fame save for the fact that he was the brother of a man who had plotted against Nero. The choice was unfortunate, because Otho had assisted Galba from the beginning and had expected that if a successor was to be named, then it should have been himself. Otho did not find it difficult to win over the Praetorians, who made him emperor and murdered Galba. Otho took the name Caesar as Galba had done, but he had more credibility as the successor of the Julians than Galba had enjoyed. Unfortunately his reign was to be very short. He had the support of several legions, on the Danube and in the east, but they were nowhere near Rome, so even if they set off to help him they would not arrive for some considerable time. Consequently he was vastly outnumbered by Vitellius's troops.

Vitellius was approaching Italy, marching a little more slowly behind two advance columns under Valens and Caecina who crossed the Alps via the Mont Genevre and St Bernard passes. Otho tried to prevent Valens and Caecina from crossing the River Po, having vacillated too long to send troops to block the passes. Between Cremona and Bedriacum, Otho's generals Suetonius Paullinus and Celsus, with very few troops, almost stopped Caecina, but ultimately failed. Suetonius advised Otho not to engage the enemy until more soldiers had arrived from Dalmatia, but Otho was concerned that the Vitellians would also build up more support and more military strength, so risked fighting near Cremona. He was defeated. He said that he did not wish to involve everyone in civil war, told his supporters to declare for Vitellius, and committed suicide.

Vitellius AD 69

The Senate acknowledged and conferred powers on Vitellius, who was still in Gaul. He prudently sent many of his troops back to their bases, but when he eventually arrived in Rome he was dressed like a conquering hero, at the head of 60,000 troops. The soldiers ran riot in the city. It was disquieting to find that Vitellius had no control over them, and nor did anyone else. The Praetorians were all dismissed and replaced with Vitellius's German troops. It did not bode well for the future, but it did provide the excuse for the governors of Judaea and Syria to start their campaign to rescue Rome from Vitellius, which was their official party line after the event.

Nero had appointed Mucianus as governor of Syria and Vespasian as governor of Judaea, where the Jewish revolt was still not quelled. The two men corresponded with each other via Vespasian's son Titus. They did not reveal their hand until July, but the supposedly spontaneous acclamation of Vespasian as emperor presumably required quite a lot of intrigue and forward planning. When they heard of Nero's death and the proclamation of Galba, Vespasian and Mucianus would have to decide what to do. Even if they disapproved of what was happening in Rome, it would not be wise to ask the soldiers to withhold the oath of allegiance to whoever was emperor since it would signal rebellion. So they played the game until they were ready, and at the beginning of July the troops in Egypt, Judaea and Syria in quick succession declared for Vespasian.

When the news of the events in the eastern provinces reached Rome, Vespasian's brother Flavius Sabinus, and his younger son Domitian, aged about eighteen, were in some danger. Sabinus had been city prefect under Nero. Galba removed him from office. Unlike other associates of Nero his life was spared, possibly because his brother Vespasian was in command of legions in Judaea, and it was not prudent to irritate such commanders. Otho reinstated Sabinus, who retained his office and kept order in the city until Vitellius arrived in the summer. Now, with Vespasian as rival emperor, Vitellius put Sabinus and Domitian under house arrest.

Meanwhile, the Flavian troops began to move towards Rome. Mucianus set off on the overland route from Syria, preceded by the legions of Pannonia under Antonius Primus, who was closer to Italy. At Cremona, Primus met Vitellius's troops commanded by Caecina, who tried to negotiate, possibly to ingratiate himself with the side that looked most likely to win. Caecina's own soldiers arrested him, and the second battle of Cremona was fought and won by Antonius Primus. Unfortunately Primus was either unwilling or unable to prevent his army from sacking the town. Had he stopped the carnage, he may have fared better under Vespasian. As Primus's troops approached Rome, Vitellius abdicated, and Sabinus celebrated a peaceful outcome, prematurely, as it turned out. It soon became obvious that Vitellius could not persuade his adherents to lie down meekly and accept Vespasian as emperor. They vented their anger and disappointment on the Flavian party, and soon Sabinus and his friends fled to the Capitol

Hill, barricading themselves in by using anything they could find, including some statues, to block access. Sabinus sent for Domitian, but not long after he had arrived, the Vitellians stormed the temporary stronghold. Sabinus was killed, but Domitian escaped, allegedly by mingling with a procession of priests of Isis, and then perhaps by hiding at a friend's house.

Fortunately, Antonius Primus arrived in time to prevent a witch hunt, but his soldiers ran riot just as Vitellius's troops had done when they arrived in the city. This outrage, combined with the sack of Cremona, cast an unfavourable light on Vespasian, who wished for a squeaky clean beginning for his reign. Antonius Primus had done more than anyone to help the Flavians to gain power, but he was sacrificed for the sake of appearances, eventually retiring to Gaul. When Mucianus arrived in Rome, he could take the credit for restoring order, all part of the Flavian mythology established after the event and disseminated by the literary work of Flavius Josephus, who was at first one of the leaders of the Jewish revolt, and afterwards a partisan of Vespasian and Titus.

Vespasian AD 69–79

The Senate accepted Vespasian's rule, making the new Emperor and his son Titus consuls, and Domitian urban praetor with consular powers. Vespasian himself did not set out from the east until peace was restored in Rome. He had halted operations against the Jews after Nero's suicide, waiting to see what would happen next. He put Titus in charge of the mopping up in Judaea, and arrived in Rome probably at the end of the year 70, though different dates are favoured by different authors.

A law was passed conferring Imperial powers on Vespasian (*lex de Imperio Vespasiani*). In accordance with normal custom, Vespasian would have dated the beginning of his reign, his *dies imperii*, from the date when the law was passed, but being too honest and too realistic about the way in which he had become emperor, he dated his reign from the beginning of July when the troops in Alexandria had acclaimed him. Some of the text of this law survives on a bronze tablet from Rome. There is debate about the lost portions and the nature of the law in general. The Senate traditionally formulated the law to confer power on the Emperors, and the people's assembly passed it. It is not certain whether the law concerning Vespasian was based on the exact texts of previous bestowals of Imperial powers, or whether it was amended because this was a special case. Some scholars have suggested that after the disastrous reign of Nero there was an attempt to limit the powers accorded to Vespasian. This seems unlikely. Vespasian would know perfectly well what was normally entailed in the conferment of power, and would not countenance any curtailment or restrictions. He required all the support that he could summon for his reign, especially the law which made it legal. He was the first emperor who was not remotely related to the Julio-Claudians. He was an Italian, or more precisely a Sabine born in the town of Reate. He was most definitely not a member of the Roman senatorial aristocracy. Worse still, in the eyes of this clique of aristocrats, he belonged to an equestrian family, not a senatorial one. His brother Sabinus had become a senator long before Vespasian, who initially seemed reluctant to improve upon his equestrian status. It was said that for a few years he had bought and sold mules for a living. He was therefore not the sort of man who would inspire loyalty among the senators. But his track record as a military man was secure. In the invasion of Britain under Claudius he had been a legionary commander and had stormed the British hill fort of Maiden Castle in Dorset, and he had served in Germany and Thrace. His appointment to the command in Judaea may have been partly as a punishment for not enthusing about Nero's literary prowess, but it was a sound choice.

The suppression of the Jewish revolt was the task of Vespasian's son Titus. He took Jerusalem in 70, destroying the Temple and subduing all but a few of the rebels, who held out for a few more years. The most famous episode of these years is the siege and eventual fall of Masada, where nearly 400

Jews killed themselves in 73 rather than submit to the Romans. Another revolt, contemporary with the rebellion in Judaea, occurred in Gaul and Germany, led by Julius Civilis, a Batavian who had served in the Roman army and been given Roman citizenship. At the beginning of the revolt he declared that he was a supporter of Vespasian, but it quickly became a fully fledged rebellion against Roman rule. Most, but not all, of the Germanic tribes of the Rhineland joined Civilis, but of the Gallic tribes, several refused to rally to his standard and remained loyal to Rome. Civilis had the advantage that the Rhine legions were very much under strength, since many men had accompanied Vitellius to Rome, so the Roman commanders had to disperse their few remaining troops to deal with attacks from the rebels. The situation deteriorated rapidly, several Roman forts were destroyed, the colonies of Cologne and Trier were captured, and as a result of these successes, more of the Gauls came over to Civilis. When Mucianus reached Rome and restored order, he gathered some of the troops that Vitellius had brought with him, and sent them back to the Rhine, commanded by Petillius Cerialis. Two more legions, one from Britain and one from Spain joined Cerialis, who concentrated on the recovery of the Rhine, while at the same time Annius Gallus with four legions operated against the tribe of the Lingones. Between them the two commanders suppressed the revolt, but the number of troops that had been assembled for the task indicates how serious the rebellion was. Civilis surrendered to Cerialis, and Vespasian strengthened the Rhine garrison.

As a prime consideration Vespasian needed to consolidate his power and to ensure that he would retain it. As Galba and Otho had done, he adopted the name Caesar, but went one stage further by also incorporating the titles Imperator and Augustus into his name. His official nomenclature was *Imperator Caesar Vespasianus Augustus*, which set the pattern for future emperors. The use of *Imperator* as a name is to be distinguished from the victory titles accrued via (allegedly) spontaneous acclamations by the troops, which were so assiduously collected and numbered by the non-military Claudius, and later by Domitian, who did much more than just accompanying his armies on campaign. All the emperors displayed on inscriptions and in official correspondence the number of times they had been saluted as Imperator, as well as using the term as part of their names.

Since the support of the military was essential to all emperors, Vespasian reconstituted the Praetorian Guard that Vitellius had dismissed, and to make doubly sure of its loyalty he made Titus Praetorian Prefect, keeping the important posts within the family. The Praetorians could make or break emperors, but so could the armies in the provinces, as Vespasian was only too well aware. The historian Tacitus would describe laconically how the secret of empire was revealed during the civil disturbances of 68 to 69, and emperors could be made in places far from Rome itself. The armies, therefore, had to be befriended and fostered. When Julius Civilis led the revolt in Gaul, it showed how nationalist feelings still predominated even after more than a century of Roman rule. Civilis was a dangerous enemy. Having served as a commander of an auxiliary unit in the Roman army, he was fully conversant with Roman military methods and how to combat them. The auxiliary troops of Republican times had been allowed to fight under their own commanders and were often disbanded when the wars ended. The same situation pertained under Augustus and the early emperors, but now the *auxilia* had to be reorganized, and made a regular part of the standing army established by Augustus. As the Empire expanded, the troops moved further away from Rome towards the edges of Roman territory. Auxiliary troops fighting close to home under their own tribal leaders could be potentially dangerous, and yet the extra manpower and expertise could not be discarded altogether. From Vespasian onwards, auxiliaries were raised from tribes around the Empire but were sent far away from their homes, and were commanded by Roman officers. After they had completed their term of service of twenty-five years, they were given pensions and also

Roman citizenship, a privilege well worth having, as shown by the fact that there were several false claims on record, usually punishable by death.

Vespasian ignored the example of Augustus, who had not monopolized the consulship after he had established himself. Vespasian and both his sons were consuls many times. The succession was secured and made crystal clear. 'Either my sons shall succeed me, or no one' said the new Emperor, and set about elevating Titus, with Domitian in second place but still given some powers. In 71 he bestowed proconsular and tribunician power on Titus. Two years later, Vespasian and Titus assumed the office of censor, reviewing the Senate and bringing in new men from Italy and some of the provinces, mostly in the west. So many men had been killed in the 'Year of Four Emperors' that there were several vacancies to be filled. As Claudius had recognized, the days of an exclusively Roman Senate and jealously guarded Roman citizenship were over. The Empire would be made stronger if it became a commonwealth, with shared citizenship sensibly bestowed, and the expansion of social mobility with attainable goals in government and the army. Probably in connection with the census, a survey of agricultural land and produce was carried out, so that tax could be properly assessed and collected, with the incidental result that a transparent record of such assessments would leave no opportunity for cheating the provincials.

The provinces were encouraged, but not forced, to urbanize and Romanize. Colonies were founded, cities were granted municipal status, Latin rights were conferred on many communities in Spain, which was ready for demilitarization. Boundaries were adjusted and new territory taken in. In the east, the main focus was always on the activities of the Parthians, especially their interest in the kingdom of Armenia. Vespasian strengthened the territories bordering on the Parthian Empire, and those on the western borders of Armenia. He placed troops in Cappadocia, and annexed Commagene, which was administered as part of Syria, where the number of troops was increased. After Petillius Cerialis, who may have been Vespasian's son-in-law, had suppressed the revolt of Civilis, he was sent to Britain in 71. The rebellion of Boudicca in 60 had put an end to further expansion for several years, and governors had been chosen whose experience was in civil and juridical adminstration rather than in military matters. The governors concentrated on the repair of the damage and fostering better relations with the Britons. Vespasian reversed the policy of non-expansion, sending troops northwards into Brigantia, covering what is now Lancashire, Cumbria and much of Yorkshire. There was a valid excuse that made this a legitimate exercise. For many years the kingdom of Brigantia had been ruled by its queen Cartimandua, who was loyal to the Romans, but dissension within her kingdom had started before Boudicca's rebellion. Cartimandua's estranged husband Venutius had been building up his anti-Roman party for some time, and was finally strong enough to force his wife out of the kingdom. Appeals to Rome from British kings were not unusual, but were not always answered. In this case, the presence of a hostile king on the northern borders of the province of Britain could not be tolerated. Cerialis's campaigns are not well documented either in ancient literature or by archaeological methods, since it is difficult to put a precise enough date on the camps and forts that are known in the areas where he campaigned. The sites could have been established by Cerialis or by his successors, or could have been used more than once. Cerialis's exploits were considered satisfactory by Vespasian, who recalled him probably in 74. He was succeeded by Sextus Julius Frontinus, who turned aside from the north to concentrate on the integration of Wales, and then by Gnaeus Julius Agricola, whose exploits were recorded by his son-in-law, the historian Tacitus, and tend to overshadow the achievements of the previous governors. He was still in command, conquering northern Britain, when Vespasian died.

The decade of Vespasian's reign was mostly peaceful. Apart from the wars in Britain, and after the suppression of the Jews, there was no serious trouble in the Empire. It was mostly the philosophers, the Stoics and Cynics, who objected to Vespasian. Some of them were die-hard Republicans longing for a return to a mythically perfect form of rule that they had never experienced except in history books, elaborated by imagination and wishful thinking. Others would have tolerated kings if only they had been chosen from the best educated men of the aristocracy, and not from a recent member of the equestrian class who had once sold mules and relied upon the army to shore up his rule. At least Vespasian did not try to dissemble about his origins or the source of his power. There was a continual needling and mostly verbal opposition to Imperial rule in general and Vespasian in particular from Helvidius Priscus, whose family and friends had tried the same opposition to Nero and paid the penalty for it. Perhaps if Priscus had evolved a coherent policy, or formulated a list of demands for better government, or even tried to engage the Emperor in discussion, he may have been treated leniently and possibly scored some successes, but his policy seemed to have been one of random broadsides whenever there was an opportunity, and puerile rudeness combined with obstruction. Vespasian held out for a long time, but in the end the only way to stop the insults and pointless challenges was to execute a few of the perpetrators. The historian Suetonius hints darkly at genuine conspiracies, without giving any details, but it is known that two men were punished in 79 for plotting. Caecina, who had been defeated by Antonius Primus at Cremona, was executed, and a senator, Eprius Marcellus, committed suicide. These blots on Vespasian's reign hardly compare with the terrors of Caligula or Nero.

At the beginning of his reign, Vespasian found the treasury empty, and set about refilling it. Caligula's extravagances had been repaired by Claudius but all the profits that had accrued were frittered away by Nero after he had detached himself from the influence of his advisers. The census that Vespasian conducted and the survey of agricultural lands and produce informed him of the tax potential of the whole Empire, and he immediately began to collect revenues. While he toured Greece, Nero had granted tax immunity to the whole of Achaea, but Vespasian reversed the decision. He also invented new taxes, the most infamous being the tax on urine that the fullers collected outside their establishments. The ammonia content was the main agent in cleaning cloth. Titus protested but had to give in when Vespasian handed him some coins and asked if he could smell anything.

In concert with raising revenues, Vespasian put a brake on unnecessary expenditure. He spent money on worthy causes, such as road building in the provinces, and repair of damages caused by the civil war. In Rome, the buildings on the Capitol Hill had been destroyed or damaged when the Vitellians attacked the Flavians, so restoration of this symbolic site began when Mucianus arrived, presumably endorsed by Vespasian. The spoils taken from Judaea, when the Jewish revolt was crushed, financed the building of the Colosseum, the colloquial name for the Flavian amphitheatre, derived from its location, near the colossal statue of Nero that had stood in the grounds of his notorious Golden House.

By the end of Vespasian's reign, the treasury was in good health, and he left a flourishing empire after the years of peace. Vespasian died in 79, in his seventieth year, at his home town of Reate in the Sabine country. He asked to be helped to his feet so that he might die upright, and famously joked 'Dear me, I seem to be turning into a god'. He was right of course, since he was deified after his death. The succession was assured. Titus had shared all the major offices with Vespasian and had carried out much of the administrative work of the Empire. He succeeded his father unopposed.

Titus AD 79–81

The Emperor Titus, who ruled for only one year and two months, is difficult to assess. As a young man he was not popular with either the senators or the populace, but by the time of his accession he had learned how to win friends and influence people. According to the ancient sources he was generous to a fault, providing games and entertainments for the people and distributing lavish presents at most of them. He said that he considered the day lost if he had not been able to give gifts. He dedicated the Colosseum, and put on games for 100 days, and when he opened the new baths on part of the site of the Golden House, he organized gladiatorial shows to celebrate the event.

Two major disasters occurred while Titus was emperor, first the terrible eruption of Vesuvius that obliterated Pompeii and Herculaneum in 79, and then the fire in Rome in 80. Even these served to emphasize Titus's generosity, since he responded by providing men and money to help the victims. After the fire in Rome he sold much of his own property to contribute to the relief fund. Apart from these disasters, Titus's reign was depicted as a golden age. He had been the full partner of Vespasian and was therefore tried and tested before he came to power, but there was some opposition to his rule, mostly from the senatorial class who at the very least felt cheated of a share in government by Titus's continued monopolization of the consulship. Nevertheless no one was executed, there were no treason trials, and informers were driven out of the city.

It may have continued in this way if Titus had lived longer, but it is worth pointing out that if Caligula's and Nero's reigns had lasted for only two years, they too may have been considered generous and enlightened rulers. Another consideration is that the ancient authors would not be reluctant to praise his virtues and to laud his short reign as a sharp contrast to that of his universally detested brother Domitian, who succeeded him when Titus died of an unknown illness in September 81. He was deified by Domitian, about a month later.

Domitian AD 81–96

After Titus's death several stories circulated that Domitian had killed him, or at least hastened his demise, but the variety of methods that he was alleged to have used to despatch Titus give the lie to the tale, all supposition and no substance. Such rumours did not impede the succession. The troops hailed him as Imperator on the day of Titus's death, and on the following day the Senate confirmed Domitian as emperor, with the title Augustus. Within a few days of his accession, Domitian awarded the title Augusta to his wife, Domitia, the daughter of Domitius Corbulo. The precedent had been set by Augustus, who awarded the title to his wife Livia, and the next Imperial lady to receive it was Antonia, who was granted the title posthumously by her son Claudius. She had been awarded it by Caligula, but refused to accept it from his hands. Agrippina took the title as part of her plan to dominate the Roman world through her son Nero. From Domitian's reign onwards it became more common for the wives of emperors to take the title.

During his reign Domitian's titles proliferated. The preamble cited him as *Imperator Caesar divi Vespasiani filius Domitianus Augustus*, indicating that he was the son of the divine Vespasian, with the same titles as his father. Domitian was also *Pater Patriae* (father of his country, a highly honorific appellation) and Pontifex Maximus. More important, tribunician power was granted to him, and he commanded all the armies, with all military and civil appointment within his gift. His rule was assured, but to make certain he followed his father's example, and was also consul for ten years of his fifteen-year reign. He usually stepped down after a few months, giving the opportunity for other men to become suffect consuls and thereby gain experience of government, but during his tenure of the office, Domitian could put administrative measures into effect.

Like other emperors who ended badly, Domitian was said to have begun well. The documentary sources are universally hostile, but Suetonius, who wrote during Hadrian's reign, reports in three separate passages that Domitian's earlier behaviour contrasted sharply with that of his later years. At first he was generous like his brother, fair minded and just. Significantly, Suetonius says that Domitian's cruelty began after the suppression of the revolt of Saturninus in 89.

Domitian was a perfectionist, who would in modern parlance be labelled a control freak. His rule was autocratic, but at least at first it arose from his desire to attend to the smallest detail of government, concerned to oversee everything and do it properly. His administration was sound and sensible. The provinces were governed well, and he seems to have tried to curb extortion, with genuine motives, but he perhaps drove it underground instead. After Domitian's death, his successor Nerva could find very little among his enactments to repeal. His silver coinage was the most pure in content of any that had gone before or was issued afterwards. His buildings had to be magnificent, two examples being the *Domus Augustana*, his palace on the Palatine Hill in Rome, and his villa at Alba, where several centuries later, the summer residence of the Popes was built. The ambition to do nothing sordid or shabby extended to the way in which Domitian represented himself. Probably in 86, he decided that his title should be *dominus et deus*, lord and god. The first part of this title was just about acceptable. Pliny addressed Trajan as *dominus* without hesitation. It is the equivalent of 'master' as workers would address their employers, except that it was interpreted as an indication of how Domitian viewed everyone from the senators to the lowliest slaves. The populace had no trouble in acclaiming Domitian and Domitia as *domino et dominae* on feast days. *Deus* on the other hand, was more suspect. Domitian was the focus of the Imperial cult, but worship of the emperors was directed at their spirit, or *genius* rather than the mortal man. It was said that Domitian demanded obeisance as well, prefiguring the third century emperors who distanced themselves from their subjects in the same way.

At the beginning of his reign Domitian treated the senators with fairness but also with indifference. He tried to pre-empt potential opposition by a studied policy of conciliation, appointing the son of Helvidius Priscus, who had been a thorn in Vespasian's side, to the consulship, to show that there were no hard feelings. He held ten consulships himself but did not restrict access to his own extended family, allowing non-Flavians to take up the office. He continued his father's policy of promoting equestrians, appointing more and more of them to administrative posts, sometimes at the expense of freedmen, who had monopolized Claudius's centralized civil service. At least one equestrian, Lucius Julius Ursus was promoted to the Senate, and then the consulship, after serving as Praetorian Prefect. Another was temporarily appointed to take charge of a proconsular province when the governor was executed for reasons unknown.

The populace were kept entertained by the usual shows and games. On one memorable occasion the Colosseum was flooded to stage a naval battle. But although he attended all the shows, Domitian incurred the displeasure of the audience because he attended to his correspondence while supposedly watching the action. He courted popularity as many emperors did by distributing cash gifts (*congiaria*) to celebrate special occasions, in this case his victories over the German tribe of the Chatti, and the Dacians and the Sarmatians.

At the end of 82 Domitian started to overhaul the mint in Rome. As a committed perfectionist he issued silver coinage of a very high standard, but unfortunately had to devalue it later in his reign. In 83 he awarded a 33 per cent pay rise to the soldiers. It was long overdue, and also very unpopular with everyone except the armies. At some point in 82 or 83 he dismissed the freedman Tiberius Julius who had served under Vespasian and Titus as financial secretary, or *a rationibus*. It is not know who replaced him, or whether this was the first appointment of an equestrian to the post. The freedman Abascantus, secretary *ab epistulis*, whose name is known from the work of the poet Statius, was also dismissed and replaced by an equestrian, Titinius Capito. The rumour grew up that Domitian could not tolerate any of the staff who had worked under Titus and Vespasian, but it is more likely that he considered each case individually and appointed men he thought best suited to the task.

The way in which local government worked in the provinces is illustrated by three municipal charters from towns in Spain, all dated to Domitian's reign. The charters were modelled on the city of Rome, documenting in detail the rights and duties of municipal officials and the ordinary people. It is clear that the municipal authorities were allowed considerable freedom of action in governing their towns, hardly supporting the image of Domitian as oppressor. He continued the work that Vespasian had begun with regard to the provinces, but perhaps with a sense of detachment rather than a genuinely benevolent attitude. He responded to crises and specific needs. When he considered that the food supply was deficient in cereals, he tried to promote the production of grain by issuing an edict that forbade the planting of new vines in Italy, and removed half of the plantations in the rest of the Empire. The law has attracted much speculation as to Domitian's motives, but it probably was a sincere attempt to increase cereal production. In the end it was not practicable, and had to be withdrawn.

The reigns of Vespasian and Titus were not noted for military activity, except for the ongoing campaigns in northern Britain, but under Domitian there were additional actions on the Rhine and Danube. The general who was responsible for the conquest of northern England and most of Scotland was Gnaeus Julius Agricola, who took over from Cerialis and Frontinus and built on their work. He was unusual in that he had served in Britain twice already, as military tribune at the time of the rebellion of Boudicca, as legionary legate of the Twentieth legion, and now as governor of the province, probably from 78 to 84, though these opening and closing dates are much disputed. Most military officers served in different provinces as they were rising to prominence, rather than in the same one at different times. Agricola's career was also unusual in that he was governor of Britain for seven years instead of the more normal three of four. His campaigns on behalf of the Flavian emperors were described by the historian Tacitus, and there are several archaeological remains that illustrate the conquest, but unfortunately it is not so easy to marry up the literature with the archaeology. For the reign of Domitian, the most important question is when and why Agricola's conquests were given up, probably only two or three years after he had fought the final battle, completed the conquest, and left the province to his successor. Tacitus describes the withdrawal of troops with great bitterness, but it is possible that Domitian had good reasons to do so.

Perhaps in 82 or more likely 83, Domitian started a campaign in Germany against the tribesmen of the Chatti, who lived beyond the Rhine. The dates are disputed and the reasons for the war are not clear. The Chatti may have been raiding the province from their homelands, but this is not documented. They were formidable enemies. According to Tacitus, who would never have credited Domitian with a genuine achievement, the Chatti differed from other tribes in that they were united and organized, and could form plans and carry them out, unlike some other tribes. In the words of Tacitus, 'other Germans go to battle, the Chatti make war'.

Domitian raised a new legion called *I Minervia* in honour of his favourite goddess Minerva. This legion probably replaced *XXI Rapax* at Bonn, which accompanied Domitian on campaign, along with detachments from the four legions of Upper Germany. The army may have penetrated far into Chattan territory. The author Julius Frontinus, who had been governor of Britain before Agricola, says that Domitian covered 120 Roman miles on this campaign, which was once taken to mean that he established the frontier line of watchtowers and small forts enclosing the Taunus and Wetterau region of Germany. However, this frontier is probably Vespasian's, developed by Domitian, so Frontinus perhaps meant that Domitian penetrated for a considerable distance into Chattan territory. There is insufficient information to be sure when and in what manner this war ended. Domitian celebrated a triumph in 83, issued a *congiarium* to the populace of Rome in 84, and by 85 he had been acclaimed *Imperator* for the fifth time, but none of these events can be securely related to the Chattan war.

Shortly after the problems on the Rhine were solved, another war broke out on the Danube frontier. Probably in the winter of 85/86, though the date is uncertain, the Dacians crossed the river, defeated the Roman army in Moesia and killed the governor Oppius Sabinus. There may be a connection with the abandonment of Agricola's conquests in Britain and the outbreak of this war, when Domitian needed troops and may have taken some from the British garrison. Coin evidence indicates that Roman troops were in Scotland long enough to receive issues of bronze coins of 86 in their pay, but there are no examples of issues of 87 from the same sites. This suggests that troops were suddenly withdrawn from the newly established forts in Scotland, perhaps because detachments were assembled for Domitian's war, either to strengthen the Rhine frontier while troops from there went to Dacia, or to go direct to the Danube. Despite the expenditure of much ink or keyboard skills, no such connection between the Dacian war and Britain has been conclusively demonstrated to the satisfaction of all parties.

Dacian territory corresponds roughly to modern Romania, with the Carpathian mountains as the stronghold. The Dacians were fearsome fighters, led by Decebalus, who had been building up a power base for some time. He had perhaps removed the original chief Diurpaneus, who seems to have started the war. These Dacian leaders were not the first to unify the tribesmen. In the reign of Augustus, the Dacians were potentially just as troublesome, under their chief Burebista. Other tribes from the vast territory beyond the Danube had successfully attacked Roman territory and been repulsed, the Roxolani in 67, and the Sarmatians in 69, taking advantage of the turmoil of the civil war in Rome. Mucianus repelled them on his journey from Syria to Italy. In the following year they attacked again, defeating the Romans and killing the governor of Moesia, Fonteius Agrippa. Vespasian sent out a new governor, Rubrius Gallus, who restored order, and strengthened the frontier according to Vespasian's orders. Domitian's problems on the Danube were therefore not new.

The reasons why the Dacians invaded are unknown. There may have been pressure from other tribes, or a shortage of lands, or they may have become alarmed at Domitian's success against the Chatti, and decided to attack before the Romans attacked them. Domitian responded as rapidly as possible, collecting an army with the Praetorian Prefect Cornelius Fuscus in command, and set off with the troops to the Danube. Little is known about the progress of the war, but between February and September 86 Domitian was hailed as *Imperator* by the troops three times, making his total up to fourteen. Victories of some kind are indicated, but probably in the following year, Cornelius Fuscus mounted what should have been a punitive expedition across the Danube and was defeated and killed. There seems to have been a hiatus while Domitian collected another army, and devoted some time to thorough preparation and reconnaissance. He may also have divided Moesia into two provinces at this time, called Moesia Superior and Moesia Inferior. The governors of these two provinces, Funisulanus Vettonianus and Curiatius Maternus, were both rewarded by Domitian, perhaps for work in stabilizing the frontier. The result of the long preparation was a victory at a site called Tapae, under Tettius Julianus, dated without conclusive proof to 88. There is no record of a peace treaty or even a proper conclusion to the war. When he was assassinated, Domitian was preparing for another Danube campaign, indicating that Decebalus had not been subdued. The Dacians may have been bought off with cash payments, since in January 89 Domitian was faced with a rebellion by the Roman commander in Upper Germany, Lucius Antonius Saturninus.

Saturninus could call upon four legions, two based at Mainz, and one each at Vindonissa (modern Windisch) and one at Argentorate (modern Strasburg). His aims are not clear, but his discontent coupled with the precedent of Vitellius's march on Rome twenty years before may have spurred him on to attempt to usurp Domitian. On his way from Rome to Mainz, Domitian summoned the single legion from Spain, *VII Gemina*, which was commanded by Marcus Ulpius Trajanus, the future Emperor Trajan. Before they reached Mainz, the commander in Lower Germany, Aulus Buccius Lappius Maximus, had attacked and defeated Saturninus. His legions received the honorary title *pia fidelis Domitiana*, but the latter part of this title was dropped after Domitian's assassination.

Retribution was swift and gruesome. Partisans of Saturninus were hunted down and killed, and although no senators were punished because there was no proof that any of them had been involved, Domitian was probably left wondering about how many of them knew about the plot. Suetonius says that Domitian became more suspicious and cruel after the revolt, which may well be true. The Emperor had tried somewhat dispassionately to foster good relations with the Senate, but he had felt quite secure with the army, and now that was shattered. From now onwards, there were to be no double legionary fortresses such as that at Mainz, because too many soldiers stationed in one place would be useful to future usurpers. Domitian also restricted the amount of money that could be held in the soldiers' savings accounts in the fort headquarters to 1,000 sesterces, because Saturninus had used all the cash at the fortresses to finance the rebellion.

As soon as the rebellion been put down, news arrived of trouble in Pannonia, where Domitian arrived probably in the spring of 89. The tribes of the Marcomanni and Quadi constituted the main threat to Roman security, but the official excuse for the war against them was that they had not sent help for the campaign against the Dacians. At about this time, Domitian made a treaty with the Dacians, which he does not seem to have arranged before withdrawing from their territory after the battle at Tapae. By the terms of this treaty, Dacia became a client state of Rome. Client kings received the title *Rex sociusque amicus*, friend and ally of the Roman people. The Dacians received subsidies and Roman assistance to build forts to defend themselves against other tribes. The payment of subsidies was a system of external control that the Romans had used before and would use throughout their history, in order to keep the leader of a tribe well disposed to Rome, and willing to control his own people. The system was employed to good effect later, in the second century, by the Emperor Hadrian to ensure peace beyond the frontiers. It was never a popular scheme with the Senate and people of Rome because it looked like tribute from a weaker state to a stronger one, and in Domitian's case the terms of the treaty caused enormous discontent, most especially because of the assistance in fort building. When the next war was waged by the Emperor Trajan, the forts had to be taken and destroyed.

One of the terms of the treaty allowed the Romans to march through Dacian territory to attack the Marcomanni and Quadi. Little is known about the course of the war against these tribes, except that the number of legions in Pannonia was increased from two to four, while no other province held more than three. Furthermore, although Domitian held a triumph at the end of 89 over the Dacians, and the Chatti, which really meant Saturninus, he held none over the Marcommani. The Danube wars were not finished, and broke out again in 92. This time, Domitian may have been engaged on two fronts, fighting the Sarmatians as well as the Marcomanni, but the evidence used to support this theory, documenting awards to military officers for their exploits in a war against Germans and Sarmatians, is not securely dated to Domitian's reign.

At the end of the war of 92 on the Danube, the Empire was predominantly peaceful. Domitian attended to the defence of the provinces, continuing Vespasian's and Titus's work. He did not annexe Dacia after the Danube campaigns and made no attempt to regain Scotland after the troops were withdrawn. The eastern provinces were quiet for the time being, since the Parthians were not aggressive, perhaps because there were now six legions to defend the frontier, one in Judaea, two in Cappadocia and three in Syria. In the west, the Rhine ceased to be the main theatre of war, while on the Danube the numbers of troops increased to meet an escalating threat. After the assassination of Domitian this threat was ultimately left to Trajan to deal with.

Most of the disturbance was now focused on Rome itself, where the reign of terror had begun. In 91, Domitian had executed Cornelia, a Vestal Virgin who had been found guilty of immoral relations with more than one man. The ancient penalty for Vestal Virgins who reneged on their vow of chastity was to be buried alive, and Domitian insisted on the strict application of the law. Allegedly it was Cornelia's second offence, so Domitian could not afford to acquit her when she merited punishment, but the barbarity of the punishment was held against him. A series of executions took place in 93, beginning with Herennius Senecio, the author of a work praising Helvidius Priscus, Vespasian's opponent. Arulenus Rusticus was next, for writing about Thrasea Paetus, related to Priscus and another opponent of Imperial rule. The younger Helvidius had written a play parodying Domitian's household, so despite having promoted him to the consulship, Domitian executed him too. The episode was particularly sordid because the senators, eager to exonerate themselves perhaps, manhandled Priscus to prison. All these victims were Stoics, related to each other by marriage ties, and the women of their families were exiled.

More senators were executed in the following years, for reasons that may be deliberately obscured in the sources, to portray them as the unpredictable whims of an unhinged tyrant. Acilius Glabrio was forced to fight in the arena, on account of his impiety, and Domitian's cousin Titus Flavius Clemens was executed for atheism. Salvius Cocceianus unwisely celebrated the birthday of his kinsman Otho, the emperor of 69, and was therefore executed for having designs on usurping the throne. Pompusianus was despatched because he read the speeches of famous generals, and went about carrying a map of the world. There were more examples, but the point has been made that executions became more and more commonplace, for improbable reasons. The victims may have been involved in plots against Domitian, but the number of executions could only foment more plots as senators and equites feared for their lives.

Domitian used to say that no one would believe him if he said men were plotting against him until he was dead. The tragedy is that when the final conspiracy was formed it started not among the senators but very close to home. It was the members of his own household staff who killed him, allegedly with the consent of his wife Domitia. No senators were ever proven to have been part of the conspiracy but the alacrity with which the aged senator Marcus Cocceius Nerva was proclaimed emperor suggests that at least some leading men were informed of the plot and were ready and waiting to act once the assassination had occurred.

Domitian was forty-five years old when he was killed on 18 September 96. He was almost universally detested, except for the populace of Rome, who remained largely indifferent. Only the Praetorians mourned his loss. His memory was damned, and the historian Tacitus made sure that he remained so for all time.

Nerva AD 96–98

The accession of the Emperor Nerva was accomplished without a hitch, so smoothly in fact that it is assumed that he must have been a party to the assassination plot and had been waiting in the wings for his stage entrance. He was not the designated heir of the previous emperor, and he was the first to be chosen by the senators and not by the army, so he had to ensure that the soldiers accepted him. The Praetorians were courted by him but eventually forced him to execute the assassins of Domitian, some considerable time after the murder had taken place.

In reviewing Domitian's administration and legislation, Nerva left most of it intact, but repealed certain harmless acts with exaggerated fuss. For the Roman populace and the troops, there were cash gifts, and the burdens of the poor were partly relieved by tax exemptions and land distributions, partly funded by a sale of Nerva's own property. Poor families in Italy were assisted by a new scheme, the *alimenta*, a three-way arrangement where the state lent to several small farmers a percentage of the value of their lands, which acted as security. Interest rates were very low, and the payments were directed to the local municipality instead of to Rome, so that the money could be used to make grants to support and feed young children until they reached puberty. Trajan took on the scheme and developed it.

Since he had no heirs and was already past middle age, Nerva looked around for an acceptable successor, and chose Marcus Ulpius Trajanus, a military officer who had served under Domitian and supported him at the time of Saturninus's revolt in 89. Nerva formally adopted him, and appointed him as governor of Upper Germany. Imperial powers were conferred on Trajan before he succeeded, so there could be no doubt as to who the next emperor should be, when Nerva died at the beginning of 98.

Trajan AD 98-117

The Emperor Trajan was the first provincial to become emperor. He was born *c*.53 at Italica, in Spain, and his family owed its success to Vespasian, who had made Trajan's father a senator. Vespasian was not a Roman aristocrat, but an Italian, and Trajan was not even an Italian, which demonstrates the expansion of Roman citizenship and social mobility in Italy and the Empire. In only a few generations from the time of Augustus, first the Italians and then provincials were admitted to the consulship, and within a short time they could also aspire to Imperial rule.

When Nerva died, Trajan was governor of Upper Germany, but he already possessed full Imperial powers. He wrote to the Senate, but did not come to the city. Instead he marched from the Rhine to the Danube, where the tribesmen threatened the province of Pannonia, and in Dacia, Decebalus was once again building up his power base. The new emperor remained in the Danube provinces until autumn 99, possibly strengthening frontier defences and reconnoitring the area, and gathering intelligence. It does not seem that he fought important battles or advanced into non-Roman territory, but Domitian had been preparing for another Danube campaign when he was assassinated, so there was some unfinished business with the tribes, but Trajan did not make a move for another two years.

He made a good impression when he returned to Rome by entering modestly on foot instead of riding at the head of troops. He was immensely popular with the regular army, so he could afford the gesture of ejecting the Praetorians who had executed Domitian's assassins. His cash gift to the guardsmen was much less than other emperors had paid but there were no repercussions. He spent two years in Rome attending to all sectors of society, not simply to court popularity, although that was one of the effects, but to show concern for the well-being of Romans, Italians and provincials. In 99 when he arrived from the Danube he gave 300 sesterces each to the Roman people, which was not unusual, but he also added more names to the lists for the free corn dole.

In 101 he embarked on the first of his Dacian wars. The years from his inspection tour in 99 had probably been spent in preparing for this war, which was a popular move, especially since he concentrated on the disgraceful treaty that Domitian had made, involving payments to the Dacians and technical assistance from Roman engineers. It is possible that Domitian himself intended to reverse this policy as soon as he was able, or there was a reasonable excuse, but it was Trajan who did so, and took the credit for it. The cause of the war is not known. There does not seem to have been an invasion of Roman territory, so it is possible that Decebalus was keeping within the terms of the treaty. But the Romans did not trust him, and they were eager to see Domitian's arrangements overturned.

Preparations for the advance into Dacia included repairing the road originally built by Tiberius on the Roman side of the Danube, near an awe-inspiring gorge called the Iron Gates. Trajan assembled a huge army of at least nine legions, or large detachments from them, since some soldiers were probably left behind as small garrisons, and a number of auxiliary units, and crossed the Danube into Dacian territory. There was a battle at Tapae, where Domitian's general Tettius Julianus first defeated Decebalus. This time there was no satisfactory conclusion, and Trajan decided to spend the winter on the Roman side of the Danube. He was attacked by the Roxolani but the Romans beat them off.

The second year of the campaign was more successful. The Romans struck at the heart of Dacian territory and fought so hard that Decebalus was forced to submit. According to the terms of a treaty that was imposed on him, Decebalus surrendered his war equipment, and promised military assistance for the Romans. It was common for defeated tribes to provide troops for the Roman army, which at one and the same time reinforced the troops of the province to which they were sent and reduced the available manpower of the tribes.

Trajan did not annexe Dacian territory, though he left some troops north of the Danube, and the Roman army of Moesia and Pannonia would monitor events. It took three years for Decebalus to rearm. When he was ready he attacked the Iazyges, who were allies of Rome, defeated and expelled Trajan's garrisons and then erupted into Moesia, in 105. Other tribes joined him. Trajan arrived as quickly as possible, and had to spend time in winning back the loyalty of these tribes so that he could advance without fear of being cut off. In 106 he built a stone bridge with a wooden superstructure across the Danube and entered Dacian territory. After fierce fighting the Romans captured the Dacian capital at Sarmizegethusa. Decebalus was nearly taken but committed suicide. Resistance collapsed, and this time Dacia was annexed and placed under a consular governor with two legions and auxiliary troops. The new province was bordered on the west by the River Tisza, on the east by the River Aluta, and on the south by the Danube. The annexation enabled the Romans to protect the Danube more easily from incursions from the north.

The victories were marked by three monuments at Adamklissi, a circular mausoleum or Tropaeum, and an altar recording the first Dacian war, and another circular mausoleum for the second war. Both campaigns were recorded in pictorial detail on the carved reliefs spiralling up Trajan's column in Rome. It had been well worth the effort. The Carpathians were rich in minerals, with lucrative iron mines, but better still they were virtually overflowing with gold and silver. Trajan held the victory title Dacicus, possibly after the first war, but this honorary description, and his unofficial title Optimus Princeps which was awarded to him early in his reign, were more than justified by the successful outcome of the second war, which so enriched the Roman state. The precious metals brought back to Rome were measured in hundreds of tons.

While the second Dacian war was in progress, the client king of Arabia Petraea, died in 105. It was Pompey who made the territory a client kingdom, and it had remained so ever since, but now the location of the country, neighbouring Syria and the Parthian Empire, made it strategically important, so instead of installing another king, Trajan ordered the governor of Syria, Aulus Cornelius Palma, to send troops in. The southern part of the kingdom formed the new province of Arabia, with a new capital at Bostra, which became the headquarters of a legion from the Syrian garrison. Trajan's newly raised legion, *II Traiana*, was sent to Syria to replace it. The northern part of Arabia was attached to Syria itself. The extra legion in the east would help to protect the frontier and strengthen the army if there were to be a campaign against Parthia.

Trajan now spent some years in Rome, where he embarked on a building programme that included the Forum that bears his name, with rows of shops, a law court, and two libraries, one for Latin works and one for Greek. The column recording the Dacian wars stood inside the new forum. Trajan's Baths were founded in the city, and he built another theatre. Roads and bridges were built to facilitate communications in Italy, the harbour at Ostia was improved and building work was carried out at other ports. The *alimenta* scheme that Nerva had established was developed, and in Rome children were added to the list of those eligible for the corn dole to ease the burdens of the poor.

In the provinces, the financial situation in some of the towns had deteriorated. As some of the leading men had become senators and took a more active part in the government of the Empire, the towns from which they were drawn began to suffer a decline in manpower, and in consequence were deprived of the skills and wealth of these men who would normally have devoted all their energies to government at home. The problem was made worse when the remaining town councillors embarked on ambitious plans to outdo each other, and other communities, in embellishing their towns and providing entertainments. Provincial governors could not direct affairs in the cities which had been proclaimed free and autonomous, and normally the emperors did not interfere with the administration of towns in the senatorial provinces, but Trajan reviewed the problems and swept all custom aside. He appointed *curatores* to take over financial affairs in some towns. The first known example is Caere in Italy, in 113, and perhaps the best known example of the direction of affairs in a whole province is Bithynia, where the Younger Pliny was sent out as governor under Trajan's watchful eye. The letters that Pliny wrote about everyday details, and Trajan's short, sometimes monosyllabic replies, bring history and administration alive.

The years of peace were ended in 113. The Parthians under Chosroes began to stir, and trouble arose as always over Armenia. Chosroes placed one of his nephews on the Armenian throne, which was interpreted as an act of war. Chosroes tried to negotiate and was refused. Trajan assembled an army and advanced to Armenia in 114. He decided against trying to control it by means of friendly kings, and annexed the whole country, but this did not solve the problem entirely. As with all Roman annexations, the border shifted to neighbouring territory, in this case to Mesopotamia, and if Armenia was to be controlled and protected, the package had to include Mesopotamia as well. About eighty years later, Severus encountered the same problem. After spending the winter at Antioch, Trajan advanced into Parthia from Zeugma, summoning troops from his allies and trying to detach the allies of the Persians from Chosroes. He overran the upper reaches of the River Euphrates and northern Mesopotamia, and then retired to winter quarters at Antioch. The next campaign took him to the Parthian capital at Ctesiphon, in 116. He annexed more territory as the new province of Parthia, and dealt with the rest of the vast Parthian Empire by fostering dissension among the claimants to the throne, bestowing the crown on yet another of Chosroes' nephews.

The annexation of such large territories was too much, too soon. There was no consolidation, and not enough manpower to garrison and administer the provinces. It all began to fall apart almost immediately. A widespread rebellion of the Jews over much of the east caused disruption and tied down Roman troops in Mesopotamia, Africa, Egypt and Cyprus, and in 117 there was trouble in Dacia as well. Quadratus Bassus, the governor of Syria, was sent to deal with it, and in his place Trajan appointed his relative and close associate, Publius Aelius Hadrianus, who had accompanied him in the Dacian wars, and to the east, though it is not known in what capacity.

When all was reasonably quiet in the east, but not pacified, Trajan decided to return to Rome. He never arrived, suffering a stroke at Selinus in Cilicia. His wife Plotina and the Praetorian Prefect Acilius Attianus were with him. He died after a few days, probably on 8 August. The short interval would allow some time for Plotina and Attianus to inform Hadrian, in Syria, and to decide what to do. Trajan had obviously groomed Hadrian for the succession, appointing him to important posts and advancing his career, but he had not formally adopted him or specifically named him as the next emperor. Hadrian therefore succeeded Trajan with only the sworn testimony of Plotina and Attianus that he had been adopted and named as heir on Trajan's deathbed. Fortunately the troops in Syria readily accepted him, and he counted his *dies imperii* as 8 August, but it was not an auspicious beginning.

Map 1. Map of the provinces of the Roman Empire in the second century, at its largest extent after the conquests of the Emperor Trajan. When Hadrian succeeded he abandoned some of the recently conquered territory and devoted his energies to consolidation and protection of the Empire.

4

Within Limits:
The Empire Enclosed
AD 117–193

Hadrian AD 117–138

The new Emperor Publius Aelius Hadrianus, was born on
24 January in AD 76, probably at Italica in Spain, where his
family had long held estates. His birthplace is disputed, an
alternative theory being that he was born in Rome. He received
the usual Roman education and while still a very young man
he developed a passion for all things Greek, which he retained
to the end of his life. He followed the normal career pattern
for Roman youths, but he was already exceptional in that
after the death of his father, he was made the ward of Trajan,
some time before the latter became emperor. Between 95 and
100 Hadrian served as tribune in three legions, and after his
marriage to Sabina, Trajan's great-niece, he entered the Senate
as quaestor. He gained his first experience of war during the
Dacian campaign of 101–102, and in the second war of 105–
106, Hadrian served as legate of *legio I Minervia*, which had
been raised by Domitian.

When Trajan began his eastern campaign in 113, Hadrian
served on the army staff and was eventually appointed as
governor of Syria, the most important province in the east.
He was clearly favoured by Trajan, but had not been properly
designated his successor, so when the Emperor died in Cilicia

in 117, Hadrian was not sure of his position until his adoption as Trajan's son was announced. It all seemed somewhat ambiguous, because Trajan had not taken this step during his lifetime, and rumours arose that the Emperor's wife Plotina had engineered the adoption after her husband had died. Since the armies accepted Hadrian, he was also accepted by the Senate and people, but even then, he was not entirely secure, since he did not have universal approval as the adopted successor of Trajan. From the very start of his reign there seems to have been a plot to eliminate him, though the details are obscure. All that is really known of the alleged plot is his response, which was to execute four senators, though he claimed afterwards that he had not ordered their deaths.

Arriving in Rome in the summer of 118, Hadrian spent a short time in the city, arranging a triumph to celebrate Trajan's victories, which may have seemed hypocritical to some senators in view of the fact that Hadrian abandoned some of his predecessor's territorial gains. In 121 the Emperor set off on the first of his many travels through the Empire, beginning with the Rhineland, and then journeying to Britain in 122. From then until 127 he travelled in Gaul, Spain, Greece, Asia and Sicily. In 128 after a brief stay in Rome he went to Africa, where he reviewed the troops and made a speech in praise of them, which has been preserved on an inscription. He spent more time out of Rome than in it, but he took many officials with him and attended to the government of the Empire while travelling. He was the first emperor to take an interest in the provinces and the troops, and in the lives of ordinary people, but even this beneficent attitude did little to increase his popularity.

Hadrian had an innate desire to tidy things up, to codify and put everything in order. Attending to the law, he tried to alleviate the burdens of the Roman citizens in Italy who had to come to Rome if they wanted to present appeals. Hadrian divided Italy into four regions and appointed four ex-consulars to hear the cases in each area, but it seemed as though he regarded Italy as just another province and the scheme was abandoned after his death. His more lasting achievement was in private law, which was dealt with by the *praetor urbanus*, each of whom issued the praetor's edict on taking up office. The edict was substantially the same as that of the preceding praetor, but changes could be made to it as the praetors dealt with new cases. Hadrian asked the jurist Salvius Julianus to codify the existing laws, and the result was the *Edictum Perpetuum*, a permanent set of laws, which henceforth could be altered only by the Emperor or the Senate.

Hadrian's interest in the arts extended to buildings, and in Rome itself he was responsible for the massive Temple of Venus and Rome which now faces the Colosseum, and for the unique Pantheon, on the site of a temple that was first built by Marcus Vipsanius Agrippa. The Pantheon still bears Agrippa's name, not that of Hadrian. Another celebrated building is Hadrian's villa at Tivoli, where he could retreat and devote himself to private study on the few occasions when he was not travelling.

His personal life was not happy. He was estranged from his wife Sabina, and had no children, and his passionate attachment to the youth Antinous detracted from his image. Like Augustus, he was unfortunate in his first choice of heir. He adopted Lucius Ceionius Commodus, who took the name of Lucius Aelius Caesar. This man was intended to be the next emperor but he died before Hadrian, who then adopted Titus Aurelius Fulvius Boionius Antoninus, better known as Antoninus Pius. The adoption was carried out on condition that Antoninus in turn adopted the seven-year-old Lucius Verus, the son of Lucius Ceionius Commodus, and the teenager Marcus Annius Verus, who became the Emperor Marcus Aurelius.

The Frontiers of the Roman Empire

Hadrian's most enduring contribution to the Roman Empire is the creation of the frontier systems. During the reign of Trajan the Roman Empire had reached its greatest extent.

With his death in 117 the period of aggressive, or accidental, expansion came to an end. Whenever the Romans had acquired new conquests they inevitably came into contact with new neighbours, who could be compliant or aggressive, according to their perceptions of the Romans. In the prevailing opinion of the Romans, whatever the mood of their neighbours, there was always an imperative for the defence of their boundaries, which sometimes led to new wars and new conquests and then new boundaries. Militaristic imperialism, trading considerations, and the search for precious metals, also played their part in expansion and annexation, but on some occasions Rome's remorseless empire-building can be classified under the heading of the search for viable and safe boundaries.

The Empire that Trajan bequeathed to his successor Hadrian was the product of several centuries of territorial expansion. This expansion had necessitated the continual evolution of the administrative system that had been designed originally to deal with a city state. Roman provincial government and military organization had been modified and adapted to cope with the steady addition of new territories. On the whole this had been a largely successful enterprise, since the Romans were comfortable with improvization, adaptation and change when necessary. After the death of Emperor Trajan, who had expanded the Empire and earned considerable popularity for doing so, Hadrian reversed this policy, calling a halt to endless conquest. One of his first decisions was to give up the recent conquests north of the Danube, and he abandoned Trajan's schemes for a war with the Parthians. It would have been unnecessarily costly in terms of manpower and cash, and another reason for turning his back on an eastern campaign was his immediate need to consolidate his power in Rome and the Empire. The execution of the four senators at the outset of his reign was an inauspicious time, and if he had then gone to Parthia to carry out the war that Trajan had planned it would probably have been a suicidal act.

His policy of ending imperial expansion made him extremely unpopular with almost everyone, because it went against the Roman ethos of *imperium sine fine*, power without end. If Rome did not continually extend her control of new lands and new peoples, the senators would be deprived of opportunity to govern and possibly exploit new provinces, the military men would be deprived of glory, and traders would be deprived of profit. Hadrian probably thought that the costs of administration and defence of a constantly expanding Empire would outstrip the resources of the Empire as a whole.

Initially, the abandonment of Trajan's conquests may not have been viewed with alarm, since it was not irreversible, but Hadrian made it clear that this was not a temporary withdrawal from the land beyond Dacia and from a potential eastern war, but a permanent state of affairs. He set about the creation of clearly marked boundaries, enclosing the Empire, and ending the expansion into areas beyond the frontiers. He wanted to consolidate within these boundaries the territory that he thought Rome could successfully administer.

From the mid-second century onwards, parts of the Empire were protected by physical barriers such as the appropriately named Hadrian's Wall in Britain, or the timber palisade in Germany. In Raetia there was another stone wall, not as massive as the one in Britain, and in parts of Africa stone walls were built to guard the agricultural lands and guide the pastoral tribes with their flocks and herds onto the designated paths. If there was no physical barrier, the Roman provinces were enclosed within plainly marked and protected boundaries which divided Roman territory from that of the various non-Roman peoples.

The purpose of the frontiers and how they worked are subject to scholarly debate. Were the frontiers designed to stop all movement, or were they designed to channel the movement of people, to watch and guard, and probably collect tolls at the same time? There is no surviving ancient record of what the frontiers were intended to do. Only the historian Eutropius, writing in the late Empire, touches on the subject by informing his readers that Hadrian built a wall in Britain to divide the Romans from the barbarians, which is not very helpful to military strategists, archaeologists or modern historians. The purpose and function of the frontiers may have been slightly different in each province, perhaps adapted to local circumstances, and the Romans may have operated in different ways at different times in the frontier zones, responding to perceived threats. Some modern historians have labelled Roman frontiers as ultimate failures, but it does not seem that the Romans thought of them in that way. Antoninus Pius, Marcus Aurelius, Septimius Severus, Diocletian, Constantine and Valentinian all repaired frontier works, or established new ones on much the same pattern as before.

There were some later adjustments, and on occasions there were campaigns that went beyond the frontiers. Antoninus Pius made some territorial advances in Britain and in Germany, but he did not depart from the established Hadrianic pattern of a running barrier with forts strung out along it. As far as the Romans were concerned the system worked and the frontiers were neither destroyed nor breached until the onslaughts of the mid-third century. Even then, the damage was repaired and the frontiers were put back into commission.

The establishment of the frontiers does not mean that the Romans would henceforth have absolutely nothing to do with the people on the other side of the boundaries. Diplomatic relations still continued, trading was allowed in both directions across the frontiers, though usually at specified locations, and client states were designated as friends of Rome. In some cases, especially on the northern frontier beyond the Rhine and Danube, the Romans promoted and supported tribal chiefs and the elite groups by means of gifts and subsidies, in return for which the local ruler would keep his people in order and friendly to Rome. Gift exchange was an established native custom for most tribes, but after Hadrian's reign gift giving was not always viewed sympathetically at Rome, sometimes falling into the category of bribes to buy peace. One of the greatest advantages of friendly relations with the tribesmen was the provision of recruits for the army. The soldiers from the Germanic tribes proved loyal to Rome and served her well, and in the straitened circumstances of the third century, the Romans would probably have been overwhelmed if they had been unable to tap into this huge resource of manpower.

For most of the time while Hadrian was emperor there was peace, in that there were no major wars such as those that had characterised the reign of Trajan. There were localized rebellions, which were put down with relatively little trouble, except for the Jewish revolts, one at the beginning of Hadrian's reign, and another more serious one from 132 to 135 under the leader Bar Kochba. The death toll on both sides was high, and the Roman victory was bitter. From 70 onwards the province of Judaea had been governed by a praetorian legate who also commanded the legion, but after the suppression of the Bar Kochba revolt the province lost its Jewish identity and was more tightly controlled, being renamed Syria Palaestina and assigned to a consular governor. The Jews were denied entry to Jerusalem. To this day, the Jews refer to Hadrian by a scatological term.

Antoninus Pius AD 138–161

Hadrian died in July 138, and was succeeded by Antoninus Pius, who was immediately presented with a problem. The Senate expressed its collective dislike of Hadrian by refusing to deify him, and proposing that all his acts should be nullified. As the new emperor pointed out, if this proposal was achieved, then he would not be emperor. The Senate backed down, deified Hadrian and awarded Antoninus the name Pius, for his delicate dealings with his predecessor's memory. The Roman Empire entered into one of the most prolonged periods of peace that it had ever known, labelled as a true golden age, in contrast to the turmoil that began shortly afterwards.

Hadrian's work in pacifying, protecting, and integrating the peoples of the Empire was one of the most important contributory factors to this peaceful and prosperous reign. There were no serious wars, only some minor actions in the provinces of Dacia, Mauretania and Numidia. The frontiers that Hadrian had established were extended, in Germany by an eastward advance for a few miles, and in Britain by a considerable drive northwards into Scotland, to the narrow gap between the Firth of Forth and the River Clyde. In each case a new frontier line was drawn, almost exactly like the lines that had just been abandoned. No new system was invented to guard the frontiers, and in Britain the advance northwards from Hadrian's Wall was very short lived, so that the Hadrianic system was quickly reconstituted.

For the twenty-three years of Antoninus's reign, there were no spectacular trials, no treasonable actions, no executions, no financial crises and no scandals, the lack of which leaves the historians, both ancient and modern, with very little to say about the period. Unfortunately, this golden age was about to become, in the words of Cassius Dio, one of iron and rust.

Marcus Aurelius AD 161–180

When Antoninus Pius died in 161, the two boys who had been adopted as his sons, Lucius Verus and Marcus Aurelius, both succeeded him, without faction or personal rivalry. They shared power equally, both adopting the title Augustus. Sharing power in this way was not a new idea. In the first century, Titus had been given the title Augustus along with his father Vespasian. In 166, Marcus Aurelius's two young sons, Commodus and Annius Verus, were both granted the title Caesar, and from the second century onwards this title was used to designate the junior partners, who were the designated successors to Imperial rule.

The reign of Marcus Aurelius was beset by various problems. Not long after his accession, Armenia came under threat from the Parthians. The control of Armenia was always a bone of contention between the two Empires, so Rome prepared for war. Lucius Verus campaigned against the Parthian regime for four years from 162 to 166, reliant upon his military officers for eventual success. Almost immediately after the conclusion of peace in the east, bands of tribesmen from across the Danube invaded the Roman Empire in 166 or 167. Marcus Aurelius and Lucius Verus marched to repel the invasion.

The tribes of the Marcomanni, Quadi, Sarmatae or Sarmatians, and the Iazyges entered Dacia, and crossed the Danube into Pannonia. The Romans had already met the Marcomanni and Quadi in the first century. During the reign of Augustus, one of the prominent men among the Marcomanni, Maroboduus, united the tribesmen and promoted himself as their leader. When he was toppled by another tribesman called Catvalda, Maroboduus was brought to Italy by Tiberius and settled near Ravenna where he remained for the rest of his life. The Marcomanni were subsequently threatened by another tribe, so the Romans allowed them to migrate and settle on the north bank of the Danube. From then onwards until their eruption across the Danube in the 160s, nothing much was heard of the Marcomanni.

The Sarmatians and Iazyges were descended from the same nomadic roots, originally located on the lower reaches of the Danube, but they moved westwards through Dacia and settled again on the Hungarian plain. Emperor Domitian launched a campaign against them in 89, and they were sufficiently pacified for Trajan to convert them into allies of Rome. In the 160s they joined with the Marcomanni to attack the Roman provinces. At one point the tribes even penetrated Italy, reaching Aquileia, which was uncomfortably close to Rome. The Romans would probably not need to read their history books to remember the invasions of the Cimbri and Teutones during the Republic, and the efforts that were necessary to repel them.

The tribesmen were not always intent on destruction and hit and run raids. Many of them wanted to settle within the Roman Empire, and Marcus accommodated them, finding lands for some of the tribes in Dacia, Pannonia and Moesia, perhaps even in Italy itself. This was neither the first nor the last such settlement as more and more tribes approached the Roman world, fleeing from fiercer tribes who flushed them out of their homes, or seeking more fertile lands on which to settle. Once they were inside the Empire these tribes often provided recruits for the Roman army.

Campaigning against the tribes who did not want to settle or were denied access to the Empire, Marcus adopted a policy of continual harassment, not allowing them to stay in one place, breaking up gatherings but preventing free movement, and restricting the places where the tribesmen could conduct their trading activities with the Roman Empire. This last measure probably hit hard, because the leaders of the tribes were often dependent upon receiving goods from the Roman world and being able to trade their own produce, so that they could control the flow of wealth to their own men and thereby remain in their eminent position as leaders. The importance of trading rights to the tribesmen is disputed, because there is no evidence for an abundance of Roman artefacts that found their way into the territory beyond the frontiers, or *barbaricum* as the Romans called it. But the withdrawal of trading rights was employed by more than one emperor in connection with tribal wars, so the Romans presumably knew that it had an adverse effect.

The wars against the northern tribes began in 166 and lasted until Marcus's death in 180, with a short respite of about three years from 173 to 176. The ultimate aim of Marcus's wars with the tribes, apart from driving them out of Italy, was perhaps to defeat them decisively and then to annexe and garrison their territory. According to the historian Cassius Dio, he planned to create two provinces called Sarmatia and Marcomannia, but whether this is true or false has been debated. If there was such a plan, it was never realized.

After the death of Lucius Verus in 169, Marcus fought most of these northern wars alone as sole emperor, while also combating other problems that threatened the Empire. Verus had most probably been a victim of the plague of unknown origin, which had first broken out in the early 160s. It killed hundreds of civilians and soldiers. State bankruptcy was another threat to stability. In a noble gesture, and to set an example, Marcus sold the Palace furniture and his personal goods.

Another unexpected threat to the regime broke out in 175. While Marcus was fighting in the north, his friend Avidius Cassius, who was governor of the province of Asia, raised revolt. There are conflicting accounts of the reasons behind the rebellion, It was said that he was wrongly informed that the Emperor had died, and in order to preserve the Empire he organized a take-over, which was of necessity termed a revolt. Other rumours blamed Marcus's wife Faustina for encouraging Avidius, because she was afraid that her husband, who was beginning to show signs of serious illness, might die, and she wished to find a champion who would ensure the succession of her son Commodus. Whatever his reasons, Avidius was declared emperor. He governed Egypt, where he could control most of Rome's corn supply, and most of the eastern provinces declared for him. After three months and six days his rule was ended and he was killed. It was a bitter personal blow for Marcus, all the more tragic since Avidius was his friend.

In governing the Roman Empire, Marcus Aurelius preserved much of the established practice of his predecessors, continuing to develop practices which had already been established, but he also initiated a new order. Social distinctions began to be crystallized, but the snobbery of the Republic and early Empire was relaxed. Augustus had inaugurated a limited social mobility that was fostered by the Flavians and by Hadrian, and Marcus finally separated social rank from noble birth. He judged people by their abilities, and appointed them to situations where their talents could be utilized to the greatest effect. Henceforth rank was bound up with the civilian or military posts held by each individual, but in order to avoid upsetting the old order he often elevated men of proven competence to the necessary social status normally associated with the appointments.

He promoted non-senators by adlecting them to the Senate, sometimes providing them with the necessary funds so that they qualified for the rank. He appointed some of them to legionary commands, and in some cases to the consulship.

Marcus's relationship with the Senate was cordial and benign. He listened to the opinions of his senators, and discussed his policies with them. The equestrians were reorganized on a hierarchical basis, with superlative labels for each stage in a man's advancement from *egregius*, to *perfectissimus*, and then to *eminentissimus*. More administrative posts were created for equestrians, especially procuratorial offices. The Imperial civil service was expanded; the finance minister, *a rationibus*, was given a higher salary and an assistant. The *consilium principis*, previously an advisory body, was granted official status, and its members received the title *consiliaris*. The city prefect was given wider juridical powers, and the Praetorian Prefects were made responsible for keeping order in Italy.

Perhaps the most far-reaching development was Marcus's increased employment of military officers in ordinary or extraordinary commands, without regard to their personal origins or status. The close interest that he maintained suggests that he noted men of tried and tested expertise. High appointments were theoretically open to everyone, ranging from the sons of freedmen, through provincials to equestrians, who might begin their careers in the army, and then progress to even higher appointments through the equestrian and senatorial posts to which Marcus promoted them. Avidius Cassius was one of the men whose career was assisted by Marcus's liberal policies. His ancestors were enfranchised provincials, but it was no barrier to his promotion as governor of Asia. Publius Helvius Pertinax, whose father was a freedman, rose from the ranks of the army, achieving the consulship in 175. A well-documented extraordinary career is that of Marcus Valerius Maximianus, an equestrian promoted by Marcus Aurelius to the Senate with the rank of praetor, and then given legionary commands in Pannonia, Dacia and Moesia. During the

Danubian wars, Maximianus was very active in a variety of special roles, including command of a fleet operating on the Danube to bring supplies to the Pannonian armies.

Maximianus's career, documented on several inscriptions, is indicative of Marcus's policies of creating special commands in wartime, allowing some of his commanders to act independently. Marcus Aurelius, the emperor who appreciated the benefits of peace and prosperity, was forced to spend most of his time fighting wars, and in the absence of a permanent staff such as those of more modern armies, he established a corps of military men with wide experience and specialist knowledge. The urgency of the almost constant wars of the later years of the second century meant that these men were engaged almost exclusively in military service, with only brief experience of civilian government posts. In the early Empire, military and civil careers were closely intertwined, but there was a gradual separation, more noticeable under Hadrian, but perhaps beginning under the Flavian emperors. The process was given greater prominence during the Danubian wars of Marcus Aurelius. Professionalism and specialization developed in the army, making it a more efficient tool, but on the other hand it gave the military officers a strong influence over large armies, whose loyalties to their commanders could be exploited. The legionary legates were closer and more real to the soldiers than the emperor, and more importantly they were the men who could offer immediate benefits, like ready money and the promise of more of it in the future.

This was the dilemma of the later Roman Empire. If defence of the Roman world was to be effective, the frontier armies were obviously essential, and it was also essential that they should contain large numbers of professional and well-trained soldiers, who should be commanded by experienced officers. As shown by the revolt of Avidius Cassius, this combination could be very dangerous if either the soldiers or the generals, or both parties, conceived a desire for mastery of the Roman world. This problem was never satisfactorily solved. Whenever the all-important succession was in dispute, it was the army and its commanders who decided who should rule, the secret of Empire, as the historian Tacitus called it, but it had never really been a secret. The endemic warfare of Marcus Aurelius's reign, too extensive to be overseen by one man, gave the Emperor no choice but to entrust various military commanders with great powers, setting a precedent for the future. Combined with the sporadic movements of the tribesmen north of the Rhine and Danube, trying to enter the Empire for raids or for permanent settlement, and the problems of the succession, the seeds of the third century crisis had already been sown.

Commodus AD 180–193

Marcus Aurelius died in 180, at Vindobona (modern Vienna), before the Danube wars were concluded. Though Marcus had started out with a colleague of equal rank, and two designated successors, Lucius Verus and Marcus's own young son Annius Verus, had both died, so in 180 there was only his son Commodus, who had been elevated to the rank of Caesar as a boy, and was made Augustus, sharing power with his father, as soon as he had reached the age of sixteen. It was the only way to avoid jealous rivalries and even civil war when one emperor died and another was to take his place. Commodus had the enormous advantage of being the undoubted heir, and as Augustus since 176 he was accepted as the next emperor. The succession of Commodus was the first true hereditary succession since Vespasian bequeathed the Empire to his sons Titus and Domitian.

After the death of his father, Commodus brought the wars with the Danube tribes to an end by diplomatic means. The peace was a long lasting arrangement, despite the fact that Commodus was severely criticised for not carrying on fighting and annihilating the enemy. It is possible that just before his death Marcus Aurelius had already come to the conclusion that he should make peace, abandoning his alleged plans for total conquest and the creation of new provinces.

The treaty that Commodus arranged with the Marcomanni and Quadi contained the useful provision that the tribesmen should immediately furnish an enormous batch of recruits for the Roman army. This method of recruitment became more common as time went on. The Marcomanni and Quadi kept the peace and honoured the terms of their treaty with Commodus, even after his death. The major problem in the Danube area arose from small scale raids, which Commodus dealt with by policing rather than campaigning. Several inscriptions record the construction of watchtowers to control the movements of robbers (*latrones*). The towers would be garrisoned by soldiers from the Roman army, backed up by more troops if trouble broke out.

In theory, Commodus had every chance of becoming a philosopher emperor like his father. He had been groomed for succession since his childhood, and Marcus Aurelius was the first emperor since Flavian times to have a son of his own for whom the succession was hereditary and absolutely unequivocal. Marcus has been blamed for allowing Commodus to succeed him, but if he had recognized his son's potential defects and had designated someone else while Commodus was growing up, it is possible that the Roman world would have divided into factions promoting their own candidates and the civil war of 193 would have broken out in 180 instead. There were alternatives to succession by natural or adoptive heirs, ranging from bribery and corruption, through the acclamation of a candidate by strong-willed soldiery, to full scale civil war. The third century was to become familiar with all of these methods of Imperial succession.

The reign of Commodus began reasonably well. There was no serious neglect of the frontiers or the army, and the provinces did not suffer under his rule. But he descended into farce and finally into terror, ending with his assassination by the Praetorian Prefect and the palace chamberlain. Commodus had been given every opportunity to learn how to govern, and he inherited Marcus's circle of advisers with considerable cumulative experience, but he soon removed them all, promoting in their places men like Perennis and then Cleander, his personal favourites. By the end of his reign he had alienated almost everyone and there were grave problems.

In 190, Commodus's favourite, Marcus Aurelius Cleander, was the most influential man in Rome. He had started out as a slave, but had been freed by the Emperor Marcus Aurelius and as was customary he had taken the name of the citizen who had manumitted him. His status as Imperial freedman gave him access to the court and Imperial family. He was made chamberlain to Commodus, and gained even more power and influence when Perennis, the more important of the two Praetorian Prefects, was executed. Cleander somehow managed to subordinate the two succeeding Praetorian Prefects to himself and rapidly became the fount of all power. Commodus made him his security chief, with a new title '*a pugione*' or 'the dagger', indicating his position of supremacy. He was privy to the Emperor's plans and policies, and he had the power to elevate and promote people to various appointments, but on the other hand with complete control over men and their careers, he could thwart people and even remove them. Everyone had to go through Cleander's efficient filter system, before he could even hope to rise to any significant post.

Eventually Cleander went too far, having alienated too many people, with the inevitable result that even well-balanced, sane men who normally distanced themselves from politics and government were by now amenable to Cleander's elimination. He was made the scapegoat for a food shortage, and when the Roman mob indulged in riots, Commodus panicked. He realized that not even Cleander could solve the problem this time, so he executed him. Towards the end of his reign, Commodus had become completely detached from the needs of the Empire and his behaviour was increasingly bizarre. It began to seem that he must be unhinged. He had ignored the advice of his counsellors, allowing his subordinates to gain too much influence over him, and made no efforts to diminish the increasing power of his favourites. He had failed to realize, or did not care, that the emperor must be the sole source of power and patronage, and that if any of his subordinates took his place in the dispensation of appointments and rewards, he would be seriously undermined. He had not achieved the fine balance that was necessary in dealing with his court circle, his military officers, the senators and the people. Of necessity the emperor had to be sensitive in the control of his close associates, preventing them from accruing too much power without stifling all hope of promotion.

Commodus was nervous in the years following the death of Cleander and became highly unpredictable. Life under Commodus was similar to that during the later years of Domitian. No one felt safe. Senators and equites alike felt threatened. The Praetorian Prefects, Regillus and Julius Julianus, were successively removed, after the latter had enjoyed a brief period as sole Prefect. A series of murders began. The senators were not just fearful for themselves but for their entire circles of *clientelae*, drawn from all ranks from the city and from the rural population, from Italy and the provinces. An individual senator could wield considerable and widespread influence, and to eradicate this influence and avoid the possibility that any one of them might try to gain control of the Empire, it was necessary to eradicate the entire circle of each senatorial victim. This may be what Cassius Dio implies when he says that many other people were killed as well as senators, even including women.

The activities of the Emperor became more and more outrageous. Identifying himself with Hercules, he devoted himself to gladiatorial pursuits, delighting in displaying his talents in public performances. At the end of his reign these gladiatorial shows were compulsory viewing. Senators were not given the option of boycotting them. They were even obliged to chant in unison, hailing Commodus as Lord, First Among Men, Victorious and so on. At one performance, Commodus cut off the head of an ostrich, waving it at the senators as if to suggest that he could just as easily cut off the heads of everyone else. Dio describes how he took refuge in chewing laurel leaves so as to disguise the fact that he was laughing – a potentially fatal reaction if the Emperor happened to see it.

This ridiculous state of affairs was lightened a little by the appointment of Aemilius Laetus as one of the Praetorian Prefects. Laetus was a native of North Africa, and had promoted the careers of some of his fellow countrymen to posts on the northern frontiers. One of these was Septimius Severus, who was made governor of Upper Pannonia in 191. He had no experience of the Rhine and Danube areas, nor of the government of a fairly large province with an army, but in Roman tradition, he took on the task without any previous training.

It was a time of great insecurity for everyone, and it was clear that sooner or later the reign of Commodus would end, probably with bloodshed. Severus was ambitious, and even if he had not planned to become emperor at this stage he would at least have given some thought as to how he might survive in a change of regime. Severus's career had begun at the age of twenty-eight, when he entered the Senate in the reign of Marcus Aurelius. He had risen slowly, taking up the normal appointments one after another. He was quaestor in Rome in 170, and had then served in Baetica, Sardinia and Africa. He was legionary legate of *IV Scythicae* in Syria, with Helvius Pertinax as governor. From 186–189 he governed Gallia Lugdunensis. His knowledge of the Empire was reasonably wide, but his career was not spectacular, and he had not seen much military action. He reached the consulship in 190 at the age of forty-five. It was not such a signal honour, since there were twenty-five consuls in that same year, giving each man about one month's experience of the office and its duties. These suffect consulships were sometimes awarded when the Emperor wished to honour some of his supporters, or when there too few candidates for the proconsular offices, so some men were promoted so that they could acquire some experience and the appropriate rank.

Severus's appointment was probably purchased from Cleander. According to Dio he was only one among many who were appointed in this fashion. In view of the events of the very near future, it is not important how Severus became consul. Poised in Upper Pannonia, Severus waited and watched. The garrison of his province comprised three legions, and the route into Italy was quite short

Sooner or later Commodus was sure to meet an untimely end. His sister had already been involved in a plot to remove him. It is not known how far in advance the Praetorian Prefect Laetus planned the assassination of Commodus, nor if he confided in anyone except perhaps a few accomplices. On New Year's Eve, 192, he and the palace chamberlain Eclectus murdered the Emperor, and shortly afterwards Publius Helvius Pertinax was proclaimed in his place. It is not certain that Pertinax was party to the plot. Dio and Herodian insist that the assassination was an *ad hoc* decision as Laetus seized his chance, and Pertinax was taken completely by surprise when he was declared emperor.

Pertinax AD 193

Pertinax was sixty-seven years old, a man of wide experience. He started life as the son of a slave, and began his career in the army. In Marcus's reign he had been elevated first to equestrian rank and then adlected into the Senate. He had been governor of Lower Moesia, Upper Moesia, Dacia and Syria. He was a sterling example of the social mobility that had begun with the reign of Augustus. In the early years of the Empire, it had been possible to rise from lowly origins to consul within three generations, but Pertinax rose from the humblest rank to emperor in one lifetime. The Senate accepted him without demur, voting him all the usual titles, including *Pater Patriae*, 'father of his country', and his wife and son were respectively offered the titles Augusta and Caesar, but Pertinax rejected these honours on their behalf. He persuaded the senators to spare the life of Laetus. Although he had worked on behalf of Commodus as Praetorian Prefect, this did not mean that he supported the Emperor and all his actions, as demonstrated by the fact that he had killed him.

Winning over the Praetorian Guard was not quite so straightforward. Pertinax was a strict disciplinarian, noted for his severe punishment of the soldiers in Britain when they had proclaimed him emperor, which was potentially a death sentence even if the chosen man decided to march on Rome and topple the incumbent ruler. Now, ironically, he was positively encouraging the Praetorians to do under coercion the very thing that he had previously punished the British soldiers for doing voluntarily. The Praetorians were given a payment of 12,000 *sesterces* per man, which they accepted but at the ceremony where they were supposed to take the oath of loyalty to Pertinax, some of the soldiers decided that a senator called Triarius Maternus suited them rather better, but their attempt to create a new emperor failed, largely because their chosen candidate fled, minus his clothes.

Pertinax set about tidying up the Imperial household, selling all the slaves whom he considered to be superfluous, and banishing the many hangers-on, but according to Herodian a few concubines soon found their way back into the palace. In the Senate, Pertinax reinstated the men who had been exiled or had fled, and he assisted the families of those who had been condemned or killed. His major problem was lack of funds, but somehow he found the cash to pay the donatives to placate the Praetorians and the Roman mob. He turned his attention to the coinage. It had been debased in 190–2, so Pertinax brought the silver standard of the *denarius* back to the level it had enjoyed in the days of Vespasian. He reduced customs dues to try to boost commercial activity, and he tried to promote agriculture by granting titles of ownership to waste lands with ten years' tax exemption. There may be some confusion in the sources, since Hadrian's laws on waste lands were still in operation, but it is also possible that Pertinax hoped to speed things up. He did not rule for long enough for any judgement to be made about the likely success of his measures and his intentions, but

Herodian thought that given time he would have changed the administration for the better, instituting 'sound and orderly government'.

Pertinax was not given time. Laetus instigated his murder after only eighty-seven days as emperor. In this instance there was no immediately obvious successor who could take up the reins of state. Pertinax had not chosen anyone as his successor and Laetus clearly did not want to be emperor himself. Not even the Praetorians, whose commanders and officers had from time to time gained a preponderant influence in political events, took the initiative in raising an emperor of their own choice. Instead they waited to see who would pay the most cash, standing by while Flavius Sulpicianus, Pertinax's father-in-law and currently Prefect of the City, tried to outbid Didius Julianus for the purchase of the Empire, but he was unsuccessful. Finally Julianus bought the Empire for the price of 25,000 *sesterces* per Praetorian Guardsman, and became the Emperor of Rome himself for a short time.

As soon as the news of the death of Pertinax reached the frontiers, the armies and their generals were ready. Early in April, Severus was proclaimed emperor by his troops at Carnuntum on the Danube. There were two other rival candidates, Pescennius Niger in Syria and Clodius Albinus in Britain. They were situated at opposite ends of the Empire, and appropriately named for the opposite ends of the spectrum, black (*niger*) and white (*albus*). Niger was proclaimed at some time before the end of May 193, while Clodius Albinus may have entered the scene somewhat later. The chronology is not established, but it does not really matter who was proclaimed before anyone else. They were bound to fight each other in a contest involving civil war. Severus decided to ignore the threats from the eastern and western contenders, and went straight to Rome to secure his position there. He had the shortest distance to travel to the capital city and took advantage of it. The proclamation of Severus as emperor cannot have been as spontaneous as it sounds, nor can it have depended entirely on opportunism. Though he was not in a position to predict exactly what would happen in Rome, Severus could still have prepared the ground very generally, by establishing a large and loyal *clientelae*, by sounding out likely contacts outside his own group of clients, and creating networks of influential people ranging from army officers, wealthy senators and equites, down to the most lowly individual with specialized knowledge or particular talents. His marriage to Julia Domna, his second wife, had been carefully arranged, not simply because her horoscope contained the brilliant news that she was to be the wife of an emperor, but also because her eastern connections were important, bringing more influential and wealthy people into Severus's circle. Networks had to be very wide, spread over as much of the Empire as possible, as well as in Rome itself, providing eyes and ears for political and military developments. Information about who was friend or foe was absolutely vital in a regime like that of Commodus, simply as a survival tool, but the network could be turned to good use when the time came. No one could predict the precise moment and consequently no one would know who would be where and in what post when the crisis came, but it was obvious that there would be a crisis, because there was no designated heir, and Commodus's behaviour was less and less conducive to longevity. It was highly likely that at some point the Empire was going to need an emperor quite suddenly, and Severus had probably thought about it long before Laetus chose and then eliminated Pertinax.

Money was the most important tool for would-be emperors. Influential and wealthy connections were essential to provide rapid access to cash. Money could buy the army and other people, at least temporarily. The next most important considerations would be to cultivate the soldiers and monitor their moods, and to investigate the opinions of the other provincial governors. Severus would need to know whether there was support for him. He did not want to be forced into a premature civil war before he had even crossed the Alps. Prepared and waiting,

Severus was probably quite ready to take over as emperor when Commodus was murdered at the beginning of 193, but the transition between old and new emperor was rapid, leaving no room for Severus to act before the accession of Pertinax. He was fortunate that he did not act too soon and then find himself in opposition to the new emperor. Severus swore allegiance to Pertinax, then waited upon events.

According to the *Historia Augusta*, the legions of the Rhine and Danube declared for Severus, encouraged by their generals, and when he established himself as emperor in Rome Severus issued coins specifically honouring many of these legions by their individual names. The evidence is not conclusive but it will bear the interpretation that Severus had thoroughly prepared the ground long before his acclamation. His investment paid off because sometime later, when civil war began in the west, the governor of Lower Germany, Virius Lupus, stood firm for Severus and opposed Clodius Albinus when the latter reached Gaul.

Since Pertinax had promised a brighter future for the Empire and it had looked as though he might have been able to stabilize the government if he had survived long enough, Severus chose to enter Rome as his avenger. He adopted his predecessor's name to demonstrate solidarity and continuity with the regime. His first coins bore the name Imperator Caesar Lucius Septimius Pertinax Augustus. It was important to disassociate himself from Commodus, but in the stance that he took as the avenger of Pertinax he was able to present himself the role of selfless leader doing his duty to the state, rather than as an opportunistic general racing to the top. Later, when he was more secure, he was forced to change his attitude towards Commodus, because he wanted to establish a firmer basis for his power by connecting himself with the house of Marcus Aurelius and Antoninus Pius.

Severus would have to overcome three potential opponents when he arrived in Rome, in the form of the legitimate Emperor Didius Julianus, the Praetorians and the Senate. It would probably be possible to deal with them separately. Julianus took hasty steps to defend himself as soon as he knew that Severus was approaching Italy. He executed Laetus and persuaded the Senate to declare Severus a public enemy (*hostis*), but the Praetorians pre-empted both Julianus and the Senate by opening up negotiations with Severus. The Senate quickly sacrificed Julianus, condemning him to death and declaring Severus emperor.

The Praetorians were eliminated before Severus entered Rome. He took them by surprise by summoning them to a meeting where they found themselves surrounded by his legions. He dismissed them all with dishonour. Since they had been the first to negotiate with him, they probably expected to be rewarded, but Severus knew how extremely fickle they were, and in any case he did not want to be placed in the dubious position of owing his power to them. He mastered them from the start. When he was ready he created a new and larger Guard, recruited from the legions and not just from Italians. The Praetorians had become very arrogant and had started to terrorize people, shamelessly abusing their privileges. The demise of the Praetorians was not regretted, except that the historian Dio accused Severus of filling Italy with unemployed Italians and disgruntled ex-guardsmen who continued to terrorize people.

The new emperor treated the Senate with studied respect. He brought his troops to Rome ready for battle, but he changed into civilian dress when he crossed the city boundary. He promised to rule like Marcus Aurelius, and guaranteed never to put any senator to death without first bringing him to trial by his peers in the Senate. He distributed cash to the soldiers and the Roman populace. Civil war was postponed for a while. Clodius Albinus was offered the title of Caesar, designating him as the next emperor. It has been questioned whether Albinus believed that Severus's offer was genuine. He must have known that Severus had two sons, but he may have reasoned that they were very young, and did not represent a threat.

Clodius Albinus is presented by the historians as somewhat naive, which was perhaps inevitable since he was ultimately defeated. If he had been the victor in the civil wars, he would probably have earned a reputation for crafty and calculated planning, waiting until the right moment had come before committing himself to battle. In reality he may have had much more common sense and been much more prescient than he has been depicted. He may have played the game as well as he could, accepting the name of Caesar gracefully, pretending to acquiesce in the arrangement while all along he was simply stalling for extra time to prepare. There was more than one choice of action. He could have given in without a fight, abdicating and perhaps being lynched by his own legions. He could have remained in Britain at the head of his own small Empire as Carausius did a century later, or he could meet Severus somewhere in Gaul or Germany and hope to defeat him there. If he made no move at all he could be sure that Severus would eventually come after him, so he could not sit still, but on the other hand he was handicapped by having to leave at least some form of secure garrison behind him in Britain before he could begin to ferry troops onto the continent. Far from being the dupe of Severus, it is just as likely that Clodius Albinus was grateful to have reached what he may have regarded as a temporary stay of execution and breathed a sigh of relief, knowing that Niger was to be the first to receive Severus's attentions.

5

Military Rule:
Emperors & Usurpers
AD 193–260

Severus AD 193–211

In the course of the third century, from the reign of Severus onwards, the Empire progressed from the Principate, a modern term derived from Augustus's use of the title *princeps*, into the Dominate, based on the title *dominus*, signifying lordship. Severus introduced into the Roman world the concept of the divinity and sacrosanctity of the Imperial household, the *domus divina*. It also signified the start of a more overtly autocratic rule.

The Elimination of Niger & Albinus

Niger was in a strong position. He could draw upon the considerable resources of the eastern provinces, where he had powerful adherents. The proconsul of Asia, Asellius Aemilianus, had declared for him, and had occupied Byzantium. Niger also controlled Egypt and could withhold the corn supply to Rome. If he was allowed to do so, food shortages would quickly diminish Severus's popularity, so speed was essential in challenging him. Severus ordered the troops in Africa to watch the western border of Egypt, and prevent the legion there (*II Traiana*) from sending help to Niger. Late in 193, having consolidated his position in Rome, Severus was ready.

He travelled overland via Pannonia and Moesia, ordering the troops in Moesia to set off ahead of him. His general Candidus defeated Niger's ally Aemilianus at Cyzicus, but the elimination of Aemilianus did not bring about the surrender of Byzantium. The city was put under siege.

Niger withdrew into Syria, but because he seemed unable to stop Severus's advance some cities turned against him, wishing to be on the right side at the end of the war. Loadicea was probably the first city to break away, spurred on by jealousy of its main rival, Antioch, where Niger set up his .headquarters. By the spring of 194, the war was over. Niger fled, but was overtaken and killed. Severus sent his head to Byzantium to demonstrate that there was now no leader to rally behind, but the city still refused to surrender until the end of 195. Severus destroyed it to set an example to other rebellious cities, but Byzantium was far too important for Roman emperors to lose, so it was rebuilt.

Loadicea, Tyre and other cities which had declared for Severus were rewarded, but those which had sided with Niger were heavily fined, especially Antioch. Niger's adherents, embracing senators, equestrians, officers and soldiers alike, were severely punished. They found refuge in Parthia, working as engineers, builders and arms manufacturers. When he discovered this, Severus stopped the punishments and concentrated instead on restoring Roman control and influence on the eastern frontier. The Parthian King Vologaeses, had been sympathetic to Niger, and the city of Hatra had helped him. There was rebellion against Roman control in Osroene and Mesopotamia, and the city of Nisibis, which had been in Roman hands since the expedition of Lucius Verus in the 160s, was besieged, but held out for Severus. Order was quickly restored. Severus converted Osroene into a province in charge of a procurator, and he rewarded Nisibis by elevating the city to the rank and privileged status of a *colonia*, or colony. It may have been at this point when Severus divided the province of Syria into two unequal parts and renamed them, the larger northern part being Syria Coele with two legions, and the smaller southern province being Syria Phoenice, with one legion. From now on, no governor would command more than two legions, reducing the chances of rebellion backed by an army.

Severus initially adopted the victory titles *Parthicus Arabicus* and *Parthicus Adiabenicus* after the defeat of Niger, but when he moved against Albinus in the west he dropped the *Parthicus* title, because of its suggestion of a Parthian victory. He wanted to ensure that he did not provoke the King of Parthia unnecessarily, and took what steps he could to secure the eastern frontier, so that he could then march to Gaul. Albinus had by now gained support in the Senate. The chronology of the breakdown of relations is not crystal clear, so it is not certain who made the first hostile move. Severus portrayed Albinus as the instigator of the war, because in 195 or 196 he declared himself Augustus, which was a direct challenge to the legitimate emperor. Severus responded by making it clear that Albinus was not destined to succeed him. He fabricated his own descent from the respected Marcus Aurelius, and solved the problem of Commodus, whose memory had been damned, by asking the Senate to overturn this decision and deify Commodus. This pacified the army, since they had no quarrel with Commodus. Severus raised his eldest son Septimius Bassianus to the rank of Caesar, renaming him Marcus Aurelius Antoninus, better known as Caracalla, a nickname derived from the Gallic hooded cloak that he habitually wore. Being groomed for succession, Caracalla was given the unequivocal title *Imperator destinatus*. Severus did not promote his younger son Geta as rapidly, but he intended that his sons should succeed him.

Albinus moved troops into Gaul and established himself at Lugdunum (modern Lyons), where he began to issue coins in his own name as Augustus. He brought troops from Britain, and recruited more in Gaul. *Cohors XIII Urbana* from Lyons joined him, but the Rhine legions refused to help. Albinus presumably did not remove all the troops from Britain, probably ensuring the protection of the cities and coasts, in case he was driven back to the island. However, there are some indications that he effected a large scale evacuation of Hadrian's Wall. Archaeological evidence reveals that the Wall garrisons of the late second century were completely changed by the third century.

In order to prevent Albinus from invading Italy from his base in Gaul, Severus garrisoned the Alpine passes, but there was no invasion. The governor of Gallia Lugdunensis left the province rather than join Albinus, and Virius Lupus, the governor of Lower Germany, attempted to stand against him. The city of Trier also held out, and perhaps other cities followed suit. The issue was decided at the battle of Lyons in February 197. Albinus conveniently committed suicide, and infamously, Severus allowed his troops to sack Lyons. The city never fully recovered. The episode demonstrated how easily a Roman army would turn against other Roman troops or against a Roman city, and it highlighted the overwhelming power of the army in co-operation with the emperor. The mutual dependence of the soldiers upon the emperor for their pay and perks, and of the emperor on the soldiers for their corporate support had never been so blatant as it was under Severus.

At some unknown date, Severus divided Britain into two separate provinces, just as he dealt with Syria, and for the same reasons, to prevent any other governor from gaining access to large numbers of troops. This division may have occurred when troops were sent back to the province after the defeat of Albinus, but some scholars prefer a later date, perhaps after Caracalla's settlement in 208, or even at some time after 213.

In the aftermath of the civil wars there was a reshuffling of personnel in provincial and central government posts, and in the army. Severus chose his provincial governors and army commanders very carefully, especially since he planned to leave Rome to attend to the unfinished work on the eastern frontier. The centre of government was wherever he was himself, but if he could trust his provincial governors and military officers in the rest of the Roman world, so much the better.

The Army

Attention to the army was a hallmark of Severus's reign. Probably in 197 he put into effect his army reforms, in particular his pay rise for the soldiers. It created great disapproval, because most Romans wanted defence at an impossibly cheap price. The last army pay rise had been granted over a century earlier by Domitian, so it was well overdue, as was the recognition of the soldiers as people, with the right to marry and reasonable prospects of promotion, which is what Severus gave them. Marriages had been forbidden to soldiers, but liaisons with local women near the camps had always occurred, so the new legislation merely acknowledged the existing situation.

Severus relied upon his government officials and the army to keep a firm grasp on Rome and Italy. He had reconstituted the Praetorian Guard, larger now than in previous reigns, and he also installed a new legion at Alba (modern Albano), not far from Rome. This was *legio II Parthica*, raised at an unknown date, but it was stationed in Italy when Severus went on campaign against the Parthians. The units of the new Praetorian Guard, combined with the new legion, provided Severus with about 30,000 men, all under his immediate control.

The Promotion of the Equestrians

Severus opened up promotion for soldiers from the ranks, and created more military commands and governmental posts for the equestrians, continuing a trend already set in motion by previous emperors. The three new legions that he raised, all named *Parthica*, were commanded by equestrians instead of senators, and he appointed more equestrians as the governors of the new eastern provinces created after the Parthian campaigns. The equestrian class in general experienced a whole new impetus under Severus. It is not valid to speak of a senatorial decline, but the influence of the senators remained static.

Severus held the purse strings of the whole Empire, he was the commander in chief of the armed forces, and was the source of all patronage and advancement. He appointed his loyal supporters to key posts. From *c.*196 Cornelius Anullinus, one of his close associates, was city prefect. The Emperor's personal friend and fellow countryman from Africa, Caius Fulvius Plautianus, was prefect of the *vigiles* from 193 to 196, and in 197 he was appointed commander of the Praetorian Guard, rapidly becoming the most infamous Praetorian Prefect since Sejanus, eliminating his colleague and enjoying sole command of the Praetorian Guard for the rest of his career.

The Parthian Campaign

Severus set off for the Parthian campaign in early summer 197. From the Roman point of view there was a pressing need to attack Parthia, since King Vologaeses had occupied Mesopotamia and laid siege to Nisibis. The city was ably defended by Laetus (not the man who assassinated Commodus). Despite the initial aggression of Vologaeses, the Parthian Royal House was weak and split into factions, which could only assist the advance of Severus's army. Vologaeses retreated as Severus aimed for the Euphrates valley, encountering no resistance at Seleucia or Babylon, and only a slight problem at the Parthian capital Ctesiphon, which he sacked.

The campaign had been a demonstration of strength to deter the Parthians from interfering in Roman administrative arrangements on her eastern borders. There was no intention of remaining in Parthian territory, and in 198 Severus set off for Rome. The army was in high spirits, acclaiming him Imperator for the tenth and eleventh time, and proclaiming Caracalla joint Augustus with his father, while Severus's younger son Geta was made Caesar.

The only resistance that Severus experienced during this expedition came from the city of Hatra, which he besieged unsuccessfully in 198 and again in 199. In order to consolidate his demonstration against Parthia, he encased the upper Euphrates in Roman provinces. In 195 he had created the new province of Osroene, and now he adopted a scheme originally proposed by Trajan but abandoned by Hadrian, of annexing Mesopotamia in 198. He installed an equestrian prefect as governor, with the capital at Nisibis and a garrison comprised of two newly raised legions, *I* and *III Parthica*, both of which were commanded by equestrians. The approaches to Syria Phoenice and Arabia were protected from Parthian attack by the Palmyrene militia, who patrolled the eastern desert on the Emperor's behalf. But the annexation of Mesopotamia as a Roman province was costly, a constant thorn in the side of the Parthian kings, and the cause of future confrontations.

Severus returned home via a tour of Mesopotamia, Syria, Palestine, Arabia and Egypt. Entering Rome as conquering hero, Severus celebrated a triumph in which his sons Caracalla and Geta played a prominent part. He also celebrated his ten year rule, his *Decennalia*, with appropriate pomp and ceremony, and distributions of cash to the people of Rome. The most durable evidence of his military achievements is the arch named after him in the Forum in Rome, close by the Senate House.

The Frontiers of Africa

After a short stay in Rome, Severus and his family, including the Praetorian Prefect Plautianus, embarked on a voyage to Africa, the Emperor's native land, where his generals had extended the frontiers, taking in more territory, rationalizing boundaries, protecting routes, and building new forts. Hadrian had done much to rationalize and stabilize the frontiers of Africa. In Numidia he had moved *III Augusta* from its base at Ammaedara to a new fortress at Lambaesis, and he had constructed watchtowers and small posts on the frontiers of Mauretania Caesariensis and Tingitana, but there was no unbroken running barrier like those in Britain and Germany. Commodus continued the frontier work by building outposts to give advance warning of raids.

Severus extended Roman territory in Africa, through his governors and generals, in particular Quintus Anicius Faustus, a native of Africa, and legate of *legio III Augusta* at Lambaesis from 197 to 201. In Mauretania Caesariensis Severus took in more territory, creating a new frontier commemorated on inscriptions as the *nova praetentura*, begun in 198 by Octavius Pudens, another African. This extension of the Empire earned for Severus the title of *propagator imperii*, attested on several inscriptions in Africa.

The Downfall of Plautianus

In 204 Severus celebrated the Secular Games. The ceremony was rooted in the Roman past, combining religious ceremonial with games and festivals, occurring once every 110 years, so that no one ever witnessed more than one celebration in a lifetime, or *saeculum*. Severus marked the occasion on his coinage, and put his whole family on display at all the ceremonies. The *domus divina*, attested on inscriptions, denoting the Imperial household as an entity, sacrosanct and unassailable, was now firmly established in Roman consciousness.

The Praetorian Prefect Plautianus had built up a vast accretion of power and his unashamed exploitation of it had made him more feared and detested than either Sejanus or Cleander. Plautianus's daughter Plautilla had been betrothed to Caracalla since 201, so the Praetorian Prefect was a member of the Imperial household. His name appears on several inscriptions alongside those of Severus and Caracalla. He treated Julia Domna with contempt, and towards the end of the second Parthian campaign he began to eliminate men of good reputation and distinguished service, such as Quintus Aemilius Saturninus, his colleague as Praetorian Prefect, and Laetus, who had been with Severus since 193, and Tiberius Claudius Candidus, the first officer to see action against Niger's troops. For a while, Plautianus was unassailable, because Severus was oblivious of the enormities, but the Emperor was finally made aware of what was happening by his brother Septimius Geta, who denounced Plautianus on his deathbed. Caracalla took the initiative, persuading his father that Plautianus had hatched a plot to remove the entire Imperial household. On 22 January 205, Plautianus was killed. Two

Praetorian Prefects were appointed in his place, Quintus Maecius Laetus, who had been prefect of Egypt 200–3, and Aemilius Papinianus, an Imperial secretary with a good reputation as a jurist.

The Expedition to Britain

The situation in Britain after the defeat of Albinus is variously depicted, ranging from one of extreme gravity to perfectly normal routine. Successive governors, Virius Lupus, Valerius Pudens and Alfenus Senecio, had carried out rebuilding and repairs to several forts in the north, but this does not mean that the repairs were necessary because of destruction by British tribesmen. According to Cassius Dio, the governor Virius Lupus was forced to buy peace from the Maeatae, who lived 'near the wall that cuts the island in half', by which it is normally assumed that he meant the more northerly Antonine Wall. Beyond the Maeatae there were the Caledonians. Both tribes were hardy and hostile, and moreover they were not subject to Rome. No one since Julius Agricola had succeeded in the conquest of Scotland, and Dio affirms that Severus now intended to conquer the whole island.

The Imperial armies, including troops from the Rhine and Danube armies, possibly *II Parthica* from Italy and detachments from the Praetorian Guard, arrived in Britain in 208 and Severus set up his headquarters at York. He brought his two sons with him to give them experience, and he was accompanied by his *comites* and chosen officials, since he governed the whole Empire from his British base.

The archaeological traces of Severus's two campaigns in northern Britain are slightly more useful than the ancient literary evidence. Severan supply bases have been identified at Arbeia (modern South Shields), at Corbridge, and at Cramond on the Forth. At Carpow on the Tay, Severus established a legionary base, where tiles of *VI Victrix* have been found. Two lines of marching camps have been traced in the north leading into Scotland, usually identified as those used by Severus's army.

There were two campaigns, the first in 208–9 led by Severus himself and the second in 210 led by Caracalla alone.

Severus's younger son Geta was left behind in York, perhaps compensated when he was finally made Augustus, the colleague of his father and brother. The Imperial family did not enjoy harmonious relations. Caracalla had an obvious wish to rid himself of his brother and it may also be true that he tried to kill Severus while they rode out together to meet the Caledonians to arrange a truce. There was hardly any need to kill him, since Severus was already ill. In February 211, on the brink of preparing a third campaign, he died at York. On his deathbed he told his sons not to disagree with each other, to pay the soldiers, and to despise everyone else.

Caracalla may have mounted a third British campaign in 211, before he concluded peace and returned to Rome. The frontier remained stable for the next eighty-five years, so whatever arrangements he made presumably had some worth. Severus may have already divided Britain into two provinces, but some scholars suggest that it was Caracalla's work, after his father's death. At about this time, Caracalla readjusted the boundaries of the two Pannonian provinces, so that there were two legions in each, as part of a consistent policy to reduce the number of legions at the disposal of any provincial governor.

Caracalla AD 211–217

Very soon after returning to Rome, Caracalla murdered Geta, perhaps at the beginning of 212. He then took refuge in the Praetorian camp claiming that he had killed Geta in self defence. The soldiers were far from happy to forget that they had sworn allegiance to Geta, but cash payments helped them to edit him out of their collective memory. Caracalla eradicated all his brother's supporters, killing a large number of people, including the Praetorian Prefect, Papinianus. All over the Empire, orders went out to chisel Geta's name out of inscriptions, and to destroy his portraits and statues. Even papyrus records were edited for any reference to Geta.

Universal Citizenship

The most famous administrative measure of Caracalla's reign, giving rise to endless discussion, is the *Constitutio Antoniniana*, traditionally dated to 212. By this edict, Roman citizenship was granted to all free born inhabitants of the Empire, and since it was usual to take the name of the man who enfranchised new citizens, after 212 there was a great preponderance of men and women all over the Empire with the family name Aurelius, from Caracalla's official name Marcus Aurelius Antoninus. The levelling effect of the *Constitutio* theoretically subjected all free peoples of the Empire to Roman law, though in practice local customs remained intact. Financially it broadened the base of the inheritance tax, paid by all citizens.

Though the act could be said to degrade Roman citizenship, in reality it had already lost its status. After 212 a new elite evolved. Instead of Romans and provincials, or citizens and non-citizens, the yardstick shifted to a distinction between upper and lower classes. The new groups were labelled *honestiores* and *humiliores*, beginning as a social distinction but soon crystallized in law. *Honestiores* were possessed of greater legal privileges than *humiliores*, for whom punishments were much more severe.

The Rhine & Danube Frontiers

For several years there had been no serious trouble in the north, but in 212–213 Upper Germany was threatened by invasions of tribesmen, labelled by the ancient sources as the Alamanni, though the use of the name in this context may be anachronistic. The term simply means 'all men', denoting a federation of different tribes who chose to adopt a non-ethnic name for themselves, though it is unlikely that the federation had been formed as early as 213.

Caracalla responded to the danger by conducting a campaign for which he appears to have prepared very thoroughly. In Raetia considerable numbers of new milestones indicate that the network of roads was repaired and increased; troops were collected from various sources, including detachments from *II Adiutrix* from Upper Pannonia and from *II Traiana* from Egypt. The campaign is not well-documented, but Caracalla's frontier policy probably combined open warfare and demonstrations of strength, possibly followed by the payment of subsidies to the tribes to keep them quiet. In other cases he may have played one tribe against another to divert their attention from Roman territory. Whatever his methods, they brought peace for two decades thereafter. Caracalla took the title *Germanicus Maximus*, and received his third acclamation as Imperator.

The East

As a dedicated admirer of Alexander the Great, Caracalla was drawn to the east, whether or not there was a need for Roman intervention. The opportunity was timely since the Parthian Royal House was still disunited, Vologaeses V and his brother Artabanus being at odds with each other. Preparing for the eastern campaign, Caracalla took over the kingdom of Edessa, which he made into a colony, intending to use it as a military base. He tried and failed to take over the kingdom of Armenia.

He marched to the east by way of the Danube provinces, attending to affairs in Dacia, making some sort of alliance and probably raising troops there, arriving in Macedonia towards the end of 214. Vologaeses diplomatically avoided all action which would put him in the wrong with regard to the Roman Emperor, so Caracalla was hard pressed to find any reason to make war. He was temporarily distracted by trouble in Alexandria, where there were serious problems, demanding the Imperial presence. Leaving the Parthian campaign to his general Theocritus, who was sent to attack Armenia, Caracalla went to Alexandria where he is credited with killing many people in 215–6. At the end of 216 he returned to the east, where the situation had changed. Theocritus's expedition had been disastrous, and Vologaeses had been replaced by his more energetic brother Artabanus V. Roman ascendancy was no longer assured. Instead of mounting a quick campaign, Caracalla tried to negotiate a marriage between his daughter and the son of Artabanus, but the offer was refused. The troops resented this ineffective inaction. Rumours began to circulate, foremost among them the prophecy that the Praetorian Prefect Macrinus would succeed Caracalla. The Emperor heard of it, and Macrinus began to fear for his life. At least, that was his story after he had murdered Caracalla, early in April 217.

Macrinus AD 217–218

The Praetorian Prefect Marcus Opellius Macrinus was the first non-senator to become emperor. He was a native of Mauretania who had survived the fall of his patron, the infamous Plautianus. He started out with three disadvantages: he was not of the correct social class, he owed his elevation to the army, and he was not in Rome when he became emperor. The rise of Macrinus ought to have created waves in the Senate and throughout the Roman world, but the senators were so relieved to be rid of Caracalla that they did not care at first that the new emperor was not of the relevant social rank.

Macrinus took the name of Severus to imbue his reign with some continuity with the previous regime. In a letter to the Senate, Macrinus announced his adoption of the Severan name and gave himself the additional titles of Pius Felix Augustus. It would have been more fitting to wait for the Senate to bestow these titles upon him, but Macrinus chose to act on his own authority. On the subject of Caracalla, everyone proceeded with circumspection. The Senate did not dare to vote for damnation of Caracalla's memory because of their fear of the soldiers, who had supported him, so Macrinus neither declared him an enemy of Rome, nor did he deify him. The episode illustrates the divergent interests of the civil population and the military, and the fact that the preponderant influence lay with the soldiers.

In keeping with Imperial practice, Macrinus was consul in 218, with Oclatinius Adventus as his colleague, but this appointment caused resentment, since Adventus's origins were even lower than those of Macrinus himself. He was an uneducated ex-mercenary who had been a member of the *frumentarii* or secret police. Macrinus made him city prefect, but replaced him soon afterwards by Marius Maximus, perhaps because of public disapproval, but more likely because Adventus was an old man who had seen long service. Other appointments of Macrinus were criticised, because he employed non-senators in positions of responsibility which more usually went to consulars, choosing suitable men for the tasks he gave them, regardless of social standing or rank. He removed Caracalla's adherents Sabinus and Castinus from their posts as governors of Pannonia and Dacia, and installed in their stead his own men Marcius Agrippa, a slave who had been convicted and banished, and Deccius Triccianus, once a door-keeper to the governor of Pannonia, rising to commander of *II Parthica* and then to provincial governor.

Macrinus inherited the Parthian war from Caracalla. Taking advantage of the preoccupation of the Roman high command, King Artabanus had seized the chance to launch an offensive against Mesopotamia. Macrinus prepared for a counter offensive, but the war was ended by negotiation. He bought peace from Artabanus, and readjusted some territorial boundaries. Despite his appointment as Praetorian Prefect, Macrinus was not a military man, but an experienced jurist, and an administrator with a wide knowledge of how the Empire functioned, and realistic about his own capabilities in conducting a war in the east. Sufficiently satisfied with the outcome of the eastern campaign, he awarded himself the title *Parthicus Maximus* in his report to the Senate.

In attempting to provide for the future succession, Macrinus bestowed on his young son Diadumenianus the name Antoninus and the title Caesar, confirmed by the Senate. In deference to the army, he finally deified Caracalla. The army was essential as the main prop for his regime, but he needed to strike a balance. Macrinus tried to curb the expenses of the army, without unduly offending the troops. While he did not attempt to withdraw any privileges, he did not celebrate the Parthian victory by gifts to the soldiers, and worse still, he reverted to the Severan rates of pay, ignoring the rise that Caracalla had awarded the army, a measure which may have pleased the Senate and people but certainly did not please the soldiers, who were accustomed to the lavish rewards given them by Caracalla. The discontented troops began to murmur.

Macrinus made a fatal mistake in failing to disperse individual army units in winter quarters. By allowing them to stay together, he made it easier for them to foment rebellion, so when relatives of the Severan family made their move, the ground had been well prepared. The Empress Julia Domna did not long survive her son Caracalla, but she had a sister, Julia Maesa, whose ambitions were no less ardent than her own. Julia Maesa's two daughters, Julia Soaemias and Julia Mammaea, each had a young son, and Maesa was determined that her elder grandson should be emperor. She persuaded the soldiers that Caracalla was the true father of Soaemias's son Varius Avitus Bassianus, and on 16 May 218 the army declared the boy Emperor, with the name Marcus Aurelius Antoninus, nicknamed Elagabalus, after his devotion to the eastern god of the same name.

Elagabalus AD 218–222

Macrinus persuaded the Senate to declare Elagabalus a usurper and enemy of the state, and elevated his son Diadumenianus to the rank of Augustus, but the troops deserted them and both were killed. Elagabalus entered Antioch early in June, paying the soldiers 2,000 *sesterces* each to persuade them not to sack the city. He wrote to the Senate as emperor, styling himself Imperator Caesar Antoninus, grandson of Severus. At the end of September 219, Elagabalus arrived in Rome, bringing with him the strange and passionate cult of the god after which he was named. As priest of this cult Elagabalus would not be persuaded to wear suitable Roman clothing, and had ordered a painting of himself in his priestly robes to be sent on ahead to

Rome and placed in the Senate House, so that everyone would become accustomed to seeing him. Despite these visual aids, the Senate and people of Rome had no inkling of the character of the new emperor, nor of the overpowering influence of the Syrian princesses.

Probably before he arrived in Rome, Elagabalus embarked on the usual round of reshuffling military and government officials, disposing of Macrinus's followers and installing his own. Publius Valerius Comazon was made Praetorian Prefect, though he had absolutely no experience. He rose even higher, quite rapidly attaining the rank of consul. He held the post of city prefect three times, which was considered positively scandalous for an equestrian who had once been condemned to the galleys. Significantly, Claudius Attalus, the senator responsible for condemning him to the galleys, did not long survive Comazon's appointment as Praetorian Prefect. Other victims were despatched as quickly, and the Senate obligingly condemned them after Elagabalus had killed them.

For the reign of Elagabalus the focus of the ancient sources is the scandals in Rome, with the result that knowledge of what was happening in the provinces is not elucidated. The enormities of the reign hold all the attention. It was not so much Elagabalus's outrageous sexual behaviour that caused offence as the fact that he was strongly influenced, to the exclusion of all else, by the unsuitable men with whom he associated, and he was unable or unwilling to shake off the controlling authority of his mother Julia Soaemias. His grandmother Julia Maesa failed to control him, but soon found a way of supplanting him by her other grandson, Gessius Bassianus Alexianus, the son of Julia Mammaea. She arranged his formal adoption by Elagabalus, who was only a few years older than his cousin. The Senate ratified the adoption, fully aware of the ridiculousness of it all. Alexianus was renamed Severus Alexander, and was made consul in 221. Before long, Elagabalus was intriguing against his cousin, but found that Alexander was too well protected by his grandmother and the Praetorians. The end was not far off. On 6 March 222 the soldiers killed Elagabalus, his mother, and many of his adherents, including Fulvius the city prefect. Once again Comazon, the only one of Elagabalus's court to survive, filled this sudden vacancy for his third term as city prefect. Marcus Aurelius Severus Alexander, still a teenager, was declared emperor.

Severus Alexander AD 222–235

Reforms and reparations were badly needed. One of the first Imperial appointments was Domitius Ulpianus, or Ulpian, as sole Praetorian Prefect, unencumbered by a colleague throughout his short-lived appointment. He was a jurist, not a soldier, but at this moment administrators and legal experts were required to a greater extent than soldiers. Ulpian was part of Julia Maesa's circle, perhaps with long established connections with the Severan dynasty. He had been *praefectus annonae* at the beginning of 222, becoming Praetorian Prefect in December of the same year. His achievements were worthy, but unfortunately he was murdered, perhaps in the spring of 223, but some sources give the date 228.

Throughout the reign of Severus Alexander, the Syrian princesses Julia Maesa and Julia Mammaea were the guiding forces in the government. Mammaea was honoured with several titles which gave her no actual political powers but extended her influence. In particular she took on the role that Julia Domna had held with regard to the army, with the title *mater castrorum*, or mother of the camp. Not content with that alone, eventually she was known as *mater Augusti et castrorum et senatus atque patriae*, indicating that her influence if not her authority extended over most aspects of Roman life, including the senate. This sort of influence worked through connections and favours, not via political procedures, but it was just as effective. The Syrian princesses took care to surround the young Emperor with the best qualified advisers, choosing sixteen of the noblest senators to guide him, acting as part of his council, or *consilium*.

Fortunately for the young Emperor and his advisers there was a peaceful interlude from 222 until 230, during which the policy of expansion and aggressive warfare was dormant, taking second place to restructuring the government. The eight or nine years before war broke out in the east enabled a new aristocracy to establish itself, and some of the old Severan notables re-emerged during the 220s, infiltrating government posts and the Imperial court.

The Rise of the Sassanid Persians

While the Romans had been concentrating on their internal problems, the Parthian Royal House was under threat from a powerful new lord, nominally a vassal of Artabanus V. This was Ardashir, or Artaxerxes, son of Sasan, of Iranian lineage. In 224 the Sassanid Persian dynasty with Ardashir at its head supplanted that of the Parthian Artabanus, after the latter was defeated and killed on the battlefield of Hormizdagan. Within a few years, Ardashir had begun to expand his empire to incorporate the states around the old Parthian kingdom. This naturally brought him into contact with Roman frontier territories. The first news of trouble on the eastern frontier reached Rome probably in 229 when the Persian king attacked Hatra. By 230 Severus Alexander was preparing for an eastern expedition, recruiting soldiers in Italy and the provinces. He left Rome in spring 231.

There was trouble among the troops when Severus Alexander arrived in the east. The Mesopotamian legions had murdered the governor Flavius Heracleo, and the Egyptian troops among Alexander's army were restless. These problems were dealt with before the campaign began. Coins were issued with the legends *Fides militum* and *Fides exercitus* proclaiming the loyalty of the army, but it was more an indication of wishful thinking than reality. Using Antioch as a base, Alexander attacked in three columns, leading the central one himself, while the others marched to the north and south, one to Armenia and then into Media, and the other towards the Persian city of Ctesiphon. The results were mixed, with huge losses on both sides, but especially to the Roman troops when they marched back through the hostile terrain of Armenia. Alexander was blamed for his slow advance and lack of support for the other two columns, and at some point there was an attempted usurpation by a certain Uranius, who was quickly suppressed.

Alexander's achievements were perhaps not as abysmal as they have been painted. The Persians remained quiet after the campaigns, not causing any serious trouble until the 240s under Ardashir's successor Shapur I. While he was still in Antioch, Alexander received news of disturbances on the Rhine and Danube. There had been attacks on the frontiers at several points, in Upper Germany, and in Raetia. Without concluding an official peace with Ardashir, Alexander returned to Rome at the end of 232. He held a triumph, and then began preparations for the war on the northern frontiers. He took with him troops which had fought in Mesopotamia, such as the archers from Osroene and the units of Moors. As part of the preparations he placed an experienced officer in command of the recruits. This was a soldier of Thracian origin who had risen from the ranks, Caius Julius Verus Maximinus, who would be responsible for training the troops for the coming campaign.

The destruction of several forts along the Taunus-Wetterau frontier in Germany has been dated to 233 or thereabouts, suggesting that this area was where the German tribes concentrated their attacks, an assumption corroborated by the fact that Severus Alexander chose Mainz as his base, launching an offensive in 234 against a new federation of Germanic tribes who were by now calling themselves the Alamanni. Alexander won a victory, but instead of pursuing the enemy and eradicating them, he began to negotiate, offering money and perhaps food and supplies. He may have assessed the situation correctly, analysing what this was that the tribesmen needed, preferring to give it to them before they came to take it, but the troops saw it differently. The Emperor's policy caused much resentment. In spring 235, Severus Alexander and his mother were murdered, and the Pannonian soldiers proclaimed as Emperor Caius Julius Verus Maximinus, nicknamed Thrax, the Thracian.

Maximinus Thrax AD 235–238

Maximinus was better known to the troops than Severus Alexander, with a proven military record. He was the first soldier-emperor to rise from the ranks, only a few decades after Septimius Severus had broadened the base of recruitment and facilitated promotions for outstanding soldiers and junior officers. Maximinus Thrax was perceived by the Senate as a barbarian, but nevertheless the senators passed the necessary decrees investing Maximinus with Imperial powers.

The new Emperor did not disappoint his supporters, immediately continuing the war against the Germanic tribes, but even in the Rhine and Danube armies, not everyone was unanimous in support of his rule. Severus Alexander's Osroenian archers set up their own emperor, a man called Quartinus, and a group of officers declared for a senator called Magnus. Neither group was successful.

Maximinus developed a healthy distrust of everyone, especially senators. His very young son was quickly declared Caesar. The immediate entourage of Severus Alexander was removed, but without wholesale murder. Some men were relegated to lower grade posts, such as the equestrian Timesitheus, one of the close associates of Alexander, who was sent out of the way to a provincial command.

By the end of 235, Maximinus was calling himself *Germanicus Maximus*, and in 236 he had transferred the army to Pannonia, basing himself at Sirmium to fight against the Sarmatians and Dacians. Inscriptions from Pannonia refer to soldiers killed in a Dacian war in the reign of Maximinus. Occupied with these northern wars, Maximinus did not enter Rome to reaffirm his rule and try to win at least some members of the Senate to his side. Instead he ignored the Senate and concentrated wholly on the frontiers, consuming vast amounts of money to pay the soldiers. The usual taxes did not prove sufficient for his needs, but to be fair to him, income had not matched expenditure for some considerable time.

Perhaps he could have limited the financial damage caused by his taxation policies, but in concentrating on the matter in hand he did not seem to care about other sectors of the community, laying himself open to charges of cruelty, greed and corruption. He complicated matters by giving the soldiers a pay rise, never a popular move because the inhabitants of Rome, secure now for many years, did not experience at first hand the threats to their frontiers and probably did not worry about it very much until there was a sudden scare, as in the reign of Marcus Aurelius when the Germans reached Aquileia in the north of Italy. To the Romans of Italy and the more peaceful provinces, the army was far away, full of semi-barbarous men who were troublesome and greedy. It was no longer a case of their own young men marching bravely away to fight in defence of the Empire, then coming home as heroic corpses or victorious heroes. When the Empire was smaller, the army was a part of the state, consisting of neighbours and friends, but now it was literally a foreign body, and despite the work that the soldiers did, the army was not appreciated, particularly when money was wrested from unwilling hands to pay for its services.

The financial dilemma had important consequences, provincial in origin but affecting the whole Empire. Some of the wealthy nobles in Africa rebelled against the extraordinarily harsh tax collections, killing the Roman procurator in Thysdrus (modern El Djem), and then realizing that in order to prevent Imperial retribution they would need an emperor of their own. The proconsul Marcus Antonius Gordianus Sempronianus was persuaded to take on the task, but since he was in his eighties, he immediately shared power with his son of the same name, both of them known to modern audiences as Gordian I and II.

Gordian I & Gordian II AD 238

From now onwards it is well-nigh impossible to establish the precise chronology of the virtually simultaneous events on the northern frontiers, in Africa and in Rome. At the beginning of April 238 the Senate confirmed the Gordians in power. In Rome the Praetorian Prefect Vitalianus, loyal to Maximinus, was killed by agents of the Gordians, and the city prefect Sabinus was killed during a riot. In Africa, the two Gordians were quickly routed and killed by the governor of Numidia, Capellianus, who was loyal to Maximinus, and who was fortunately not interested in seizing power for himself. The Empire was now officially leaderless.

Maximinus, outlawed by the Senate, gathered his troops and marched towards Italy. Another emperor had to be found, but the Senate compromised by electing two of them, Marcus Clodius Pupienus Maximus and Decimus Caelius Calvinus Balbinus, as if the new emperors were regarded as consuls, each checking and balancing the other. When the people and the soldiers of the Praetorian Guard agitated in favour of the thirteen-year-old Marcus Antonius Gordianus, the nephew of Gordian II, the Senate recognized the boy as Caesar, conceding that he would be the successor of the two senatorial emperors.

As Maximinus approached Italy, Balbinus remained in Rome, while Pupienus marched north to meet the outlawed emperor, and won a victory of sorts. Maximinus's army, besieging Aquileia, was disaffected, because food supplies were low and morale was even lower. Eventually the soldiers of *II Parthica*, thinking of the safety of their families at Alba, not far from Rome, decided to kill Maximinus and his son. Pupienus took over all the troops, keeping the German contingents as his bodyguard. He sent the others back to their bases and returned to Rome. His employment of German guards made the Praetorians uneasy, in case he planned to dismiss them and install the German units instead. In the event, the experiment with two equal emperors failed because of mutual jealousies and their inability to win over the Praetorian Guard, who brutally tortured and then murdered both Pupienus and Balbinus, and declared Gordian III Emperor.

Gordian III AD 238–244

The main sources for the history of Rome now expire altogether or lose themselves in fantasy, so only an outline can be given of the events of the next few years. Besides the soldiers, the nobles also rallied to Gordian, as did the populace, possibly because his accession brought a temporary peace after a long period of unrest, and measures were taken to put right the several wrongs that had plagued the state since the reign of Caracalla. Attempts were made to improve the finances of the inhabitants of the Empire without compromising the state treasury. The ranks of the sycophants and informers were considerably thinned, and control of the army was tightened up. *Legio III Augusta* in Africa was disbanded for its part in the defeat and deaths of the first two Gordians, but without the legion to keep order and to take charge of defence, trouble broke out afresh in Africa. The governor of Mauretania, Caesariensis, had to restore order.

Gordian III was a teenager, hardly of an age to rule by himself. By 241, the most important man in his entourage was Timesitheus, who was appointed Praetorian Prefect and to all practical intents and purposes directed policy and military matters. The Imperial peace did not last long over the whole Empire. Internal as well as external troubles beset the provinces. In some areas there was dissension between the civilian population and the soldiers, as the famous inscription from the Thracian village of Skaptopara (in Bulgaria) demonstrates. In 238 the villagers petitioned Gordian III to protect them against the depredations of the soldiers of the nearby garrisons, who descended upon them demanding *hospitium* (in Greek *xenia* or *xeinie*), literally 'hospitality' but implying much more than that. It was not exactly an illegal procedure, having its roots in Republican and early Imperial practice when soldiers were quartered not in barracks but in official lodging houses, but in the case of Skaptopara it descended into blatant exploitation, because the soldiers took whatever they wanted without paying for it. Gordian referred the villagers to the provincial governor. The complaints of the inhabitants of Skaptopara may have been symptomatic of similar problems elsewhere.

Externally, there were ominous signs of disturbance in the Empire. In the west, coin hoards deposited in the years 238–244 indicate some kind of trouble, usually interpreted as unrest originating from incursions of tribesmen from beyond the Rhine. It seems that there was some destruction in north-west Gaul, and in some parts of Germany, where coins and other objects were buried between 241–244 at Kösching and Gunzenhausen, and the fort at Künzing was destroyed. Further east, Pannonia was quiet and untroubled, but in Moesia and Dacia the Carpi and the Goths had erupted into Roman territory. The Emperors Pupienus and Balbinus sent the general Menophilus to restore order in 238. He brought the tribes to terms and arranged a treaty, which was more favourable to the Goths, who received subsidies, than to the Carpi, who did not. It may have been a deliberate ploy to set one tribe against another.

In 239 the Persian King Ardashir took advantage of his enemy's preoccupation, attacking Dura Europos on the Euphrates, and possibly capturing Hatra. He overran the greater part of Mesopotamia, threatening Syria. A gap in the coinage of Antioch from 240–241 implies that he may have attacked or even taken the city. In 241 in Rome, preparations for war were begun. In the same year, Timesitheus became Praetorian Prefect, and his daughter was married to Gordian III.

Before Timesitheus could begin the war with Ardashir, he was forced to attend to the Goths and Germans in Illyricum. After a short war against them in 242, Timesitheus concluded peace, probably recruiting defeated tribesmen for the eastern campaign. He and Gordian III arrived in the east probably in the last months of 242, thus delaying the start of the Persian campaign until the spring of 243. By now Ardashir had raised his son Shapur as his colleague, and the latter may have taken over Edessa. Timesitheus wrested Osroene from Persian control, and after a battle at Rhesaena the Persians left Nisibis and Singara, but at this high point of the war Timesitheus died. The Romans did not recover from the blow, though Gordian III and the Praetorian Prefect Marcus Julius Verus Philippus (Philip the Arab), followed the original plan and marched to Ctesiphon. Events are now clouded in obscurity. From unknown causes, Gordian III died. Philip was blamed for his death, but there are four different versions in the ancient sources for Gordian's demise, so it seems that even the historians were not sure of the facts.

Philip the Arab AD 244–249

Philip was declared emperor by the troops. He said that Gordian's death was from natural causes, and treated the dead emperor with the greatest respect, transporting his ashes to Rome, insisting upon his deification, and negotiating carefully with the Senate, gaining recognition as emperor in the process. Meanwhile he had to extricate the army from the clutches of the Persians. He negotiated peace, by means of an indemnity to the Persians of 500,000 denarii, and giving up control of Armenia. He retained control of Osroene and Mesopotamia. Philip issued coins proclaiming that he had made peace with the Persians (*pax fundata cum Persis*) but the fact that he had bought his way out of a tricky situation was not well received at Rome, so despite his proud statement on his coinage, he is accused of hastening back to Rome without settling the east. The accusation is unfair since Philip placed his brother Priscus in command as equestrian prefect of Mesopotamia. Documents show that Priscus was also governor of Syria, and an inscription reveals that he held the title *rector Orientis*. This does not signify an actual office, but it does indicate that he held wide ranging powers over the eastern provinces.

When he arrived in Rome, Philip made his son Caesar, and later he elevated him to Augustus in 247. The Emperor's wife, Otacilia Severa, was named Augusta. As a further insurance policy for his regime Philip deified his father Marinus, even though he had never been emperor. This was an unprecedented measure, but it was perhaps less artificial than trying to claim descent from any of the previous emperors, none of whom had been particularly admirable or worthy as ancestors.

Philip enjoyed good relations with the Senate, and from the outset of his reign he reaffirmed the old Roman virtues and traditions. From 246–7 he fought the Carpi and Quadi on the Danube, taking the titles *Germanicus* and *Carpicus Maximus*. In 248, back in Rome, he celebrated the Secular Games, always a significant festival for the Romans, marking their development and power over the centuries, but this time the celebrations even more meaningful, since it was the first millennium of Rome, an occasion worthy of celebration, highlighting the fact that Rome if not the Empire had existed for 1,000 years. There were theatrical and musical events, spectacles in the Circus and the amphitheatre, literary and artistic displays. Strictly, the Secular Games were not due to take place for over sixty years, but the ritual religious purifications associated with the Games were probably felt by some to be long overdue.

As part of his dealings with the Goths, Philip stopped paying their subsidies in 248, with the result that by 249 the tribes had formed a coalition, united in adversity to Rome. They invaded Moesia and Thrace, and laid siege to the city of Marcianopolis. Two revolts also broke out among the Roman army commanders in the north and the east. One of the usurpers, Pacatianus, had been given an extended command over Pannonia and Moesia, though it is not specified exactly where his authority lay. His command is symptomatic of the need to combine the armies of more than one province in order to defend large areas, because the enemies of Rome now ranged far and wide, moved rapidly and could not be dealt with by one provincial governor acting alone and keeping within his own defined territory. The corollary to this requirement was that usurpation was rendered more feasible when such commands over large areas and large numbers of soldiers were instituted. Pacatianus issued coins during his brief reign, as did Jotapianus, the other usurper who was declared emperor in the east, in 248 or 249.

Philip lost his nerve and offered to resign, but the Senate made a show of solidarity, shored up by a senator called Caius Messius Quintus Decius, who declared that the revolts would be short lived. He must have sounded confident and convincing, since Philip entrusted to him the defence of Moesia and the Balkans, and the command against Pacatianus. The results were mixed. Decius put down the revolt but was declared emperor by his troops. Civil war followed, despite Decius's attempts to avert disaster and come to terms with Philip. Two Roman armies, one from Rome and the other from the Danube, converged on northern Italy. The location of the final battle is disputed, but wherever it was fought, Decius was the victor and Philip was killed. Complications about the succession were avoided when Philip's eleven year old son was murdered by the Praetorians in Rome.

Decius AD 249–251

Decius was confirmed as emperor towards the end of 249. He started off by attempting to reunify the Roman Empire. As one of the means of doing so he reaffirmed the old Roman religion, not just reinvigorating the cult practices and rituals, but also attending to the restoration of the temple buildings and their internal and external decorative elements. An inscription from Cosa bestows on him the title of *restitutor sacrorum*. As a consequence of his policies he outlawed the cults that he saw as most threatening to unity, chiefly Christianity. Philip had been tolerant towards the Christians, earning himself a reputation in the process, completely unfounded, that he was the first Christian emperor. His reign was the calm before the storm, and the new persecution surprised the Christian community.

It came in the form of an order to sacrifice to the gods of the Empire, rigorously enforced throughout the Roman world. Compliant participants were issued with a certificate to prove that they had obeyed the order. Many people crumbled in the face of the authorities and did as they were told, but perhaps some of the Christians rendered unto Caesar what was his due, privately continuing undeterred in their Christian beliefs. The edict had the advantage of singling out those who were not prepared to conform, and executions followed. The Pope Fabian was among the first to be killed, on 20 January 250. Other trials and executions took place all over the Empire; some people ran away and found refuge in lonely places. The trials embraced not just the lowly adherents, but was aimed at the chief officials of the Church, so the name of Decius has been preserved as the arch-tyrant in the works of the later Christian authors, whose writings have lost nothing in the way of umbrage with the passage of time.

For the persecuted Christians it was seen as divine retribution when the Carpi attacked Dacia and the Goths invaded Moesia in 250. Decius was granted the name of Trajan by the Senate when he became emperor, so the parallel with the erstwhile conqueror of Dacia will have been apparent to anyone with a sense of history when he cleared the Carpi from the Roman province, earning himself the title *restitutor Daciarum*. His campaign had begun well, but he faced a more resolute enemy in the Gothic leader Cniva in Moesia and Thrace. The Goths made camp in front of Nicopolis, and whilst they could not be said to be experts in siege tactics, they had learned a lot on their travels, and they later succeeded in taking Philippopolis. Decius could not dislodge them, so he waited for them to move off in search of food. Meanwhile he made his son Herennius Etruscus, who was already Caesar, his colleague in his regime; his younger son Hostilianus was in Rome with a respected senator, Publius Licinius Valerianus (the future Emperor Valerian) in charge of the civil administration while Decius himself led the army. The presence of a respected senator delegated by the Emperor did not prevent the Roman mob from raising a candidate of their own, Julius Valens Licinianus, to replace Decius, whose name they removed from inscriptions in the city.

Decius was probably too embroiled in the struggle in the Danube provinces to notice that he had been usurped. In 251 the Goths began to move northwards, so Decius followed, fighting battles but unable to bring them to final confrontation until he reached the Dobrudja. He risked battle at Abrittus (modern Razgrad in Bulgaria) and was killed. His dynasty did not survive, since his son Herennius Etruscus may have been killed in one of the earlier skirmishes. There was now a power vacuum which the legions were not slow to fill, declaring for the governor of Moesia, Caius Vibius Afinius Trebonianus Gallus.

Trebonianus Gallus AD 251–253

It was rumoured that Gallus had stood by while Decius fought, or even that he had actually betrayed the Emperor and had gone over to the Goths. When he made peace with the Goths it certainly seemed that he favoured them. He resumed their subsidy payments and allowed them to go free, taking their booty and prisoners with them. He did not feel strong enough to defeat them decisively, and he needed to go to Rome to establish himself in power. He eventually adopted Decius's younger son Hostilianus and raised him alongside his own son Volusianus, making them Caesars and then Augusti.

The most immediate crisis was the plague of 252–3. Hostilianus succumbed to it, leaving Volusianus and his father as emperors. Gallus was powerless to raise morale. Making little progress against the Goths, it also seemed that Gallus could not solve the problems of actual or potential invasions from across the Danube and that he was not prepared to deal with the threat to the eastern provinces, where the Persian King Shapur I took Nisibis. Gallus may have made preparations to conduct a campaign from Antioch, where the mint began to issue a large quantity of *antoniniani*, the coins used to pay the soldiers, as if in preparation for a gathering of troops. But Shapur moved more quickly than the Romans, and captured Antioch, where the Roman coinage was interrupted in 263. In these circumstances the inhabitants of the affected provinces naturally look to someone in the immediate vicinity who can help them without delay. The usurper Uranius Antoninus, Priest-King of Emesa, seized power to organize defence against the Persians.

The Revolt of Aemilius Aemilianus

The Danube frontier was hardly less pressured, so there the troops chose the governor of Lower Moesia, Aemilius Aemilianus, as emperor. He put an end to the subsidies to the Goths and defeated them in battle. Aemilianus realized that his claims would be received in a much better light if he adopted a respectful attitude towards the Senate. Regardless of the fact that Trebonianus Gallus was the legitimate emperor, he sent a letter to Rome suggesting a division of responsibilities. The Senate should exercise supreme power, and he would be the general in chief commanding the Danube and the east.

Gallus sent his general Valerian with the Rhine legions against Aemilianus who was marching on Rome, but the legions proclaimed Valerian as emperor. Valerian perhaps reasoned that he might as well fight on his own behalf, instead of trying to support an emperor who seemed to be rapidly losing control of the Empire. The soldiers killed Gallus and Volusianus, and soon afterwards Aemilianus was eliminated by his troops, leaving Valerian as sole emperor. He set about confirming his power immediately. The Senate bestowed the title Caesar on his adult son Publius Licinius Gallienus. When Valerian arrived in Rome he made Gallienus his colleague as Augustus. Now at last there were two emperors who would be able to deal with the problems in the two halves of the Empire at the same time, Gallienus taking the west and Valerian going to the east as soon as he could, to combat the Persian menace.

The Joint Rule of Valerian & Gallienus AD 253–260

In 253 Shapur I turned his full attention on Armenia, killing King Chosroes, whose son Tiridates fled, leaving Armenia wide open to Persian domination. The Romans soon recovered their losses. On his arrival in the east Valerian set up headquarters at Antioch and started rebuilding the city. The mint reopened, and damage to the surrounding Syrian territories was repaired. From 253 to 255 the situation in the threatened provinces of both east and west slowly improved. Gallienus celebrated victories over the Germans in Illyricum. By 256 it seemed that Rome was in the ascendancy again, until the new threat from the Franks broke out in Gaul and Germany. Gallienus left the Danube provinces, installing his son Valerian the younger at Viminacium as Caesar, while he established his headquarters on the Rhine frontier at Cologne. He opened a mint there, which soon began to issue coins naming Gallienus as *restitutor Galliarum*, the restorer of the Gallic provinces.

In May 258 Valerian arrived in Antioch, while at the same time Gallienus was threatened by a usurper called Ingenuus, whose troops had proclaimed him emperor in Illyricum. It is probable that Gallienus's son, the younger Valerian, was killed in this revolt. Personal disaster was followed by Imperial crisis, on three fronts if not four. Valerian was fully occupied in the east fighting against Shapur I, and Gallienus was re-establishing his authority over Illyricum, but now there were more invasions by the Goths threatening the Black Sea coastal cities, and the Alamanni were restless on the frontiers of Germany and Raetia. The defence of all the western provinces at the same time was impossible. Gallienus had placed his younger son Saloninus at Cologne as the new Caesar, while he returned to northern Italy and set up his headquarters at Milan, where he established a mint. Disasters piled up one on top of another. In the summer of 260, Shapur captured Emperor Valerian, perhaps by treachery. The Persians were now free to dominate the entire east, because there was no one to stop them. Usurpers appeared in several places, because in the absence of Imperial troops, self-help on the frontiers had become the only alternative. At Carnuntum the soldiers chose Regalianus to lead them against the Iazyges and Roxolani. In the east Callistus (also called Ballista in some sources) and Macrianus took charge of the remnants of Valerian's defeated army. Neither Macrianus nor Callistus declared themselves emperors, but Macrianus proclaimed his two sons, Titus Fulvius Junius Macrianus and Titus Fulvius Junius Quietus, as Augusti. In Gaul the governor Postumus was declared emperor. An inscription found at Augsburg shows that the domain of Postumus extended over Raetia as well as the Rhine frontier and the Gallic provinces; Britain was with him and Spain came over to him later.

Emperor Gallienus was backed into a corner in Milan, with only a fraction of the armies of the Empire at his disposal. With these troops and reduced resources he faced multiple problems. There were three usurpers in different parts of the Empire, in command of sizeable armies. The Persians were at liberty to raid the whole of the east, and for the first time in Roman history an emperor had not only failed to check them but had been ignominiously captured. The Goths were on the rampage in Moesia and Thrace, having learned how to use boats for successful hit and run raids on rich cities, and the Franks and Alamanni and other assorted tribes were poised to attack the Rhine and the upper Danube. Gallienus was forced to use the limited resources that he had at his disposal. Lateral thinking, continual adaptation to circumstances, and changes in operational and organisational methods were the first priority, if Rome and the Empire were to survive.

6

Hard Times:
The Empire Fragments
AD 260–284

Gallienus Sole Emperor AD 260–268

After the capture of Valerian by the Persians, Gallienus ruled alone. From his reign onwards, the Roman world entered upon a period of change, and though the changes may not have been intended to be permanent, by degrees they became entrenched and in some cases irrevocable. Deprived of the troops and the revenues of the western and eastern areas of the Empire, and therefore forced to make the best use of what was immediately to hand, Gallienus adapted old established methods and produced something new, sometimes sacrificing hallowed traditions if they were not suited to his current circumstances. Gallienus reformed the army and the administration, but these reforms evolved from emergency measures rather than as a result of a co-ordinated policy. For most of his reign Gallienus was barely one step ahead of disasters, and was not granted the luxury of forward planning, but his achievements laid the foundations for the development of the later Roman Empire.

Remaining sole emperor, Gallienus did not appoint a colleague to replace his father. He could not spare troops for a military expedition to rescue Valerian without risking usurpation at home or invasion from the northern tribes, nor did he have access to sufficient wealth to offer a ransom payment. Gallienus's apparent lack of filial devotion derived from necessity, since the state had to take priority.

The Army Reforms

Gallienus had more need than most of an efficient and loyal army. In the west, all the legions of the Rhine and in Gaul, and most of the civilian population of these provinces supported the Gallic usurper Postumus. In the east, the Persians were stronger than they had been for many years, and if it had not been for the energetic defence of the east by the Palmyrenes under their leader Odenathus, the Persians would probably have taken over all of the eastern Roman provinces.

Hemmed in on east and west, Gallienus adapted to circumstances. Fiscal and social policy, political and military traditions, everything in fact, were all subordinated to the needs of the army. He started by welding together the troops that were with him, issuing the so-called legionary coinage with which to pay them. Using the evidence from the distribution of the coins, various authors have attempted to identify the troops of the motley collection that was Gallienus's army. The Praetorians and seventeen different legions feature on the coinage, but they were probably vexillations rather than whole units, since none of Gallienus's coins have been found at the home bases of the legions in question. The core troops available to Gallienus in 260 were those which he had collected together for the Rhine campaign in the 250s, including the Praetorians and *II Parthica* from Italy, accompanied by vexillations from the legions of the provinces of Britain, the Rhine and the Danube, together with some auxiliary units.

Gallienus proclaimed the loyalty of the army via the legends on his coinage. He devoted attention to the welfare of the soldiers, and to their monetary rewards as far as possible within his limited resources. The career prospects of ordinary soldiers were improved, so that through distinguished service in the army, each man could look forward to the possibility of promotion the highest social rank.

Map 2. Map of the Roman Empire about AD 260, after the defeat and capture of the Emperor Valerian by the Persians. His son and co-ruler Gallienus was confined to Italy and the Danube provinces, deprived of the armies and revenues of both eastern and western portions of the Empire.

The most famous, but least well documented change that Gallienus made to the army was to create a mobile cavalry army. In the straitened circumstances of the 260s there was a pressing need for rapid response and increased mobility. Based in northern Italy, Gallienus needed to be able to reach the Danube provinces, and to guard the Alpine passes. It has been said that he based himself and the mobile cavalry at Milan to prepare for invasion by Postumus, but in 260 a more realistic consideration was the presence of the Alamanni poised to descend into northern Italy. Milan and the plain of the River Po constitute good horse country, with good grazing and cavalry-friendly terrain. There is good access from Milan through the Alps northwards and eastwards to the Danube, and westwards to Gaul.

The separate cavalry army of Gallienus was a new development. The horsemen were not brigaded in auxiliary units based in the frontier posts, or attached to any provincial army. Operating as a distinct unit, the cavalry had its own commander, Aureolus, attested in more than one source. He was answerable directly to the Emperor. The cavalry was formed from the troops that Gallienus was able to muster after the loss of the Gallic and Rhine provinces, comprising *alae* and *cohortes equitatae*, and the *equites Dalmatae*, which may have been regular units, named after the province of Dalmatia where they were based, or more likely they were Dalmatian tribesmen recruited for their skill in horsemanship. In addition, Gallienus's mobile army contained the legionary cavalry, called the *promoti*, perhaps denoting an upgrade in status as they transferred from the legions to the cavalry army.

The Byzantine chronicler George Cedrenus says that Gallienus was the founder of the mobile cavalry army, familiar to ancient writers from the fourth century, but Cedrenus may have applied the term anachronistically. It cannot be stated categorically that Gallienus's cavalry army was the forerunner of the later mobile armies, because it is not certain how long it survived after his death. An inscription dating to the reign of Claudius Gothicus may refer to the mobile cavalry, since a distinction is made between the *vexillationes adque equites*, or the detachments and the horsemen, suggesting that the cavalry differed from the vexillations and did not fight under the same standard. The mobile cavalry was perhaps used to good effect by Claudius Gothicus against the Goths, and then by Aurelian, but it seems that after about 285 it was no longer at Milan, and subsequently it is not attested as a separate entity. It may have been disbanded, leaving Diocletian and Constantine to discover its usefulness all over again.

The Protectores

The title of *protector* first appeared in the joint reigns of Valerian and Gallienus. The *protectores* were drawn from diverse units and followed diverse careers, so they were not formed into a specific unit, making it unlikely that Gallienus intended to form a new bodyguard. *Protector* did not denote a rank, but it was a mark of distinction, proclaiming an acknowledged loyalty to the emperor. It was not awarded to senators, so it is possible that Gallienus wanted to establish a new kind of aristocracy of military men with proven ability. The suggestion that the *protectores* were members of a staff college is supported by the fact that at least one man was designated *princeps protectorum*, implying that there was a group who worked together and one of them was regarded as the leader. Some of the more distinguished *protectores* went on to higher offices, so that it is clear that the conferment of the title was a indication that such men were marked out for splendid careers.

The Gallic Empire

Probably in 260 when the capture of Valerian by the Persians was known in the west, Marcus Cassianus Latinius Postumus, governor of Lower Germany, was proclaimed emperor by his troops. The Rhine army had no confidence in the ability of the legitimate emperor to protect the provinces from invasion, and chose the man whom the soldiers thought most capable of doing so. The Gallic Empire was firmly based on Roman institutions. Consuls were elected annually, the emperor assumed tribunician power each year, and he protected himself by means of a Praetorian Guard.

Postumus remained in power for a decade. The two Germanies, the whole of Gaul, with the possible exception of Narbonensis, then Britain and Spain joined him. He set up headquarters at Cologne, and attended to the repair and defence of the Rhine frontier and its hinterland. He promoted himself just as Gallienus did, advertising his successes, issuing good quality coinage that proclaimed him restorer of Gaul (*Restitutor Galliarum*) and the bringer of security to the provinces (*Salus Provinciarum*).

The restored provinces, somewhat battered, were restructured according to current needs. Archaeologists have shown that many if not all the frontier forts on the Rhine and through Germany were abandoned after 260, and there is evidence of widespread destruction. City authorities began to think very seriously of strong walls and fortified gates. The magnitude of Postumus's task occupied him fully for many years, perhaps preventing him from turning his attention to Rome and the struggle for supreme power over the whole Empire. It is debatable whether he ever intended to usurp Gallienus, who never officially recognized him, but no amount of discussion as to Postumus's ambitions can solve this problem.

Gallienus on the other hand tried to win back the Gallic Empire, perhaps on two occasions, in 261 and possibly in 265–266. He controlled the exits from the Alpine passes to protect the route into Italy, and he may have succeeded in regaining control of Raetia, but ultimately he failed and had to withdraw when he was wounded at Trier. Neither Postumus nor his successors marched on Rome to fight it out with the legitimate emperor, but further conflict was inevitable.

Odenathus & the Kingdom of Palmyra

When the senior Emperor Valerian was taken prisoner by Shapur I, the Roman army was extricated by Macrianus, an equestrian who had been put in charge of logistics and supplies for the campaign as *praepositus annonae expeditionalis*. He later broke with Gallienus, proclaiming his two sons Augusti, eventually marching on Rome with the younger Macrianus, leaving the other son, Quietus, with Callistus or Ballista in command of the eastern provinces, based at Emesa. Gallienus's general and cavalry commander Aureolus defeated the two Macriani in Pannonia, and possibly after this defeat the citizens of Emesa eliminated Quietus. Ballista disappeared. The Palmyrene Odenathus pursued Shapur as the Persian army headed back across the Euphrates laden with booty.

Palmyra owed its existence and its wealth to its fortunate geographical position, at a well-watered location in the desert, where crops could be grown, animals raised, and the inhabitants could conduct their long-distance trading ventures. It was not only a trading city in its own right, but a place of high culture with an established nobility, of which Odenathus was one of the foremost members. His father Hairan had been granted Roman citizenship by Severus, and on inscriptions Odenathus calls himself Septimius. He was raised to senatorial rank, and by 258 he was of consular status (*vir consularis*).

Debate centres around the relationship between Gallienus and Odenathus. In 260 Gallienus was in no position to refuse the help of Odenathus against either the Persians or the usurpers. Odenathus had little choice except to take charge of the eastern provinces. Sandwiched between the Empire of Rome in the west and the rising power of Shapur and the Persian Empire in the east, it was possible that the Palmyrenes could turn either way, and it was thought by later chroniclers that Odenathus initially made overtures to Shapur before he began to act on behalf of Rome. Since Gallienus could not afford to mount a campaign of his own to win back the east, the better option was to allow Odenathus to continue as he had begun. Unlike Postumus in Gaul, Gallienus officially recognized Odenathus, possibly granting him a military command as *dux Romanorum*, leader of the Romans. This title is not definitely attested for Odenathus, but since Vaballathus, his son and successor held the title, it is assumed that it derived from Odenathus and that he was placed in command of troops in the east. It is not clear exactly how his command operated with regard to the existing military officers in the eastern provinces, and the provincial governors. With the sanction of Rome the Palmyrenes had for some time provided a military force under their own commanders, with which they patrolled the desert between Syria and the Euphrates, so Odenathus would have controlled these troops, but the major question is whether or not Odenathus was also placed in command of the Roman government personnel in the east, and all the available troops. It is likely that the arrangement with Gallienus may have allowed Odenathus a certain freedom of action within defined parameters.

In 262–3 and again in 267, Odenathus launched campaigns against Persia, reaching Ctesiphon and liberating Nisibis from Persian domination. In respect of these victories Gallienus took the title *Parthicus Maximus*, granting to Odenathus the title *corrector totius Orientis*. As with his title of *dux*, the inference is drawn from the titles displayed by his son Vaballathus, and not from direct evidence concerning Odenathus himself. Precisely what the title implied is not known for certain. It is reminiscent of Priscus, the brother of Philip the Arab, who was put in charge of the eastern provinces with the title *rector orientis*. Significantly, Odenathus was not granted official Roman posts such as proconsul, prefect or *praeses*. He awarded himself the title king of kings, but this did not signify that he intended to take over the Empire. The title was customary in the east, and since he had charge of the eastern provinces, Odenathus adopted a title that would be meaningful to the eastern population.

When the Goths invaded Roman territory in Asia Minor, Odenathus hurried to repel them, but before he had completed his task he was assassinated along with his eldest son, by one of his own men, in 267 or 268. The circumstances are obscure. The exact date of the assassination is unknown, and more than one murderer is named in the different ancient sources, including Gallienus himself as the instigator of a plot to remove the Palmyrene leader.

After the death of Odenathus and his son, it is possible that Gallienus could have reunited the eastern provinces with the rest of his Empire, but invasions by the northern tribes across the Danube preoccupied him. Zenobia, the young, energetic and ambitious wife of Odenathus, stepped into the power vacuum in the name of her young son Vaballathus. According to the ancient sources, she defeated the Praetorian Prefect, Heraclianus, allegedly sent by Gallienus to take charge of the east, but since Heraclianus is named as one of Gallienus's assassins in 268, this expedition, if it took place at all, may have been organized by one of Gallienus's successors. Since Gallienus failed to regain control of the east, he was regarded as a failure. It was Aurelian who brought the Empire back together.

The Equestrians & the Senators

Severus had promoted equestrians as military commanders and provincial governors, and Gallienus took the policy even further, appointing equestrians, including military men who had risen from the ranks, to high commands which had previously been the almost exclusive domain of the senatorial class. He employed men whom he knew and trusted, usually professional soldiers who had concentrated almost exclusively on the army and had not served their time simply in order to advance their political careers. In the early Empire ambitious senators usually combined their urban and civilian posts with a term of service with the army, as tribunes in a legion, then later as legionary legates, but these military appointments were merely stepping stones to a more glorious political career.

Gallienus preferred to put experienced equites rather than senators in charge of legions, not as *legati* but as *praefecti*, as in Egypt from the time of Augustus, where the equestrian commander was called *praefectus legionis*. Severus also appointed equestrian *praefecti* as legionary commanders of the three new Parthian legions. Gallienus built on these precedents, installing equestrian prefects at the head of all the legions in the provinces where his control was unchallenged. The post of legionary legate was not swept aside. The full title for the equestrian commanders, *praefectus agens vices legati*, reflects the fact that the prefect was acting as substitute for the legate.

Equestrians were also appointed as governors of some of the provinces. He had no influence in the Gallic provinces, but in the east, it seems that Gallienus still controlled the appointment of governors, while the Palmyrene Odenathus co-ordinated defence. There were precedents for equestrians as temporary governors, for instance when the original governor died or was killed and there was a need for someone to take over until a new governor could be appointed. The usual title, *agens vice praesidis*, made it clear that the equestrian substitute possessed full authority to act on behalf of the provincial governor. From about 260 onwards, Gallienus appointed equestrian *praesides* to certain provinces, not as temporary substitutes, but as authentic governors.

After 250, fully documented senatorial careers decline in number, and by about 262 the senatorial governors had disappeared from the Imperial praetorian provinces. Exactly how the change was put into effect is not elucidated. It cannot be said that Gallienus was motivated solely by his hatred of the Senate when he appointed equestrians as legionary legates or as *praesides*. The senatorial governors of large provinces with two legions were not affected, principally because equestrian prefects and not senators commanded the troops. The provinces to which equestrians were appointed were those which were threatened by the tribesmen from beyond the frontiers, or where there was internal unrest. Gallienus made no changes in the provinces where no troops were stationed, nor in the senatorial provinces, where he allowed senators to continue as proconsuls.

It has been suggested that Gallienus put an end to senatorial military careers, but in fact the military interests of the senators had been declining for some time. By the mid 250s, the military *tribuni laticlavii* had disappeared. A career pattern based on almost exclusively military or exclusively civil appointments had already begun to manifest itself as early as the reign of Hadrian, contributing to the development of specialization and professionalism, in administration and especially in the army. During the Marcommanic wars, Marcus Aurelius had found it difficult to find a sufficient quantity of suitable senators with military experience, but even after Gallienus's reforms, it is unlikely that all senators were divorced from the army. Nonetheless, senatorial participation in the government of the Empire diminished. The junior magistracies disappeared, except the quaestorship, and equestrians carried out many functions in administration and finance. The Emperor controlled the army, the finances, and significant appointments, so very little was left for the Senate to do. After Gallienus's reforms there were changes in the normal career pattern, the *cursus honorum*. The appointment as governor of a praetorian province usually paved the way to the consulship and then to further appointments. Divorced from posts in Imperial praetorian provinces and from commands in the army, senators had to find alternative routes to the consulship. From the mid-third century a spectacular senatorial career depended upon a good relationship with the emperor, a situation to which Gallienus was probably not entirely unsympathetic.

Finances

Gallienus had the army almost exclusively in mind in his monetary and financial policies. For a long time, income had failed to match expenditure, and there was no budgetary system in the modern sense. In the mid-third century there was an escalating degeneration in the Imperial finances. One response was to debase the currency and issue more of it, and both Valerian and Gallienus consistently adopted this procedure. The result was a rise in prices, the full effects of which were not apparent until after Gallienus's death, beginning around 270.

Cash payments to the army and some taxes were partly transmuted into payments in kind. The central treasury provided partial payment for the troops, but requisitions in kind fell most heavily on those areas where the troops were operating. Some areas could be denuded in a prolonged continuous war, or if successive short campaigns were fought over the same terrain before the next harvests could be brought home. Direct taxation, the source of much of the state revenue, fell most heavily on the wealthy landowners in Italy and the provinces. With regard to the payment of the army, Gallienus founded several mints near the various military headquarters, at Milan, Sirmium, Siscia and Smyrna, which reduced the risks involved in transporting coin across the Empire.

A major problem was that the values of the coinage were not standardized, so in general people judged the worth of the gold *aureus* upon what it actually weighed, not upon what Imperial power said it was worth. In the short term, the consequences of Gallienus's financial policies were satisfactory. The army was well rewarded and functioned as the Emperor wished, and the rest of the Empire managed as best it could. In the long term the policies were disastrous, and Gallienus did not survive long enough to reverse them.

Gallienus's Achievements

The chronology of events in the reign of Gallienus is far from clear. The Alamanni were soundly defeated near Milan in 260, and caused little trouble for several years after the battle. The revolt of Regalianus in Pannonia was ended when he was killed in an invasion by the Iazyges and Roxolani, while that of Macrianus was dealt with by Aureolus in the west and Odenathus in the east. Gallienus's general Theodotus put down another attempt at usurpation by Aemilianus in Egypt, in 261–2. Gallienus quelled an attempted mutiny in Byzantium at about the same time. Once these upheavals calmed down, by 262 Gallienus had re-established control over most·of the Empire save for the extensive territories still loyal to Postumus. Though the east was still in the hands of Odenathus, the Palmyrene ruler was nominally Gallienus's chosen deputy.

During the few years of relative peace between 262 and 265, Gallienus found time to devote to philosophy, promoting his favourite Plotinus. He encouraged literature and the arts, and visited Athens where he was made exarch of the city and was initiated into the Eleusinian mysteries. His self indulgence in leisure pursuits was represented in the later sources as gross negligence.

Towards the end of 266 Gallienus marched to the Danube to fight the Goths. The first campaign produced no tangible result, and in 267 it seemed that the whole of the Roman world from Moesia to the Mediterranean was at the mercy of several tribes. The Goths poured across Moesia into Thrace, and the Heruli threatened Athens, Sparta and Corinth. Another group laid siege to Thessalonika. The Emperor and the army could not be everywhere at once, and the provincial troops were not sufficient in number to meet the invading bands and drive them out. Self-help was the only answer. Various communities built walls around their cities and sometimes it was necessary to arm the civilian inhabitants and lead them to war. An inscription from Augsburg refers to civilians fighting alongside the troops, and in Athens the defence was conducted by the civilian Dexippus, who resisted valiantly but still failed to save his city from capture, a fact which is subsumed in the rhetoric of his account of the episode.

Gallienus concentrated on Illyricum, where he defeated a group of Heruli, incorporating the survivors into the Roman army. He defeated another group at Philippopolis, but was unable to follow up the recent victory, because news arrived that the commander of the cavalry, Aureolus, had raised revolt in Milan. Leaving his general Marcianus in command of the campaign against the Heruli and the Goths, Gallienus marched to Italy, and besieged Milan. In July or August 268 a plot was hatched, led by Heraclianus, to assassinate Gallienus. The commander of the Dalmatian cavalry lured the Emperor outside his tent by announcing that Aureolus was approaching with his army; not waiting for his bodyguard, Gallienus dashed out unprotected, and was killed.

The ancient sources are hostile to Gallienus, masking his real achievements in holding together the remnants of the fragmenting Empire and fighting off usurpers and invasions. It was only under Aurelian that the Empire was pulled back together, but without the efforts of Gallienus, there may have been no Empire to reassemble.

Claudius II Gothicus AD 268–270

The new emperor was Marcus Aurelius Claudius. The army officers supported him, but the troops were not happy, and he had to disburse lots of cash to persuade them to accept him. Claudius was an Illyrian army officer whose career had blossomed under Gallienus, becoming one of Gallienus's closest advisers and most experienced generals. There was apparently no stigma attached to his association with the previous emperor, so it does not seem that there was a conspiracy to remove the whole court circle and the top generals, and then start again with a new faction. Claudius's role in the assassination of Gallienus is not clear. The sources tend to whitewash him because Constantine claimed him as one of his ancestors, so all hints of a less than perfect life were expunged from the record.

Since Claudius was emperor for only a short time, he had no chance to undertake sweeping reforms or to establish coherent policies in the military, financial or social spheres, but the fact that he did not reverse any of Gallienus's policies suggests that the reign of his predecessor was not as dire as it was later portrayed. Claudius's relations with the Senate were at least cordial, but the retrospective favour shown him by Constantine may have improved and embellished the historical record. Careful to observe the formalities, Claudius went to Rome, where he persuaded the Senate to deify Gallienus. By this act, Claudius implied that the murder of Gallienus was illegal, but there was no witch hunt. Only Aureolus was put to death.

Claudius sent the prefect of the *vigiles*, Julius Placidianus, to bring the Gallic Empire back into the Imperial domain, and this officer won over part of Gallia Narbonensis and regained control of the Rhône valley, but failed to reintegrate all the provinces into the Empire. The bulk of Claudius's army was committed to the struggle against the Goths and the Alamanni. The Goths had discovered seaborne transport and were raiding the Mediterranean coastal cities. Claudius entrusted the prefect of Egypt, Tenagino Probus, with a fleet based in Greece to sweep the seas clear of the Goths and to protect the coasts.

Probably at this moment Zenobia, the widow of Odenathus, decided to take advantage of the preoccupations of the Romans to extend her control of the eastern provinces. Her armies swept into Egypt, defeating Tenagino Probus, who committed suicide. The Palmyrenes were now in command of most of the east, and of the bulk of Rome's corn supply, though there is no evidence that Zenobia deliberately disrupted the transport of grain from Egypt.

The Goths were still causing destruction on the Danube and in Greece, and had put Thessalonika and Marcianopolis under siege. Claudius claimed a victory over them at Naissus, but the Goths were not decisively defeated. The Alamanni had been quiet since their defeat in 260, perhaps because they had made a treaty with Gallienus, which they regarded as a personal arrangement between two chiefs. When Gallienus was assassinated the agreement came to an end. Claudius defeated the tribesmen near Lake Garda, taking the title *Germanicus Maximus*. In summer 270 Claudius was at Sirmium, preparing a campaign against the Juthungi and Vandals in the Danube provinces, but he died of the plague that broke out in that year. For a short time his brother Quintillus stepped into the vacancy as emperor, but he did not have the support of the whole army. The rival contender, Aurelian, was proclaimed by his soldiers, and carried all before him.

Aurelian AD 270–275

The origins of Lucius Domitius Aurelianus are unknown. His elevation from obscurity to supreme power was a result of social mobility based on military prowess. When Claudius died Aurelian was on campaign, probably against the Juthungi and Vandals. He was one of the most important officers in Claudius's entourage, and his proclamation as emperor was not a complete surprise. One of his first acts was purely practical; he seized the mint at Siscia, where he struck gold coins to enable him to pay the soldiers.

Aurelian had achieved a reputation for determination and energy, earning the nickname of *manu ad ferrum*, hand on hilt. Before the end of his reign he had earned a reputation for cruelty as well. Aurelian's priorities were to conclude the wars with the tribesmen. The Juthungi were on their way out of northern Italy, heading for home with their booty. Aurelian caught up with them in Raetia. He refused to grant them a peace treaty, but allowed them to continue homewards unmolested, if they would provide soldiers for the Roman army. In the campaign against the Vandals Aurelian devastated the territories all around them to starve them into submission, then he extracted 2,000 cavalry for the army, and made peace, giving food to the remaining Vandals so that they could return home.

When a temporary peace was restored Aurelian journeyed to Rome. The ancient sources indicate that one of the first problems that Aurelian dealt with was the revolt at the mint in Rome. There was a great deal of corruption among the mint workers, who were probably lining their own pockets. Aurelian made an initial attempt to reform the finances in the early part of his reign, and sometime later in 274 he began a more thorough reform of the currency and the financial system.

The attempted usurpations of Septiminus, Domitianus, and Urbanus, were quickly detected and eradicated. Suspicion was all that was necessary to condemn them, and whether they were guilty or not, the point was made that Aurelian would not tolerate opposition. It seems that all of these potential troublemakers appeared and disappeared early in Aurelian's reign, perhaps all of them in 271, possibly even before he arrived in Rome. As mentioned above, chronology is not one of the strong points in the documentation of the period from Gallienus to Diocletian, and for Aurelian's reign it is especially confused.

The Emperor needed to consolidate his supremacy over the Senate and people of Rome. Though the Roman mob no longer possessed the coercive power that it once had, it was always a wise move for new emperors to cultivate the goodwill of the populace, so Aurelian disbursed 500 denarii to each citizen in Rome, and cancelled debts to the Treasury, making a bonfire of all the records and gaining much popularity as a result. On the other hand he raised taxes, damaging the rich. The senators bestowed the usual powers on him, but the Senate as a body was weakened under Aurelian, losing the privilege of issuing bronze coinage, and its legislative powers disappeared as the Emperor evolved into totalitarian ruler and lawgiver.

News arrived that the Juthungi and the Alamanni were moving again, joined by the Marcomanni. The sources vary with regard to the tribes with which Aurelian fought, sometimes calling them all Scythians. Throughout the early part of Aurelian's reign there were rapidly changing military actions and wide ranging movements of troops. In 271 the Juthungi reached Milan. Aurelian chased the tribesmen from battle to battle in northern Italy, defeating bands of warriors in at least three different places, at Fanum Fortunae, Metaurus, and on the Ticinus near modern Pavia. The mobility of the tribesmen made it difficult to pin them down. After defeats they simply split up and then regrouped.

When some semblance of order was restored by running the tribesmen to ground, Aurelian returned to Rome and proclaimed a German victory. He knew well, as did everyone else, that his victories did not mark an end to war. He had gained a temporary respite, nothing more, and Rome was still vulnerable.

For centuries, the city of Rome had stood supreme, without protective walls, having long ago outgrown the old Servian walls enclosing the early city. Now in the late third century circumstances were much different. It had been demonstrated that the frontiers could not withstand determined onslaughts by large numbers of tribesmen. The prime purpose of the frontiers was to discourage attacks, controlling the tribes by a combination of alliances, gifts and subsidies, by patrolling, intelligence gathering, psychological intimidation and occasional aggressive wars. Once the tribesmen were across the Alps, however, the road to Rome was open. Aurelian called a meeting of the Senate to discuss the project of building a wall round the city.

Civilian workers were mobilized, because there were not enough soldiers to spare for building the wall. The circuit was too long to defend adequately, but the intention was not necessarily to enable the city to withstand a prolonged siege. The tribesmen did not generally attempt to besiege cities, because they did not have the ability to supply themselves for a long time in one place. They preferred to make hit and run raids, and move on. The walls of Rome were not finally completed until the reign of Probus, but even so they were built remarkably quickly, by incorporating several buildings within the circuit, and by the fact that the new walls did not take in the full extent of the city.

The Palmyrene Campaign

Aurelian turned to the reunification of the Empire. While he had been occupied on the Danube and also with the problems in Rome, he acquiesced in what amounted to a shared rule in the east with Zenobia's young son Vaballathus. Coins issued by the Alexandrian mint, on the orders of Zenobia, display the head of the Roman Emperor on one side, and on the other that of Vaballathus, but at this point Vaballathus had not assumed Imperial titles. Aurelian tolerated the situation but Zenobia knew that confrontation with the Emperor was inevitable. When he started to mobilize, Zenobia broke with him decisively, awarding to Vaballathus the titles Imperator Caesar Augustus, and calling herself Augusta, a direct challenge to Aurelian which he could not ignore.

Already on his way to the east in 271, Aurelian was waylaid by the Goths for a short time, but after his victory he marched towards the east, wintering at Byzantium in 271, and moving into Asia Minor in spring 272. Meanwhile one of his generals had reconquered Egypt, and by August 271 the Alexandrian mint was coining for Aurelian alone, indicating that Egypt was once more incorporated into the Empire. Aurelian swept through Asia Minor and into Syria. At Immae, about 40 km east of Antioch, he fought a battle with Zenobia and her army, commanded by her general Septimius Zabdas. Aurelian resorted to a ruse to draw the Palmyrene heavy armoured cavalry (nicknamed *clibanarii*, literally 'ovens') into an ambush. He ordered his Moorish and Dalmatian horsemen to turn tail and run when they saw the *clibanarii*. The stratagem worked. The heavy horsemen tried to pursue and were defeated. Zenobia evacuated Antioch, leaving a Palmyrene garrison at Daphne nearby, but it did not hold up Aurelian for long.

The final battle was at Emesa. After his victory there Aurelian marched after Zenobia to Palmyra, and blockaded the city. During the action he was wounded by an arrow, but not seriously. Since supplies were not abundant in the middle of the desert, Aurelian came to a successful arrangement with the tribes who opposed Zenobia. The tribesmen provided supplies for the Romans and helped to secure his communications.

Palmyra was not possessed of a complete circuit of walls and

Above left: 1. The famous statue of Augustus from Prima Porta in Italy, now in the Vatican Museum. In 20 BC Augustus arranged for the return by the Parthians of the Roman standards captured from the army of Marcus Licinius Crassus in 53 BC. It was a diplomatic coup of the highest order, achieved without going to war, and Augustus had the event commemorated on the breastplate of his statue.

Above right: 2. Statue of the Emperor Tiberius, the son of Augustus's wife Livia. He was the eventual successor of Augustus, having been overlooked in favour of other younger men. All Augustus's chosen successors died before Augustus himself, leaving Tiberius a reluctant and misunderstood emperor. The principle of bequeathing political and military power was not firmly established when he took over, and he did not have the 'people skills' that Augustus had developed. Tiberius tried to conciliate the senators, but only succeeded in making them mistrustful of him, and in the end his reputation was soured, despite all that he had achieved for Rome while fighting battles for Augustus against tribesmen and mutinous soldiers.

3. View of the Flavian amphitheatre in Rome, better known as the Colosseum, the largest amphitheatre in the Roman Empire. The columns in the foreground belong to the Temple of Venus and Rome, built by the Emperor Hadrian. The Colosseum takes its name from the colossal statue of Nero which was demolished to make way for the new amphitheatre. In AD 70 the new Emperor Vespasian began to build this vast monument, still under construction when he died in AD 79. By then it was three storeys high, and the Emperor Titus added the fourth storey, formally opening the building in AD 80. It was repaired several times in the third, fourth, and fifth centuries, revealing its importance to the Roman people and successive emperors. The photo shows a section of the outer wall on the left, still at its original height, and the ruined interior wall. There was an earthquake in 1349, when portions of the outer wall tumbled down, the stones providing a quarry for other building works in Rome.

4. Interior of the Colosseum, minus the original flooring. The underground passages would have held gladiators and animals, which could be hoisted up into arena above, but the structure seen today dates from the fourth century, and the first century arrangements are not known.

5. The arch of Titus at the end of the Forum Romanum, where the road from the Colosseum joins the Via Sacra coming down from the Palatine Hill. It was built to commemorate the conquest of Judaea and the capture of Jerusalem in AD 70 by Vespasian's son Titus, who was emperor from AD 79 to 81. Titus died before the arch was finished and the inscription records him as Divus, divine, after his deification by his brother Domitian, who succeeded him in AD 81 and dedicated the arch, probably in the following year. Since the arch once formed part of the medieval defences of Rome, it suffered considerable damage, but it was taken apart and sensitively restored in the nineteenth century.

6. The old-style facade of the Pantheon in Rome, still showing the inscription recording the building erected by Augustus's friend Marcus Vipsanius Agrippa. Behind the classic portico with its eight granite columns is the Rotunda, built by the Emperor Hadrian and his architects. It is a circular building with a hemispherical, coffered dome, an architectural and engineering achievement that would tax even modern builders with their more advanced equipment and materials. The name Pantheon indicates that the temple was dedicated to all the gods. In the middle ages it was used as a Christian church.

7. View of some of the shops in the apsidal sector, or hemicycle, of Trajan's Markets in Rome. These shopping centres, built on different levels on the slope of the Quirinal Hill, prefigured the modern malls by 2,000 years. They lie opposite Trajan's Forum, which housed Trajan's column, recording in a sculptured spiral the two Dacian wars of AD 101 to 102 and 105 to 106. There was also a temple to the deified Trajan, set up by his successor Hadrian, the basilica, and two libraries, one for Greek and one for Latin works.

Above left: 8. Hadrian's mausoleum on the bank of the Tiber in Rome. Like the mausoleum of Augustus, it would probably have been surrounded by a columned arcade, and topped with a conical roof. The foundation stones were laid in the AD 120s, but the building was not completed until AD 139, by Antoninus Pius, a year after Hadrian's death. The ashes of Hadrian and his wife Sabina, and those of most of the families of Antoninus Pius and Septimius Severus were housed in this mausoleum, but no trace of them has survived. The Emperor Aurelian incorporated the mausoleum into the city walls of the late third century. The modern name of the monument, Castel Sant'Angelo, derives from medieval times, when the mausoleum was used as a fortress and prison, and a papal refuge. It is linked to the Vatican by a corridor built in the thirteenth century.

Above right: 9. Copy of a statue of the Emperor Hadrian, executed in the Greek style. The Emperor is dressed as military conqueror, and trampling a barbarian. The original is from Crete, this copy is in the Museo della Civiltà Romana.

Above left:10. Reconstructed stone-built watchtower of the German frontier. Earlier timber towers running along the line of part of the German frontier may have been built in Flavian times by Vespasian or Domitian, but it was Hadrian who consolidated the frontier and marked it by a continuous palisade with watchtowers like this one accompanying it.

Above right: 11. Statue of Marcus Aurelius on the Capitoline Hill in Rome. This is the bronze original, which was removed in the 1980s and taken inside the museum for better protection from the elements. A copy now occupies the pedestal. Marcus Aurelius had persecuted the Christians because of their political intransigence, but his statue was preserved because in medieval times it was thought that it was a portrait of Constantine, the founder of the Christian Church.

12. A well-preserved section of Hadrian's Wall at Walltown Crags in Northumberland, England. The Emperor visited Britain in AD 122 and perhaps surveyed the route of the wall himself, as part of his policy of calling a halt to further expansion and attending to the consolidation and protection of the parts of the Empire that could be feasibly held. The new British frontier was 80 Roman miles long, running from Bowness on Solway in the west, to Wallsend on the River Tyne in the east. For much of its central sector it followed the north-facing heights of the geological feature known as the Whin Sill across the Pennines. It took several years to build, and was subject to changes of plan, the final form comprising seventeen forts, fortlets known as milecastles (a modern term invented for the buildings) situated 1 Roman mile apart, and two towers, or turrets between each milecastle. It has been labelled 'overkill' by modern historians.

13. The so-called Maritime Theatre at Hadrian's Villa at Tivoli in Italy. This is just one part of the massive villa covering several acres. It is sometimes called the library. The interior buildings stand on a circular artificial island with a moat all around it, and a colonnade running round the outer perimeter. The building provided a private apartment for Hadrian to retire from the world for a short time, on the few occasions when he was not travelling all over the Empire.

14. Preserved remains of one of the milecastles on Hadrian's Wall, at Cawfields in Northumberland. There were two gates, one on the north side through the Wall and one on the south. On either side of the central road connecting the gates, there were usually barrack blocks, and the full complement of the fortlet was probably one century of eighty soldiers. When the Antonine Wall was built further north in Scotland, by Hadrian's successor Antoninus Pius, some of the forts and the milecastles soon went out of use as fully occupied garrison posts. They were not fully reoccupied when the frontier was once again brought back to the line of Hadrian's Wall. Some of the milecastles were used for metal working or other occupations.

15. The Hadrianic frontier in Germany was built of timber, of which there was a plentiful supply, unlike the north of Britain, where stone was plentiful but trees were scarce. This is a reconstructed section of the frontier in Germany, showing what the palisade may have looked like, with a ditch in front of it. There was a series of small forts, called *Kleinkastelle* in German, approximating to the milecastles of Hadrian's Wall, situated just behind the palisade. There were also watch towers at short intervals to guard the frontier – see the photo of the reconstructed stone-built watchtower of the German frontier.

Above left: 16. Portrait of Caracalla, showing considerable similarity to other busts and statues of him. This is the emperor who granted Roman citizenship to all free-born inhabitants of the Empire in AD 212. The new citizens took his family name Aurelius, demonstrating the fabricated connection of Severan dynasty to the house of Marcus Aurelius. From the early third century onwards Aurelius became the most common name in the Empire.

Above right: 17. The Emperor Caius Julius Verus Maximinus, or Maximinus Thrax, the Thracian. He was proclaimed emperor by the soldiers after the murder of Severus Alexander, but he ruled for only a short time from AD 235 to 238. His reign is regarded by some historians as a turning point in Imperial history, since Maximinus was the first emperor with no family connection to any of the Imperial houses, and he had no senatorial background. He was not even regarded as a true Roman, despite Caracalla's edict granting citizenship to all free-born men. Maximinus had joined the army and risen from the ranks, the first soldier to become emperor. Courtesy Ny Carlsberg Glyptotek, Copenhagen.

Above left: 18. Portrait head of Gallienus, joint emperor with his father Valerian from AD 253 to 260, and sole emperor from then until 268. During his reign the Empire nearly fragmented, with an independent Gallic Empire ruled by Roman generals in the west, comprising Gaul, Spain, Britain and Raetia, and the Palmyrene kingdom in the east, where the Palmyrene noble Odenathus and then his widow Queen Zenobia tried to hold the provinces together and to defend them. At the same time the Empire was threatened by tribesmen in the Alps and on the Danube, but Gallienus received no credit for stemming the tide and keeping the central part of the Empire free from invasion. Courtesy Ny Carlsberg Glyptotek, Copenhagen.

Above right: 19. Head from the colossal marble statue of the Emperor Constantine, on display in the courtyard of the Palazzo dei Conservatori in Rome. The statue was once housed in the western apse of the Basilica of Maxentius in the Forum Romanum. The Basilica was completed by Constantine himself. He may have been originally portrayed wearing an oak wreath, as suggested by the alterations to his hairline visible on the carved head. He radiates calm and confidence, with his gaze fixed on otherworldly concerns. The statue was about 10 metres high, but not much of it survives – apart from the head seen here, the remains of one arm, one foot, the right hand and a knee are also on display.

Above: 20. The arch of Septimius Severus in the Forum Romanum in Rome, with its inscription recording his victories and titles, and those of his son Caracalla. The inscription states that the arch was set up by the Senate and People of Rome on the occasion of the restoration of the Republic, not literally, since the emperors still ruled, but the civil wars with the two usurpers Clodius Albinus and Pescennius Niger had been won by Severus. The panels over the smaller flanking arches, two on each side, all very much worn away, represent significant events of the Emperor's campaigns. The two panels on the side shown here, facing away from the Forum Romanum, portray scenes from the Parthian war, specifically the attack on the city of Seleucia and the capture of Ctesiphon.

Right: 21. One of the towers of the gate at the legionary fortress of Castra Regina (modern Regensburg) in Germany, which was strongly fortified after the destruction caused by the Marcomanni in the late 160s AD. A building inscription dated to AD 179 records the construction of defences with gates and towers (*vallum cum portis et turribus*). The gateway resembles the Porta Nigra at Trier which also dates to the late second century, and as at Trier, the Regensburg gate would originally have had two towers flanking two arches. The gate survived because it was incorporated into the Bishop's Palace at Regensburg.

Above: 22. Provincial towns also started to think about building walls in the later second century. At Caerwent (Venta Silurum, capital of the Silures) in Wales, earthwork fortifications may have been erected in the second century, replaced in stone in the more turbulent late third century, when other towns in Britain were being fortified. This is the best preserved of several projecting interval towers of the south wall of Caerwent. The towers were probably added after the walls had been built, most likely in the mid-fourth century.

Left: 23. Late Roman tower at Comagena (modern Tulln) in Austria, a rectangular fort on the right bank of the Danube, named after its garrison, the *ala I Commagenorum*. The first fort on this site was probably founded by Domitian, with earth and timber ramparts, which were rebuilt in stone by Trajan. It was partially destroyed on two occasions in the third century, and again in the second half of the fourth century. In the late Roman period several forts on the Danube had projecting drum towers added to the walls, but it is rare that they survive to this height. It is known as the *Salzturm*, the Salt Tower.

Above right: 24. By the late second century AD the inhabitants of some towns and cities of the western Empire were starting to build defensive walls. This is the Porta Nigra, or Black Gate, at Trier (ancient Augusta Treverorum) in Germany, viewed from the north, outside the defences. The road through this gate led to Mainz. There were originally four gates but only this one survives, because it was used as a Church in the medieval period, and an apsidal chapel was added to the tower on the left of the photo. The interior of the building was never completed, perhaps because the finer details of building work were interrupted by the troubles of the third century.

Centre: 25. Part of the defences of Senlis in France. The walls and towers are very similar to those at Beauvais, Soissons and Amiens, indicating that there may have been a corporate programme of fortification in Roman Gaul, most likely under the Emperor Probus who reigned from AD 276 to 282. The invasions of Franks and Alamanni in the AD 260s had caused tremendous destruction, and the Emperor Aurelian and then Probus made strenuous efforts to repair the damage. The projecting drum towers at Senlis were spaced 30 metres apart, with the bases of each tower filled up solid to the level of the wall walk, so that it would have been very difficult to break through. Sixteen of the original twenty-eight towers survive. The two depicted here were incorporated into the twelfth-century Royal Palace, and one tower had a fourteenth-century oratory added to it. Photo J.T. Taylor.

Below right: 26. The Great Court or peristyle in Diocletian's Palace, Split. The arch supported by four granite columns marked the division between the private and public areas. This was the main reception area, a rectangle flanked by columns leading up to the arch, where Diocletian and his officials would make their public entrances. The court was built in the florid eastern style customary in Syria and Asia Minor, where many of the workmen came from.

Above left: 27. The Tetrarchs in total harmony, a sculpture in the Piazza San Marco in Venice. Photo David Brearley.

Above right: 28. The Roman Empire could not have been created or maintained without the army, the study of which has now grown into monumental proportions. One of the more fortunate habits of the Roman army was the predilection for erecting informative gravestones, often with a portrait of the individual in armour and carrying weapons. Even when the tombstones do not include a portrait, the text normally gives the name of the man, his parentage, the units to which he had belonged, his rank, his age at death, sometimes the cause of death, and the number of years he had served. This tombstone is a modern copy, displayed at the museum at Xanten in Germany. The soldier, Pentaius son of Pedilicus, was a standard bearer in *cohors V* Asturum, depicted with his standard in his right hand, and an animal skin over his shoulders. He died aged thirty, having served for six years. The lettering would have been painted in red in Roman times, and the soldier himself may have been presented in glorious colour, with details that cannot be portrayed in stone.

29. The Horrea Epagathanea at Ostia, just one of the warehouses in the town. In this case the owners are known because they left their names on the inscription above the door, Epagathius and Epafroditius. There were shops at the front of the building, which survives in part up to the second storey. The door leads into a courtyard surrounded by columns, with a floor of the black and white mosaics which are a common feature of houses and business premises in Ostia.

30. The arch of Constantine viewed from an upper storey of the Colosseum. Like the arch of Severus in the Forum Romanum it has a central arch flanked by two smaller ones. It was dedicated in AD 315 on the tenth anniversary of Constantine's reign, and celebrates the defeat of Maxentius at the battle of the Milvian Bridge in AD 312, though the inscription in the top central panel merely mentions the defeat of the tyrant, without naming Maxentius. Some of the relief sculpture dates from Constantine's day, but much of the arch was assembled from reused panels and roundels from other monuments, traditionally from the reigns of Trajan, Hadrian and Marcus Aurelius, with the original emperor re-carved to look like Constantine.

31. A street scene in Ostia in Italy, showing the multi-storey apartment blocks, some of which are preserved up to the second or even third level. According to legend, Ostia at the mouth of the Tiber was founded by King Ancus Martius, or Marcius, to provide a harbour for Rome. The town was fortified in the fourth century BC, temples and houses began to appear in the third century and by the first century BC the warehouses, for which Ostia is famous, had been established. Claudius built the harbour north-west of the town, and Trajan enlarged it, so Ostia functioned for a long time as the port for Rome, and much of the food supply was brought in through the town.

32. The Basilica of Maxentius, running along the right side of the Via Sacra as it descends from the Palatine Hill into the Forum Romanum in Rome. It was begun in AD 307, and completed by Constantine after AD 313. In style it departed from the usual aisled basilica design, and resembles the various monumental bath buildings in construction. Only half of the building survives, the other section having been destroyed probably in the ninth century when there was a serious earthquake.

33. The Basilica at Trier (ancient Augusta Treverorum) in Germany, built by Constantine on the site of an older palace, which may have been the headquarters of the procurator of the provinces of Belgica and Upper and Lower Germany. When Trier became one of the provincial Imperial capitals, a new administrative building was needed, where the emperor held court and gave audiences. It was to be on the grand scale, very imposing, tailored to fit Constantine's self-image, and it is the largest surviving late Roman building of its type. In the twelfth century the ruined hall became the residence of the archbishops of Trier, and it was restored to its former glory in the nineteenth century, when it was converted into a church. Photo J.T. Taylor.

Top of page: 34. Cavalry soldiers usually opted for large imposing tombstones, sometimes showing the horseman riding over a stylized long-haired barbarian. Others like Longinus Biarta, depicted here, represented themselves enjoying the afterlife in the top panel (not shown here) and as cavalryman in the lower panel. There is considerable detail in this relief sculpture. Longinus is probably exercising his horse, with all its trappings, on a long rein, with his shield slung over the saddle, which is clearly displayed. It used to be thought that the Romans did not use saddles, but enough evidence has now been assembled to be certain that they did. There were no stirrups, but the horns of the saddle kept the rider in place. This tombstone from Cologne is very similar to other two-part tombstones, in particular the one for Marcus Aurelius Durises from Mainz, which is also divided into two panels, showing the horse in the lower one in very similar pose to that of Longinus. Perhaps there was a pattern book of designs to choose from.

Centre: 35. Finely detailed black and white mosaics adorn many of the floors of buildings in Ostia. The artist was obviously familiar with elephants.

Right: 36. Wall painting of a charioteer in Ostia, one of a pair still in situ on the first floor corridor walls of the apartment block which is named after them, the House of the Charioteers.

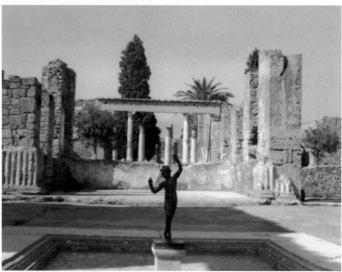

37. The House of the Faun at Pompeii, arguably the most famous and one of the most sumptuous houses of the city, if not of the Roman world. The house was originally a modest Samnite dwelling, converted into a large mansion in the second century BC. The dancing faun stood in the larger of the two *atria*, which led into the dining room, and then into one of the two peristyles, a rectangular enclosed garden surrounded by an arcade supported by columns which can be seen in the photo. The house is renowned for its art work, wall paintings and mosaics, one of which is the famous mosaic showing Alexander in battle against Darius, King of the Persians. It is now in the National Museum of Naples.

Opposite page top: 38. The peristyle and garden of the House of the Vettii at Pompeii. It was owned by two brothers, Aulus Vettius Restitutus and Aulus Vettius Conviva, who redecorated the house after the earthquake in AD 62, making it famous for its wall paintings in Pompeian Fourth Style. Photo J.T. Taylor.

Top of page: 39. A *thermopolium* at Herculaneum, an equivalent of a fast food cafeteria and wine bar, of which there were several extant examples at Pompeii and Herculaneum. The shop counters were usually arranged in an L shape, or like this one round three sides, equipped with sunken terracotta pots called *dolia* from which a variety of hot and cold food was served. Some establishments had rooms where customers could sit down to eat and drink. Photo J.T. Taylor.

40. Triumphal arch at Orange (ancient Arausio) in France. It dates from AD 26 in the reign of Tiberius, commemorating the suppression of a revolt in AD 21. It is the first known example to employ three arches, and looks a bit top heavy with two attic storeys. The panels depict heaps of captured arms and armour. Photo J.T. Taylor.

41. The Romans were excellent water engineers. This photo shows the famous Pont du Gard, part of the aqueduct that supplied water from the source at Uzès to the city of Nimes (ancient Nemausus) in Provence, France. It was built *c*.19 BC in the reign of Augustus, probably under the supervision of Marcus Vipsanius Agrippa. Photo J.T. Taylor.

42. The arch at the ancient town of Glanum in France, possibly dating to the end of the reign of Augustus. It is not well preserved, having lost the upper sections. The carved figures show captured arms and armour, and Gaul personified as a woman, in submissive pose. Photo J.T. Taylor.

43. The Roman aqueduct at Segovia, Spain. The people and the cars provide the scale for this truly massive piece of architectural engineering. Photo J.T. Taylor.

44. The north facade of the Porte de Mars at Reims (ancient Durocortorum) in France, the largest arch in the Roman world. The arch was incorporated into the Roman city defences, and used as the north gateway. The other three gates have disappeared. In medieval times the Porte de Mars was covered in earth to form the base of a castle, only being rediscovered in the seventeenth century. As a result of its mistreatment it has lost its upper storey, and the carvings are extremely worn, but the sculpture is important for the so-called reaper relief on the inside of the central arch. This depicts a reaping machine, a wheeled vehicle with long teeth at the front, pushed by a horse and guided by a man. The teeth ripped through the crop and pulled off the heads, which were collected in a basket. Considerable doubt attached to the interpretation of this carving, but it corresponds to a description of such a machine written by Pliny. Doubt was dispelled when another relief was discovered in Belgium, showing the same kind of reaper. Photo J.T. Taylor.

45. Amphitheatre at the *canabae legionis*, or civil settlement outside the legionary fortress at Carnuntum on the Danube in Austria, between the modern towns of Petronell and Bad-Deutsch Altenburg. It was excavated in the nineteenth century and there are sufficient remains to identify the entrances and seating. There was also an amphitheatre for the legion outside the fortress, but nothing can be seen of it today.

46. The water supply was essential not only for hygiene but for the many public baths in Rome itself and the cities of the Roman Empire. This photo shows part of the baths of Caracalla, on the south side of the Aventine Hill in Rome. The ruins survive to considerable height. The baths were opened in AD 217 and functioned at least until the fifth century. They were constructed on a symmetrical plan. The central feature was the massive circular hot room *(caldarium)* with its domed roof, supported on eight piers, two of which can be seen in the photo. The rest of the structure has disappeared, but its outline is still visible on the ground. On either side and behind the *caldarium* was a vast complex of rooms and open courtyards, and the whole was enclosed within a rectangular porticoed enclosure. The baths of Caracalla, like most others in the Empire, fulfilled several functions, the equivalent of a modern leisure centre, with spaces for exercise, recreational pursuits and libraries. There is a regular summer season of opera performances at the baths.

soon fell to the Romans. Zenobia fled once again, heading for the Euphrates and Persia, but she was captured. Her ultimate fate and that of her son is unknown. Some sources say that she soon died, or committed suicide, but others insist that she survived to be paraded through the streets of Rome in Aurelian's triumph, then was allowed to live in Italy, respectably married to a Roman senator. The house where she lived was pointed out to fourth-century Roman tourists.

Soon after the Romans left Palmyra, there were two revolts: one in Egypt led by Firmus, a wealthy merchant at Alexandria, and another in Palmyra, led by Septimius Apsaeus, who produced a relative of Odenathus and Zenobia called Antiochus, and proclaimed him king. The reappearance of Aurelian at Palmyra was so sudden that the Palmyrenes were taken by surprise. When he captured the city this time, he razed it. There would be no resurgence of Palmyrene power. Next it was the turn of Egypt. Alexandria was treated very severely and Aurelian took revenge on the Egyptians by raising the taxes. At the end of these campaigns Aurelian promoted his image as restorer of the east, *Restitutor Orientis*, as his coins proclaimed him.

The End of the Gallic Empire

For nearly ten years, the Gallic Emperor Postumus had governed well. He had repaired and defended the Rhine frontier. His coinage was of a better and more reliable quality than the legitimate Emperor's and he had held out against the attempts at reconquest by Gallienus and his deputies.

Dissension began in 269 with the revolt of Laelianus. Postumus defeated him, only to face another usurper, Marius. While engaged in the struggle against the latter, Postumus was killed because he refused to allow his soldiers to sack the Roman city of Mainz. Victorinus, who had been Postumus's colleague in the consulship in 268, was proclaimed emperor in October or November 271, but was quickly assassinated.

For a while his mother Victoria filled the power vacuum and brought to the attention of the troops, supported by substantial amounts of cash, the senatorial governor of Aquitania, Esuvius Tetricus, who was declared emperor and set up headquarters at Trier. He was recognized in Britain and the whole of Gaul, save for Narbonensis. Spain wavered and then joined him, as did the city of Strasbourg, but there the inhabitants soon changed their minds and declared for Aurelian. Invasions across the Rhine and along the coasts continued unabated. Some German tribesmen penetrated as far as the Loire. The only response that Tetricus could make was to abandon forts and withdraw the troops. At least some of the coin hoards in northern Gaul must relate to this period of endemic insecurity.

Aurelian mobilized against Tetricus perhaps late in the year 273 or early in 274. The opposing armies met at Châlons-sur-Marne, but it is not even certain if there was a battle. Whatever happened, the Gallic Empire came to an end probably in March 274, when the mint at Lyons changed from coining for Tetricus and began to issue coins for Aurelian, declaring him the restorer of the east, and indeed the restorer of the world. The Empire was unified once more, not without certain false starts. A usurper called Faustinus was proclaimed emperor at Trier, but the rebellion was soon quelled. Britain returned to the fold voluntarily. In Gaul the army was split up and put into different garrisons, and Aurelian's reliable kinsman Probus was put in charge of the reconstruction and defence of the frontier zones. Tetricus survived, and was given an official post as *corrector Lucaniae*, preserving his fortune and his status intact.

The Evacuation of Dacia

The date when Aurelian took the troops out of the Dacian provinces (modern Romania) is not known. The case for 272–3 is perhaps the most convincing, just before the campaign to quell the Palmyrene revolt. A buried hoard discovered in Romania, consisting of over 250 coins from the mints at Milan, Cyzicus and Siscia, contains nothing later than 272. In order to turn his attention to the Palmyrene revolt, Aurelian had to abandon the campaign against the northern tribes before he had achieved victory and a full settlement, so rather than leave behind him a threatened province, it is probable that Aurelian evacuated Dacia and brought the troops out at this juncture. He placed the population on the right bank of the Danube and created a new province called Dacia, carved out of territory that had belonged to the two Moesian provinces. Before 285, this new province was split into two smaller ones, called Dacia Ripensis and Dacia Mediterranea.

The territory of the old Dacia to the north of the Danube was now open to the Goths and Carpi. Though there is no firm evidence, Aurelian may have arranged a treaty with the tribes whereby they acted as defenders of the evacuated territory and kept it free from other incursions. How many of the civilian population came out of Dacia in the wake of the army is unknown. Many people would remain in their homes. Epigraphic evidence speaks for a continued Romanized population after the evacuation of the later third century.

Aurelian's Reforms

Superlatives began to enter the titulature of the Emperor from 274 onwards, after he had reunified the Empire and he had become in truth the restorer of the world, albeit a world that was somewhat different from the Empire of Hadrian and Severus. The frontiers that were once so clearly marked were now a little ragged, and territory had been lost north of the Danube. Nonetheless the situation was such a vast improvement on the previous two decades. On inscriptions Aurelian, conqueror of the Carpi, the Germans, the Arabians, the Persians and the Palmyrenes, is described as eternal, invincible, the personification of Hercules, divine, and finally a god and lord in his own right, *Imperator deus et dominus*. This godly status may have been thrust upon him, in return for his services to the state, but he took to it well. He began to wear a diadem, and demanded obeisance from his subjects. Obviously he had learned a lot in the east, where such behaviour was normal. Aurelian took his role as saviour of the state very seriously. It was important that Romans should believe in him, and that enemies should fear him. The time of rough soldier-emperors sharing their soldiers' meals, marching with the lads, caring little for politics and statesmanship, was over. The emperor needed to be all things, military commander, politician, statesman, psychologist, performer, and god. For this it was necessary to be remote, lofty, ideal rather than real, creating echoing distance between ruler and ruled. Aurelian knew how to do it, and would have been more than a match for Constantine.

Although the Empire was reunified territorially, there were many things to put right within the state. Inflation had reached ridiculous proportions; the monetary system had foundered, and it required a strong hand to set it on course again. Aurelian had attempted a partial reform in 271, but he had not been totally effective. In 274 he began again. Unification brought in its wake increased revenues, and new taxes were raised. Aurelian taxed the wealthy men of the Empire, justifiably in his view since everyone ought to contribute to the well-being and defence of the Empire. The flow of precious metals from all parts of the Empire was resumed, sufficient to enable Aurelian to reform the coinage. He adhered to the traditional bronze, silver and gold currency, but the right to issue bronze coinage was wrested from the control of the Senate. Aurelian tried to withdraw all the old silver *antoniniani* of negligible weight. He eradicated the bad coinage in Rome and Italy, but not in the provinces.

The food supply of the Roman plebs also claimed Aurelian's attention. He reorganized the corn dole for the city, distributing loaves of bread instead of grain, and adding salt and pork to the rations, as well as oil, and wine at a reduced cost. These arrangements continued under successive emperors. The substitution of a bread ration for the corn dole was an innovative step. It involved a series of operations all under the supervision of the *Praefectus Annonae*, covering collection of the goods and transport by sea and by land, storage, processing and distribution. Grain was levied from Egypt as part of the taxation system, and delivered to the bakers free of charge; the weight of the loaves was increased but the price was held for the benefit of those who could afford to buy. The distribution of wine revitalized the struggling viticulture of Italy, and the transport of all the various goods was a boon for the shippers, the *navicularii*. The rudiments of the guilds and corporations of the later Empire derive from this reform of Aurelian's, but he probably did not intend to impose the inflexible rigidity that developed as part and parcel of the state control of the *annona*.

Religion was another sphere where Aurelian's reforming zeal introduced changes. The old gods had not been neglected by previous emperors, but there was a certain lack of coherence and cohesion in their policies. Aurelian introduced Sol, the sun god, as the supreme being. In the east he had seen the unifying force of the sun as a divinity, which. all people, civilians and soldiers, Romans, Italians and provincials, could believe in without betraying their other gods. There were precedents in the reign of Claudius Gothicus, whose coinage had featured the sun god, and Aurelian's coinage accentuated the attributes of the sun god, with legends such as *Sol Invictus, Sol Conservator, Sol Dominus Imperii Romani*, celebrating the unconquered sun, the saviour of the state, and the lord and master of the Roman Empire. Since no cult could function without the focal point of a temple, Aurelian built one in the seventh region of Rome. It was consecrated in 274, an extremely ornate building that housed the trophies from Palmyra. The priests of the cult were drawn from the aristocracy, so that the bruised prestige of the upper classes was revived by the knowledge that the control of the state religion, if not of the state itself, was in their hands. Aurelian's religious policy was to restore old values in a new guise, to unify the Empire, to exclude no one except the most intransigent. He did not persecute the Christians or the

Jews. He regarded himself as earthly but divine intermediary between the supreme god and the people of the Empire, but was granted little time in which to develop the theme of one state, one god. Constantine finalized that, on his deathbed.

The End of Aurelian's Reign

The defeat of Valerian by the Persians was still unavenged, and Aurelian was now in a position to prepare a campaign. It was an opportune moment to attack the Persians. Towards the end of 272 King Shapur I died. His successor Hormizd did not long survive him, dying at the end of 273 or at the beginning of 274. The new king, Vahram, had much to do to keep his Empire together and had no time for an aggressive campaign against Rome.

In the summer of 275 Aurelian set out for the east. He assembled his army in Illyricum, and declared war on Persia, but he never reached his objective. On the march through Thrace the Emperor Aurelian was assassinated. The sources are garbled, naming more than one man as the murderer. One story is that a list was discovered, or fabricated, of officers who had fallen out of favour, so they struck before they were eliminated. The fact that there was no candidate, ready and waiting in the wings to take over the moment that Aurelian was dead, supports the suggestion that the conspirators acted suddenly, in blind panic. There may also have been a few officers who were glad to rid themselves of both the Emperor and the need to go and fight the Persians.

Aurelian's promising career was terminated before he had been granted the opportunity to follow up his successes in pulling the Empire back together, or perhaps before he threw away all his credit by losing the war against Persia. He deserved his title *Restitutor Orbis*, Restorer of the World. He had built on the unacknowledged work of Gallienus and Claudius Gothicus, and had paved the way for Diocletian, who absorbed most of the credit that was really due to his predecessor.

Tacitus AD 275–276 & Florian AD 276

The soldiers were very displeased at the murder of their emperor and made it clear that they did not intend to proclaim any of the generals in Aurelian's place. There was no heir, nor was there an obvious successor marked out by Imperial favour during Aurelian's reign. The important generals were dispersed in various parts of the Empire, so for a short time the Roman world was poised for complicated civil wars as the leaders of various armies fought each other until one of them emerged victorious. But this time there was no war. The sources all agree that the soldiers sent to Rome to ask the Senate to choose an emperor. The seventy-five-year-old senator Marcus Claudius Tacitus was persuaded to shoulder the task. He was in Campania when his name was put forward as emperor. His previous career is unknown. He was probably a middle class equestrian who had been adlected to the Senate.

The Emperor Tacitus was not a military man, but he spent most of his short reign fighting the Goths, earning the title *Gothicus Maximus*, for a victory or victories that have escaped documentation. He died after a mere six month reign, at either Tyana or Tarsus, perhaps because he had appointed one of his relatives called Maximinus to command in Syria, and Maximinus proved too severe, so the soldiers rebelled. The army declared for Tacitus's half brother Florian, who was Praetorian Prefect in the campaign against the Goths. At the same time Probus, commanding in Syria, Phoenicia and Egypt, was also declared emperor by his troops.

The east was almost wholly behind Probus. The conflict between the two Imperial candidates ended at Tarsus, where Florian decided to face Probus, but his soldiers were not accustomed to the eastern climate and their health declined. In direct proportion to their suffering, their commitment to the cause declined. Probus had only to wait, without giving battle. Florian's troops killed him, or perhaps suggested very strongly that he should commit suicide.

Probus AD 276–282

The reign of Probus was longer than that of Aurelian, and almost as important for the reconstitution of the Empire, but the source material is sparse. Probus's coins display his titles, making the usual claims that the emperor is invincible and unconquered, but the coinage does not help to establish dates for recorded events. The result is that the salient factors of Probus's reign can be described in broad outline based on the dubious foundation of a few overlapping statements in the works of the ancient authors, but the causes of events, and their consequences, can be reconstructed only with the help of speculation.

Probus benefited greatly from the achievements of Aurelian, but he inherited some unfinished business. The Rhine and Danube were still under threat despite Aurelian's victories, and the Persian campaign, aborted on the Emperor's death, was not regarded as redundant. Much of Probus's energies went into flushing the tribesmen out of Gaul and the Rhine frontier zones. It was said that he rebuilt sixty cities which had been damaged in Gaul, and re-established some of the Roman forts. There were wars on more than one front. Probus was victorious with the help of his generals against the Franks on the Rhine; he fought the Vandals and Burgundians, and carried the war into territory beyond the frontiers and was said to have established forts *in solo barbarico*, on barbarian territory. It was said that no less than nine barbarian kings submitted to him.

Beyond these brief notices very little detail is known. The identity of the nine kings, the tribes they represented, and the location of the forts that he established, cannot be listed. It can only be said that the Romans had returned, however briefly, to the ascendancy. Little of this energetic activity can be securely dated; it is probable that the campaigns in Gaul and Germany occupied Probus from his accession until the end of 278, and that in the new season beginning in the winter of 278–9 he turned to the Danube.

Probus had other ways of dealing with the tribes, apart from fighting them. He settled some of them in Roman territory, including 100,000 Bastarnae in Thrace. While these settlements potentially secured peace for at least one generation, providing a good source of recruits for the army and a partly Romanized zone between the Empire and the tribes outside it, the schemes did not always produce the desired results. The Franks were given lands, probably in the Danube area, but they were restless, and were soon on the move, sweeping through Greece, and then sailing to Sicily and Africa, pillaging their way round the coast, through the Straits of Gibraltar and back to the Rhine and their original homelands. This expedition typifies the sort of problems that Probus had to deal with, small-scale actions in localized zones, all of them nonetheless very disruptive, dispiriting and demoralizing. People were forced from their homes and resorted to brigandage. It was by no means a new problem; from the Republic and throughout the Empire infamous rebels and gangsters entered history, sometimes earning a grudging respect. There was considerable trouble in Egypt caused by the Blemmyes, tribesmen who had always been ready to harass the province from time to time. The rebellion was squashed by Probus's generals.

Several usurpers appeared in the east and in Gaul, but they were extinguished very quickly. A general called Saturninus was declared emperor, either in Egypt or more probably in Syria; the sources are confused as to exactly where his command lay and where he chose to stage his rebellion. It seems that the eastern troops killed him before Probus reached the scene. At Cologne there were two potential emperors, Bonosus and Proculus, who were both eliminated seemingly without much trouble. What does emerge from these scantily described events is that over most of the Empire Probus's government was working well enough. Governors of provinces and military officers did their loyal duty to the Emperor, communications were secure, the focal point was still Rome, and the army was ultimately successful when engaged in pitched battles, in suppressing other Roman generals, or in guerrilla warfare against plundering tribes.

Probably in 281, Probus celebrated a triumph. For the time being he had achieved peace over the Empire, dealt with usurpers and brigands, and could turn his attention to more peaceful pursuits. He encouraged vine growing in Gaul, Pannonia and Moesia. He employed his soldiers to plant the vines in some areas, and also set them to work on drainage projects in the Danube provinces. The fact that he had soldiers to spare for such tasks, testifies to the success of the long campaigns from the 270s to the early 280s. Probus is said to have remarked that very soon the Empire would have no need of its armies, a proud boast that satisfied the war weary inhabitants of Rome and the provinces, but not news that the army wished to hear. If Probus had promised to reward the soldiers for long service, pension them all off with lands, money, slaves, and everything they could wish for, perhaps he would have survived longer. Scepticism on the part of the Roman army was not without justification; in all periods before and since, and in all places, soldiers have often been treated in the same fashion, lauded when there is something to be saved from, reviled when they fail, and discarded without a thought when the danger is past.

Perhaps the army need not have been concerned for its future, since Probus had decided upon a Persian campaign. While he was otherwise engaged on the northern frontiers he had come to a peaceful if temporary arrangement with the Persians, compatible with both sides because King Vahram, beset by internal problems, was not in any position to fight the Romans. After the successful campaigns against the northern tribes, Probus was in a position to attack, but he was killed by his soldiers, at Sirmium.

Carus AD 282–283,
Carinus AD 283–285 & Numerianus AD 283–285

Dissatisfaction in the army probably had a long incubation period before it came to a head with the murder of Probus. The Praetorian Prefect Marcus Aurelius Carus, commanding troops in Raetia and Noricum, rebelled before Probus was killed. He was declared emperor by the soldiers, and it was said that Carus took power without reference to the Senate. His elder son Carinus, who came to northern Italy early in 283 for his marriage, may have contacted the Senate on his father's behalf. However, it is true that from the reign of Carus onwards, the role of the Senate in bestowing formal powers on the emperors was curtailed, and there was never any reversal of the trend thereafter.

Carus was an experienced military man. By the late third century it had become a prior necessity for the emperor to have a military background, and Carus was determined to take up the projected Persian campaign as soon as he could. He possessed what should have been a distinct advantage in that he had two sons and ought to have been able to secure the succession and found a dynasty that might have ensured peace and prosperity, building on and bringing to completion the work of Aurelian and Probus. Carus elevated Carinus and Numerianus to Augusti, Carinus early in 283 to take charge of the western provinces when the Persian campaign began, and Numerianus towards the end of the Persian campaign, perhaps in conjunction with the first victories. When Carus died the existence of two Augusti, one in the east and one in the west ought to have ensured a smooth transition of power, but it did not, nor did it cause a premature and irretrievable split into two separate Empires. Carinus in the west governed clearly demarcated territories with distinct boundaries, while Carus and Numerianus conducted the Persian campaign, but the arrangement was not a prefiguration of the division of the later Empire; it was more like a reiteration of the situation when Gallienus was left in charge of the west and Valerian embarked on his disastrous eastern war.

Carus fortunately met with considerably more success against the Persians, whose regime was not as strong as it had been under Shapur I. King Vahram II was still trying to establish his authority over his Empire, so he did not put up much of a fight, allowing the Romans to march into Seleucia and Ctesiphon almost unopposed. The title *Parthicus Maximus* was awarded to Carus.

At this juncture, Carus, who was in his sixties, died unexpectedly. He was probably killed by his Praetorian Prefect Lucius Aper. This ambitious individual was the father-in-law of Carus's son Numerianus, who also died during the withdrawal from Persia. Aper said that the young Emperor was suffering from an eye complaint and consequently had to travel in a closed litter as protection against light and dust. When the corpse began to emit an unsavoury aroma, Aper's subterfuge was discovered. This tale borders on the ridiculous, and all sorts of explanations are possible. Perhaps if Carus had indeed died accidentally or from disease without any assistance from Aper, then it would have been doubly difficult for the Praetorian Prefect to try to make the soldiers believe that the Emperor's son had suddenly died of disease as well. Perhaps Aper panicked and was unable to decide what to do, but he must have known that he could not travel very far in a hot climate with a dead emperor in a closed litter. A soldier called Diocles, the commander of Numerianus's guard, began to suspect that something was wrong.

7

Another World: The Empire Transformed AD 284–324

Diocletian AD 284–305

When it was discovered that the Emperor Numerianus was dead, the army declared for Diocles, proclaiming him Augustus on 20 November 284. Soon after becoming emperor, Diocles changed his name to Gaius Aurelius Valerius Diocletianus. For the remaining part of the year he made himself consul with a senator called Caesonius Bassus as his colleague. The Praetorian Prefect Aper was executed by Diocletian himself, fulfilling a prophecy made by a Gallic wise woman, that he would kill a boar (*aper*) and then become emperor.

Carus's elder son Carinus was still the legitimate emperor in the west, but he was opposed by a usurper called Julianus, who had been appointed *corrector Venetiae* in northern Italy. Diocletian simply had to wait until one or the other emerged victorious, and then fight the survivor, in this case Carinus. Their armies met in the valley of the Margus, near modern Belgrade. The Praetorian Prefect Aristobulus killed Carinus and the troops went over to Diocletian. It was probably by prior arrangement, since Diocletian confirmed Aristobulus in office as Praetorian Prefect, and made him consul for the rest of 285.

Diocletian was prevented from going immediately to Rome to have power conferred on him by the Senate, because he was involved in a struggle against the tribesmen of the Quadi

Map 3. Map showing the principal cities where the Imperial court set up headquarters at various times. During the third century the Roman emperors began to base themselves in large cities of the Empire rather than in Rome, so as to be close to the threatened areas. The presence of the emperors and the Imperial entourage brought prosperity to these cities, and the emperors were responsible for repairs, improvements, and new buildings.

and Marcomanni. He devoted his attention to the restoration of the frontiers and the re-establishment of law and order in the provinces, for which tasks he needed the co-operation of administrative and military specialists. He had served in the army, but he was by no means an experienced general, so he needed help. He had no sons, so it was advisable to designate his colleagues and successors. Joint rule had an established history, but it had usually been kept in the family. Marcus Aurelius had shared the burden with Lucius Verus and then with his son Commodus; the Severans had followed the same example, and the Emperor Carus had tried to establish a dynasty by giving his sons the title Augustus.

After the battle of the Margus, Diocletian appointed his fellow soldier Marcus Aurelius Maximianus as his Caesar. Maximian added Diocletian's family name Valerius to his nomenclature. The earthly association of the two men was equated with a partnership of the gods, Diocletian taking the name Jovius, the chief Roman god Jupiter, and Maximian that of Herculius, Jupiter's assistant. As a matter of urgency, the partners split up to attend to tasks at opposite ends of the Empire. From 285 until 288, Diocletian was occupied on the Danube, and then in the east, while Maximian took charge of the west.

Parts of Gaul had been overrun by a group of bandits called the Bagaudae, composed of displaced peasants, deserters from the army, and a collection of desperate people whose fortunes had been ruined by the invasions of the tribesmen from across the Rhine. The Gallic bandits of the third century were produced by a society in which an honest living was impossible to achieve, and everyone had to fend for himself. It is unlikely that the Bagaudae aspired to ruling the Empire, or even a part of Gaul. Maximian's successes against them are not fully documented, largely because the campaigns were better classified as police work rather than conquest.

By 286 Maximian was able to begin to concentrate on eliminating the Frankish and Saxon pirates who threatened

ORIENS

PONTICA

ASIANA

THRACIAE

MOESIAE

PANNONIAE

ITALIA

SUBURBICARIA

VIENNENSIS

GALLIAE

BRITANNIAE

AFRICA

HISPANIAE

Map 4. Map of the administrative units called Dioceses, containing several provinces, created by Diocletian.

the coasts of Britain and Gaul, and the Rhine mouth. The commander of the fleet in Gaul, Marcus Aurelius Carausius, achieved some success against them on both sides of the English Channel. It is not known whether he had been appointed by Carus and Carinus, or whether the appointment was made by Maximian soon after he took up his own command. Despite his victories, Carausius began to acquire a shady reputation. Rumours began to circulate that he knew when the Frankish raids would take place, and he waited until they had collected their booty, then captured them on their way home. It was said that the stolen goods went into his own coffers, and he was using the money to pay the Frankish soldiers that he had recruited. Maximian could not let this situation go unchallenged but the wily Carausius decamped to Britain, protected by his fleet and coastal defences, and in unchallenged possession of Britain. Maximian could do little to dislodge him.

Most of the evidence for Carausius's British Empire, or *Imperium Britanniarum*, derives from his coinage, which was of good quality. A sound coinage was a pre-requisite if the army and the influential people in Britain were to have any faith in him. He issued coins in 290, proclaiming that he ruled with 'his brothers' (*Carausius et Fratres Sui*), and depicting the heads of all three Emperors. The brotherly sentiment was not shared by Diocletian and Maximian, who never formally recognized Carausius or his claim to Britain and the coast of Gaul.

The Forts of the Saxon Shore

Anyone who wished to make war on Carausius had to gather a fleet, cross the English Channel, and then do battle with his experienced sailors, and the soldiers of the coastal forts. The Saxon Shore forts are known to modern archaeologists by their collective name, which suggests that they were part of a homogeneous defensive system along the south and east coast of Britain, of long established antiquity. None of this is true. The Saxon Shore was probably not labelled as such when Carausius created his British Empire. The forts were not built all at once as part of a unified system for coastal defence. The fort plans differ from each other, and they were built at different times, originally for different purposes, between 250 and 300. The title Saxon Shore is attested in a late Roman document called the *Notitia Dignitatum*, which lists the garrisons and titles of the commanding officers all over the eastern and western Empires. By the time the British sections of this document were compiled there was a corporate system utilizing all nine of the forts on the British coast. The command extended to the coasts of Gaul as well, just as Carausius in his day controlled Boulogne.

It has been suggested, not without dispute, that it may have been Carausius who welded the so-called Saxon Shore forts of Britain into a functional whole. He had to defend Britain and himself against the pirates and the Imperial Roman fleet, so perhaps more than any of his predecessors who governed Britain, he required a strong defensive line of forts to guard and keep watch over the potential points of access to the island.

Before Maximian could attempt to recover control of Britain, he had to drive the Franks and the Alamanni out of Gaul and the Rhineland. Carausius was not necessarily considered a threat to the safety of Gaul. He had not shown any desire to make a bid for the whole Empire, but since Diocletian was not prepared to condone the independent rule of Britain, war was inevitable.

The potential threat posed by Carausius has been viewed as one of the most important factors in the elevation of Maximian to the rank of Augustus. One consideration may have been that Diocletian needed to find a way of binding Maximian more closely to himself, with the promise of adequate rewards, to pre-empt the possibility that he might join forces with Carausius. The loyalty of Maximian had to be secured, and he would have to be granted considerable power to enable him to operate independently and with credibility while Diocletian attended to his own problems in the eastern half of the Empire. Though it has been suggested that Maximian became Augustus at the very beginning of Diocletian's reign, it may have been in 286 that Maximian became Diocletian's full partner in Imperial rule.

In January 287 Maximian was at Trier, having fought the Franks and Heruli on the coast of Gaul and around the Rhine mouth in the previous year. During a series of campaigns that lasted until 288, he cleared the tribesmen from Gaul and the Rhine frontier. He received the submission of King Gennobaudes and all his people on the lower Rhine, and he settled Friesians, Franks and Chamavi between the River Waal and the Rhine, with obligations to protect their new lands from attack by other tribes, and to provide recruits for the Roman army.

While Maximian fought in Gaul and on the Rhine, Diocletian had defeated the Sarmatians on the Danube in 285 and then marched to the eastern frontier, where he had successfully completed a diplomatic mission and made peace. He was thus relieved of the necessity of gathering a campaign army for a war against Persia, and perhaps was able to spare manpower for a war in the west. Bringing troops with him he joined Maximian, probably at Mainz, and then embarked on a joint campaign against the Alamanni. Maximian operated from Mainz and Diocletian from Raetia, probably burning and destroying crops and food supplies as they went. By these brutal but effective methods Diocletian and Maximian regained control of the *Agri Decumates*, which had been overrun by tribesmen after the fall of the frontiers during the reign of Gallienus.

The Danube & the East

Immediately after his accession, and again four years later, Diocletian was embroiled in wars against the Sarmatians and other tribes in the Danube area. The tribesmen asked for lands inside the Empire, but Diocletian refused to allow them to settle. The problem was to recur in the later Empire as more and more tribesmen found the Roman world a better and richer place to live than their own lands.

Journeying to the east via Thrace and Syria, in 287 Diocletian came to an agreement with the Persians. The successful expedition of the Emperor Carus had paved the way for a peaceful settlement. The Persians were willing to negotiate, since their internal discord had not been solved. Diocletian strengthened Rome's position in the east, taking back the province of Mesopotamia and reorganizing the Syrian frontier, and installing the pro-Roman Tiridates on the throne of Armenia. This non-violent settlement of the east conserved manpower and resources, which Diocletian needed in the west in a combined offensive with Maximian against the Alamanni.

The campaign began in 288. Diocletian was probably based in Raetia, striking into the Alamannic territories while Maximian attacked from Mainz. By the following year, the Sarmatians had regrouped, and another war loomed. No details survive, but victory for the Romans was probably rapid. Inscriptions show that Diocletian took the title *Sarmaticus Maximus* four times during his reign, the second time after the campaign of 289.

Except for the embarrassment of Carausius, who still held Britain and controlled Boulogne, by 291 the Empire was more stable than it had been for many years. Diocletian and Maximian celebrated their successes, but in Milan, not in Rome, because in the north of Italy they were nearer to the Danube provinces and the routes through the Alps. Their choice of venue highlighted the fact that Rome was not conveniently situated to enable the emperors to deal with threats to the frontiers. Rome remained supreme as an ideological concept, but the government revolved around the emperor, and now more than ever before the presence of the emperor was necessary in the war zones. From Diocletian's reign, Imperial headquarters were set up in several cities all over the Empire, and Rome began to decline in importance.

The Tetrarchy AD 294–324

The term tetrarchy was used in the Greek world to describe a territory divided into four areas, and is employed in modern times to describe the rule of four men that Diocletian imposed on the Roman world in 293. It was a response to circumstances, though no one knows when or how Diocletian conceived of the idea. For some years it had been clear that a single individual could not simultaneously direct the wars, fight all the battles, suppress usurpers, and also govern the Empire. Diocletian's answer was to create two senior emperors each with the title Augustus, and two junior emperors called Caesars, to attend to the different parts of the Empire, and also to provide undoubted successors. The two Caesars were Maximian's son-in-law Constantius, who adopted the name Flavius Valerius Constantius, and Galerius, who became Gaius Galerius Valerius Maximianus. The new names illustrated family connections with the two Augusti, further reinforced by marriage alliances. As a young soldier, Constantius married Helena, a tavern keeper's daughter from Naissus. They had a son, Constantine. When his career began to revolve around the Emperor, Constantius divorced Helena and married Theodora, the step-daughter of Maximian, probably in 289. It is not known when Galerius divorced his wife and married Valeria, Diocletian's daughter.

The four men who ruled the Empire were all Illyrians, and all military men. Diocletian chose men he knew from his own circle. The two Augusti both held the title Imperator, and the office of Pontifex Maximus. The Caesars were not given the title Imperator and did not share the high priesthood, but all four men shared the same victory titles, whether or not they had participated in the relevant wars. Constantius was equated with Maximian and adopted the name Herculius while Galerius was associated with Diocletian and became Jovius. Constantius took precedence over Galerius in official documents.

The creation of four emperors did not necessarily involve a fourfold division of the Roman world. It might seem from their attachment to certain groups of provinces as if each Caesar and each Augustus controlled an allocated portion of the Empire, marked out by official boundaries and a capital city as their headquarters, but at the turn of the third and fourth centuries the four emperors were assigned to regions as and when they were needed, and not to specific areas as part of a fixed geographical plan.

The sources for the decade or so after the establishment of the Tetrarchy are not as abundant as they are for the earlier Empire, but what emerges from the available information is that the Empire was fully stretched at certain times, with wars of reconquest or aggressive punitive campaigns going on in the east and west while the northern frontiers were harassed. For the first few years Diocletian and Maximian recede into the background while the younger men went on campaign, but they reappear on the war front in 296–7.

Immediately after his elevation to the rank of Caesar in 293, Constantius launched an attack on Carausius, winning back control of Boulogne and the coast of Gaul. Despite the fact that the loss of his Gallic port reduced Carausius's credibility and led to his assassination by one of his officers called Allectus, Constantius did not follow up this success with an invasion of Britain until 296, being diverted to Germany to fight against the Alamanni.

Galerius in the meantime was in Egypt, where a revolt had broken out, probably as early as 293. There was also some action on the Danube against the Sarmatians in 294. Literary references indicate that Roman forts were built in barbarian territory opposite Aquincum and Bononia (*in Sarmatia contra Acinco et Bononia*). These forts have been interpreted as bridgeheads guarding the approaches to the main forts on the

Roman side of the Danube, but others see them as forts built well inside Sarmatian territory, suggesting after a successful campaign, Diocletian occupied the territory of the Sarmatians, building forts to keep them under surveillance. Unfortunately there is as yet no archaeological proof of the whereabouts of these forts.

During the course of 294 there was disturbing news from Persia, where the warlike King Narses had seized power. He sent an embassy to the Romans, and for a while there was no action, but in 295 the Persians invaded Armenia and ousted Tiridates. This was a classic move, and it was not a situation that the Romans could tolerate for long, so after his operations in Upper Egypt, Galerius embarked on a war against Persia in 296, as Constantius was preparing to invade Britain. Diocletian was occupied in a struggle with the Carpi on the Danube and Maximian came to the Rhine to relieve Constantius of the task of guarding the area.

In the campaign against Narses, Galerius suffered a humiliating defeat. Constantius on the other hand, aided by his Praetorian Prefect Asclepiodotus, defeated Allectus and massacred the Frankish mercenaries who had fought for Carausius. According to Constantius they were about to sack London, and he saved the city from its fate. He issued the famous medallion from the Trier mint, proclaiming that he had 'restored the eternal light' to Britain (*Redditor lucis aeternae*). Given that Carausius had governed well for several years, looked after the interests of the merchant and land-owning classes, and issued a high quality coinage, there may have been some inhabitants of Britain who questioned whether they had really been in such terrible darkness.

During the next two or three years the theatre of action shifted from the west to the African and eastern provinces. Maximian campaigned in Mauretania, and Diocletian suppressed another revolt in Egypt, involving a prolonged siege of Alexandria that prevented Diocletian from joining Galerius in the renewed Persian campaign. It is testimony to the ability and goodwill of the army and the efficacy of Diocletian's system that the Empire was able to sustain warfare on several fronts at the same time. The long range movements of the army are illustrated by the Danubian troops that Galerius took to the east, and the German units that accompanied Maximian to Mauretania. The supply of food, armour and clothing, and above all of recruits to keep the army up to strength taxed the resources of the Empire, but the loyalty of the troops and their adherence to the ideology of Rome and the Emperor did not seriously break down.

The next four years saw an upsurge in Rome's fortunes and the achievement of peace on most frontiers. The siege of Alexandria was over by the summer of 298, and by the following year the Persians had been defeated. Negotiations followed. Diocletian travelled to Nisibis where he and Galerius formulated a treaty with the Persians, highly favourable to Rome. Tiridates was re-installed on the Armenian throne and Mesopotamia was recovered once again. Apart from the political significance of the treaty, it also carried great economic importance; all trade was to pass through Nisibis, which was under Roman control. The achievements of Galerius against the Persians were recorded on a triumphal arch at Thessalonika, Galerius's headquarters. Significantly the arch was not erected in Rome.

The pressure of the tribesmen on the frontiers was increasing. Galerius was soon occupied on the Danube fighting the Marcomanni and the Carpi, and Constantius was engaged on the Rhine against the Franks. Peace seems to have been established by 303. In that year Diocletian and Maximian went to Rome to celebrate their twenty-year rule, their *vicennalia*. The celebrations were recorded on the coinage; on one issue the Romans were exhorted to rejoice (*Gaudete Romani*), an instruction which practically begs for the addition 'or else'. There are some hints that while in Rome Diocletian persuaded Maximian that it would be politic for the two of them to renounce their powers together and let their junior partners progress from Caesars to Augusti, taking new Caesars of their own. It is said that Maximian swore to uphold Diocletian's plan, in a ceremony in the Temple of Jupiter.

Diocletian was already ill, and left Rome as soon as he could to return to his headquarters at Nicomedia. At the beginning of 304 he collapsed. At some unknown date, probably after this crisis, Maximian went to meet Galerius. Constantius remained on the Rhine watching the Franks. If Maximian hoped to forge some sort of alliance with Galerius to maintain his position as Augustus, he renounced it in 305 when Diocletian abdicated, and stepped down. Constantius and Galerius became Augusti. Diocletian retired to the famous palace at Split, while Maximian went to Lucania in southern Italy. They had both retired, but significantly they established themselves in the western and eastern halves of the Empire, but close enough together to be able to communicate.

The new Caesars were Severus in the west under Constantius, and Maximinus in the east under Galerius. Both men were colleagues of Galerius, which gave him the edge if it came to squabbling with Constantius. Severus was an experienced military officer from Pannonia; Maximinus had served in the Imperial guard. If Constantius and Galerius could achieve the same harmonious relationship as Diocletian and Maximian, with their Caesars able to take on the wars or administrative tasks that they could not attend to themselves, there was no reason why the system could not go on for several decades. But there were two other members of the Imperial households who had been overlooked. Maximian's son Maxentius, and Constantine, the son of Constantius, would soon tilt the balance.

Diocletian's Reforms

One of the advantages of Diocletian's long reign was that military, administrative and financial reforms could be set in motion, tested over time, and brought to conclusions. There is a lack of contemporary evidence for any of these reforms; most of the literary, epigraphic and papyrological information derives from the immediate post-Diocletianic period or more often from the reign of Constantine, with the result that it is difficult to disentangle the authorship of the original reforms. The only statement that can be made with certainty is that after the reign of Diocletian the Roman world was irrevocably changed.

Diocletian adopted some of the precedents that his predecessors had set. Aurelian had introduced the concept of the remote and sanctified emperor. Diocletian replaced Aurelian's sun god with Jupiter and Hercules. The cloth of gold, the diadems, the *adoratio* or obeisance, all remained and were refined into a deliberately elaborated system. The emperor-god found ready acceptance in the east, and in the west the sacrosanctity of the emperor had been established by Severus.

The Army & the Frontiers

Source material for Diocletian's reconstruction of the frontiers is so slender and so general that all that can be said is that he rebuilt forts on the Rhine and Danube and on the frontier from Egypt to Persia, but it not possible to name them, because in many cases it is difficult to distinguish the work of Diocletian from that of his predecessors or his successors. Diocletian may have consolidated the work begun by Probus on the new frontier connecting the Rhine and the Danube. In the east, the frontier road called the *Strata Diocletiana* is the classic Diocletianic or Tetrarchic frontier system, consisting of a road marking the boundary, protected by closely spaced forts, backed up by fortifications in the hinterland. Forts themselves began to change their appearance in the later third century, diverting from the classic playing-card shape of the earlier Empire. Gateways were blocked up, sometimes by projecting towers allowing for better surveillance of the walls.

U-shaped towers were built at intervals along the walls, and on the Danube distinctive fan-shaped corner towers were built, allowing for greater protection of the defences. It is possible that this work is part of the Diocletianic refurbishment of the frontiers. The Emperor probably also attended to the various road posts, watchtowers, and fortified harbours, repairing existing structures and building new ones. Such features had always been part of the Imperial defence system where interior policing and exterior protection were necessary.

There was no corporate policy for the fortification of the cities of the Empire, where initiative was left to the inhabitants. From the reign of Gallienus there had been an increasing number of cities which had acquired walls to protect them against threats from invading tribesmen, or lawless bands such as the Bagaudae in Gaul, and on occasion from rebellious Roman troops. The wall-building is indicative of the lack of faith in the ability of the central government to protect the provincial population.

The Roman army at the beginning of Diocletian's reign was essentially the same army that had defended the Empire from the first century onwards, with the exception that the cavalry had increased in importance. Campaign armies were drawn from the frontier units, as they had always been in the early Empire, but campaigns had become more frequent and more prolonged. There had been an army in the field somewhere in the Empire almost without interruption from the reign of Marcus Aurelius, increasing the possibility that the commanders might use their troops to raise rebellion.

Diocletian attended to the command structure of the frontier armies. He sent back to the frontiers the vexillations and mixed troops that comprised the campaign armies. He may have split existing auxiliary units into smaller groups, dividing them up between different forts, and newly created auxiliary units may have been smaller than the older ones. The newly raised legions may also have been reduced in size, perhaps only 1,000 strong. This makes it easier to understand how Diocletian could afford to add over thirty new legions to the existing thirty-four that he inherited. Some of the existing legions may have been divided into smaller groups. In the fourth century on the Danube, the soldiers from *legio III Italica*, raised by Marcus Aurelius, were distributed over five different forts, and also contributed a unit to the campaign army. This may mean that the legion was divided into six groups of 1,000 men, so in effect there was no reduction in size of the old legion. The legionary fortress at El Lejjun, in modern Jordan, was not large enough to hold a legion of 6,000 men, but the smaller forts nearby could have held detachments. The evidence from these and other sites is not conclusive, but it is a strong possibility that the old legions remained at their original strengths, while the new ones that Diocletian raised were only 1,000 strong.

Before Diocletian's reign there was no permanent campaign army ready to march to threatened zones. By the fourth century, the Roman army had been split into two groups, the frontier units, and the mobile armies, the *comitatenses* of the later Empire. The antecedents of this mobile army are obscure. After 260 Gallienus created a cavalry army and placed it under a single commander, but it is not known for how long this separate army survived, so it cannot be demonstrated whether there was a direct connection between Gallienus's cavalry and the later mobile campaign armies.

The role of Diocletian in the formation of the *comitatenses* is debated. The argument revolves around the *comitatus*, or groups of friends and picked soldiers that accompanied any emperor on campaign. There is no doubt that such a body went on campaign with Diocletian, and probably also with each of the other Tetrarchs, but it is less certain how the *comitatus* functioned. Whether it was an embryonic mobile cavalry army or simply a bodyguard at this stage is not established.

In broad general terms it can be said that Diocletian reconstituted the frontiers. He probably did not establish the mobile army, which was more likely Constantine's contribution to the defence of the Empire; nor did Diocletian create the static troops called *limitanei* which formed a separate frontier force, tied to the land. This term should be treated with caution, since the ancient authors from the fourth century onwards used this term to describe frontier troops of the earlier periods, which is misleading.

In the sphere of administration, Diocletian did set the trend for later years in that he finally separated military and civil posts. Henceforth, except for a few small provinces where the governor was also the military commander, all armed forces were under the control of the *dux*, (plural *duces*) literally meaning leader. The *duces* were equestrian officers, whose authority often extended over more than one province, creating a unified command over frontier zones, regardless of who the civilian governors were. The military commander and the governor had to co-operate with each other with regard to supplies, but the duties of the *dux* were purely military and the duties of the *praeses* were purely civilian, judicial and fiscal. It meant that the wide ranging work load for governors and military officers was lessened, demanding less broad-based diversity and more specialist knowledge. Later emperors did not see fit to make radical alterations to the division of military and civilian commands.

One other military reform can be attributed to Diocletian. Though they are first attested only under Constantine, it was probably Diocletian who established the *scholae* or Imperial guards. The Praetorian Guard still existed, but its power was much reduced, and did not long survive the accession of Constantine.

Finance & Taxation

The Roman Empire derived its income from taxes, spoils of war, the produce of mines and so on, but the economy was predominantly agriculture based, so if production declined, the income from taxation also declined. As for expenditure, by far the largest expense was the upkeep of the army and the buildings associated with it. Defence did not come cheaply, a point which Severus recognized when he increased army pay. The inability of the state to pay the troops increased during the third century, with the result that arrears of pay became the accepted norm, and in some cases payment in kind was substituted for cash payments. Weapons, clothing and food were originally paid for out of the soldiers' wages, but in the third century, these essential items became part of a soldier's pay. When the cash payment system broke down, hungry troops in need of food and clothing requisitioned whatever they lacked, which translates in many cases as stealing. This sort of abuse set the provincials against the army that was supposed to protect them, and landowners and city councillors protested that the state would bankrupt them.

It was necessary to find some method of tax assessment that spread the burden fairly and ensured that all provinces contributed to the defence of the Empire. Italy had for long enjoyed exemption from the tax burden, but this came to an end with Diocletian's reforms. The city of Rome itself was exempt, including territory around it up to a radius of 100 miles. In a predominantly agricultural economy, taxation was based on production, which varied from region to region, depending on the quality of the soil and the type of crops produced on it. Diocletian introduced a system of assessment based on an agricultural unit of production called the *iugum*, which varied in size according to the type of land and crop, and the amount of labour required to produce enough for one man to make a living. The labour (*caput*, literally meaning head) was also assessed; it was not strictly a poll tax, relative to the numbers of people on a farm or estate; for instance a woman's labour was sometimes assessed as half a *caput*. The *iugatio* and *capitatio* were inextricably related, and both were needed to make the fair assessment of taxes due from an area. Livestock was also included in the assessments, as the *capitatio animalium*.

For the purpose of assessment a census had to be conducted every five years. When the annual requirements for the state were set, the Praetorian Prefects were responsible for apportioning the amounts to be collected from each province. The municipal councils were then charged with the collection of the taxes. Any shortfall had to be made up by the members of the councils. City and town councillors could be rapidly impoverished if production declined. It became a matter of urgency to find people to cultivate vacant lands. Various emperors had tried to solve the problems of deserted land, sometimes offering incentives to farmers in the form of tax exemptions to help them to get started.

Diocletian attempted to reform the currency and to tackle the problem of inflation by curbing prices. The coinage had suffered during the third century, and Aurelian's measures had not solved the problem entirely. He had tried to fix the value of the coins and therefore their purchasing power, but traditionally coins were worth only as much as their metal content. While coins were issued with less and less precious metal, good coins were hoarded and disappeared, and prices inevitably rose. Diocletian issued better quality coins. In an effort to put a stop to escalating price rises, Diocletian issued the famous edict *de pretiis*, on prices. In the preamble, Diocletian reminds inhabitants of the Empire that wars have been fought on their behalf, the barbarian invasions and internal unrest have been successfully tackled, and tranquillity has at last been achieved. The edict goes on to list in minute detail products and their recommended retail prices that must not be exceeded. But it is easy to make laws and quite another matter to enforce them. The price edict did not work, and was allowed to sink into oblivion.

Control of Products & Services

Supplies for the army and the administrative staff were not fully provided for via the taxation system. Money payments did not die out altogether but a large proportion of goods were requisitioned. Mines and quarries had been under partial state control since the early Empire, but now, if privately owned manufacturing businesses possessed the slightest relevance to

Map 5. Map of the provinces of the later Empire. As well as creating the Dioceses, as an extra tier of administrative units for the government of the Empire, Diocletian split up the provinces into smaller units, giving them new names or simply numbers.

the army, they were taken over by the state. Factories producing arms and armour, textiles and clothing, were managed by military personnel. Skilled craftsmen were conscripted to work at their trades and in the fourth century it became compulsory for craftsmen to join a guild or corporation and to train their sons in their specific skills. No one was allowed to move to another profession or to another area to find work. The consequent loss of personal freedom gradually extended to all walks of life.

The rural population was no less constrained. Agricultural workers were compelled to stay on the land, and the produce was taxed. Bad harvests and insecurity drove many small farmers off the land, forcing them to ally with influential, wealthy people to enable them to survive bad harvests, or fight off the tax gatherers. Landowners needed workers to ensure that their farms were staffed and fully stocked, so a strong relationship was forged between the landowners and the farmers, the *coloni*, who were eventually tied to their patrons, almost like medieval serfs. Sometimes landowners and the military authorities competed for manpower.

Central administration of the Empire was also highly regimented, as demonstrated by the contemporary term for it, *militia*. Service in the army was distinguished from the civil service as *militia armata*, armed service. The administrators were organized in ranks, just like the soldiers. Separate departments to deal with specific sections of the administration had existed since the early Empire, and had grown and expanded as the Empire grew. Diocletian divided the administration into departments called *scrinia* after the boxes used to carry the relevant documents for each section. Officials called *magistri* were placed in charge of each section, not necessarily new personnel, but the existing ones were perhaps issued with new names. The *magistri* were members of the Imperial council, the *consilium*, which may have also been called the *consistorium*. It is not known when the *consistorium* was instituted, but whatever it was called, Diocletian's council was closer in spirit to the late Roman consistory than it was to the Imperial *consilium*, which was a circle of advisers, with no official appointments and constantly changing personnel. Diocletian's *consilium/consistorium* was the government, embracing administrators and department heads, all directed by the Emperor himself. Diocletian was the last Emperor of the Principate and the first Emperor of the Dominate.

Provincial Reorganization

Diocletian made two major alterations to provincial administration. As a preliminary measure he grouped together several existing provinces into new administrative units which he called dioceses, governed by equestrian officials called *vicarii*, which means 'substitutes'. During the early Empire a *vicarius* was sometimes appointed as a temporary substitute for a provincial governor. Diocletian adopted the title for permanent appointments, representing an extra tier in the administrative hierarchy. The *vicarii* were senior officials, supervisors of the provincial governors and responsible to the Praetorian Prefects, though the emperors could and did communicate with them directly.

The next step was to reduce the size of individual provinces. Severus had begun the process. Pannonia and Britain had each been split into two provinces, and Aurelian had created the two Dacian provinces out of parts of Moesia. Diocletian made further divisions, so that the number of provinces almost doubled. Consequently the number of officials also increased, giving rise to criticism that there were more officials than taxpayers. As mentioned above military and civilian commands were now separated, with the equestrian *duces* responsible for all the troops in the province, even if the governor was a senator. In some cases the *dux* commanded troops of more than one province. Only in a few cases in the smaller provinces was the governor also in command of troops.

The date of the changes in provincial administration cannot be ascertained. The document known as the *Laterculus Veronensis*, a list of dioceses and the *vicarii* in charge of them, and of the provinces and their governors, is the nearest evidence available for the Diocletianic system, but some of the entries have been shown to be Constantinian in date, obliterating the original arrangements under Diocletian. The provincial reorganization was probably carried out over a prolonged period, but it is not known how it was done. If it is correct that the dioceses were created before the provinces were divided, the *vicarii* may have undertaken the duties of the governors as they were replaced, until new officials were appointed.

The benefits of the subdivision of provinces were that each governor could devote more time to supervising the cities, transport and communications, the food supply, and to hearing judicial cases. They could exercise a tighter control over tax paying provincials. Control was the order of the day, as was the prevention of rebellion; some authors state that the creation of smaller provinces was designed to make it more difficult to usurp the emperor, but in the fourth and fifth centuries usurpation as a regular Roman recreational activity did not cease.

The Persecution of the Christians

Diocletian revived and strengthened the old Roman religion but did not go so far as to enforce universal observance. The first onslaught against religious sects came with the attacks on the Manichaeans, who were firmly entrenched in the eastern provinces, and were numerous in Egypt and north Africa. They followed the teachings of Mani, who was considered a heretic by the Mazdean priests of Persia, but the Manichaeans flourished because King Shapur had forbidden the persecution of religious groups. The Romans suspected that the Manichaeans were sympathetic to the Persian kings, and that they were the agitators behind the Egyptian revolts against Rome. In 302 Diocletian visited Egypt, and issued an edict against the Manichaeans. The text is known; how it was put into effect is not elucidated.

Imperial attention then turned to the Christians. For some years there had been isolated examples of Christian intransigence, particularly with regard to the army. In 295 a certain Maximilian appeared before the proconsul of Africa because he refused to enlist in the army. A purge of the army was attempted to remove any Christians who might refuse duty. A refusal to serve in the army was subversive. If it spread, recruitment for the armies all over the Empire would be compromised, and if the Christians were to be officially excused from military service, there was nothing to stop men with an aversion to the army from undergoing a miraculous conversion to Christianity, and then refusing to serve.

In 298 a Christian serving in the army, a centurion called Marcellus, refused to take part in the celebrations in honour of Maximian, which presumably involved sacrifice to the emperors as gods, or at least to Jupiter and Hercules. Devotion to the chief gods of Rome was dangerously compromised, and the matter of sacrifice became the litmus test of a Christian's attitude to Imperial rule. Most religious groups who were accustomed to the worship of several gods or aspects of gods under different names, would not find any difficulty in sacrificing to the emperor or to the gods of Rome. The Christians, unfortunately, could not tolerate gods other than their own, and their missionary spirit meant that they were not content to live quietly in the background without drawing attention to themselves and their beliefs.

At the beginning of the fourth century the emperors applied themselves to eradicating Christianity. The blame for the anti-Christian policy is laid at Galerius's door. He was in a strong position after his victories in the east and on the Danube, and was said to have been violently anti-Christian throughout his career. Those who wish to exonerate Diocletian fall back on the assumption that he merely yielded to pressure from Galerius. The first edict was issued on 23 February 303, at the festival of the Terminalia at Nicomedia. The church was destroyed and fires broke out twice in the Imperial palace.

Galerius ostentatiously left the city rather than be murdered by the Christians. Others said that he had started the fires himself to put the blame on the Christians and provide the excuse for persecuting them.

In the summer of 303 another edict was issued, aimed at the clergy, who were to be imprisoned. The prisons were soon overflowing. Another edict was issued ordering compulsory sacrifice to the gods, so that the die-hards would be weeded out. The edict was not strenuously applied over the whole Empire. The west escaped lightly because Constantius and Maximian did not share Galerius's zeal for burning people alive. Maximian limited his efforts to closing churches and confiscating books, and Constantius did even less to eradicate Christians. The uneven treatment of the Christians ensured that the edict could never achieve its goal; it was enforced rigorously in some parts of the Empire, but in other areas the officials did nothing and simply reported that everyone had sacrificed as instructed. At the time of Diocletian's retirement, the Christian problem had not been solved.

The Rise of Constantine AD 306–324

From the moment when Constantine came to power, recorded history depends almost totally upon the version that this ambitious ruler endorsed, little tempered by alternative sources. He rewrote the past to suit the present, and carefully orchestrated the history of his reign. Some cardinal facts are obscure, for instance it is known that Diocletian retired in 305, persuading Maximian to do the same, but no one knows exactly when Diocletian died. He ceased to play a major part in the political arena after his abdication, his presence influenced Galerius sufficiently to invite him to the conference at Carnuntum in 308, where he tried to persuade him to take power again, or at least to arbitrate among the rival factions that had grown up in the few years that had elapsed since the two Augusti had retired.

When the two new Caesars were proclaimed in 305, Constantine was at the court of Galerius at Nicomedia. His father Constantius was about to start his British campaign, and allegedly sent for his son because he was ill, which may be true, since Constantius died within the year. Galerius seemed reluctant at first to release Constantine, probably reasoning that he would lose his bargaining power with Constantius if he allowed his son to leave. Constantine thought that he was under threat, and proceeded as fast as he could to the west, melodramatically killing or maiming all the horses whenever he changed to fresh mounts at posting stations, so that he could not be pursued. It is indicative of the man.

Constantine arrived at his father's camp on the northern coast of Gaul, just as the British campaign was about to begin. Father and son proceeded to the far north of the island, but archaeology has little to show for this campaign. Only very slight traces of Constantius's progress are visible, and none of the many temporary camps in Scotland have been authoritatively assigned to this campaign. The similarities with Severus's British wars have been highlighted by several authors, especially since both emperors took their sons with them, and both died at York. The reasons for the war and what Constantius may have achieved in Britain is overshadowed by the fact that the army declared Constantine emperor in July 306, perhaps with a little encouragement from Constantius, and not a little from Constantine himself. The hereditary principle had not died out as far as the army was concerned and Constantine was not about to pass up the opportunity and nobly revert to the Tetrarchic principle of non-dynastic promotion. He tried to reconcile his new status with Galerius, and wrote to him to say that he had no choice but to concur with the wishes of the troops. Galerius compromised and made him Caesar.

In October 306 Maxentius, the son of Maximian, was declared emperor in Rome itself, with support from senators and the praetorians. There followed a scramble for survival in which alliances were made, broken, and made again. Galerius sent Severus to retrieve the situation, while he and Maximinus looked on from their respective parts of the Empire. Maximian reappeared, either on his own initiative, or perhaps he was invited to become emperor again by his son. Severus failed to dislodge Maxentius, and was besieged in Ravenna, where he committed suicide. Even Galerius, the conqueror of the Persians, was forced to leave Italy in the hands of Maxentius.

Maximian offered to ally with Constantine, who married Maximian's daughter Fausta in 307. There may have been a promise to make Constantine Augustus. At this stage, although Maximian was Constantine's senior partner, in fact he was nothing more than a usurper, so Constantine's dependence upon him cast a dubious light on his career, and he carefully disassociated himself from these less than perfect beginnings as soon as opportunity arose.

After Galerius left Italy, Maximian quarrelled with his son and tried to depose him, but Maxentius could call upon considerable support in Rome, and Maximian was forced to seek refuge with Constantine at Trier. For some time, Constantine remained in northern Gaul, attending to the Rhine frontier. A campaign or campaigns against the Bructeri are recorded, and there was activity at Cologne where Constantine built a bridge, and had perhaps begun to build the fort opposite the city at Deutz, though the archaeological evidence suggests that it belongs to a slightly later period.

While Constantine and Maximian were in Gaul, Galerius arranged a meeting with Diocletian on 11 November 308 at Carnuntum where an inscription from the Mithraeum records the reconciliation of emperors. The Tetrarchic system was repaired, but not for long. Diocletian would not be persuaded to rule the Empire again, and Maximian was forced to retire once more. Constantine was relegated to the position of Caesar, along with Maximinus. The vacant slot for another Augustus was taken by Licinius, a colleague of Galerius. Maxentius was not even considered.

By 310, Constantine had rid himself of Maximian, who had allegedly begun to intrigue against him. Constantine marched to southern Gaul, besieged his erstwhile ally at Marseilles, where Maximian allegedly committed suicide. Constantine now purged himself of all connection with Maximian and sought for more respectable ancestry, insisting on the divinity of his father Constantius, and attaching himself to the house of Claudius Gothicus. Licinius countered by claiming descent from Philip the Arab. Hereditary power had a longer history than Tetrarchic principles. At about the same time as he created his new lineage, Constantine also departed from the Jovian-Herculian religious support structure, and turned instead to Apollo Sol Invictus, both sun gods. Constantine was emerging as an independent entity.

In the year 311 fate took a hand in the inexorable rise of Constantine. By the end of that year Severus and Maximian had already been eliminated, and it is possible that Diocletian had died, though some scholars have argued for 313 or even 316. It is well attested that Galerius fell ill and died in 311, probably in April or May. Before he expired he reversed the persecution of the Christians, issuing the edict of toleration that restored Christian places of worship and reinstated the clergy. By 311, only three emperors, Licinius, Maximinus and Maxentius, were powerful enough to oppose Constantine, but fortunately for him the three were far from united against him. None of the four rulers of the Roman world trusted each other, so there was a period of watchful suspicion while they decided who would ally with whom. Licinius was betrothed to Constantine's half sister Constantia, so in theory he was allied to Constantine, but if he suddenly threw in his lot with either of the other two the balance would tilt.

In 312 Constantine decided to move against Maxentius, who now ruled Italy and the African provinces, with all their agricultural resources at his disposal. After securing the Rhine, Constantine mobilized. The causes of the civil war are in reality the intolerance of one emperor for the other, and the grudges they held. Even though he had quarrelled with his father, Maxentius still wanted to avenge his death, since Maximian had more than likely been murdered by Constantine. On the other hand it was clear to contemporaries that Constantine wanted to rule the whole Empire, so he now represented himself as the saviour of Rome from the tyrant and usurper.

He marched from Gaul to the Alps with a conglomerate army that has never been fully documented, smashing through the troops sent to guard the Alpine passes by Pompeianus, Maxentius's Praetorian Prefect. He stormed the town of Susa (ancient Segusio) where Maxentius had placed a garrison, but his own troops were held back and there was no bloody massacre or looting. It was an important point, and attests to Constantine's iron authority and command of his soldiers. This was going to be portrayed as a war to save Rome and the Empire from the unsuitable elements who had taken control, so it would have been extremely detrimental to the cause to behave in a worse fashion that the supposed tyrant Maxentius. At Turin where Constantine's troops defeated the guard that Maxentius had placed there, the town was once again spared. Assured of lenient treatment, other towns welcomed Constantine. Milan opened its gates to him. His eventual arrival at Rome was assured.

Maxentius decided to meet him outside the city, even though he had strengthened the Aurelian fortifications. It was a mistake to let Constantine get so far without stopping him, and when he had arrived it was a mistake to offer battle so soon, but Maxentius had already lost some of his popularity, despite his studied promotion of Roman values and traditions, partly because his building programme was proving expensive. If he had risked a siege of Rome he would merely have lost even more support in proportion to the length of time the siege went on, and when the food was running out and Constantine offered a better choice, his fate would have been sealed. So Maxentius met Constantine at the battle of the Milvian Bridge and lost. His troops were backed into the Tiber and he was drowned along with many of the soldiers. His death was convenient because now that he was removed Constantine could portray him as a tyrant, and more importantly everyone could choose to believe the propaganda without the embarrassing living reminder that he or she was betraying the erstwhile emperor. Besides there was an inevitability about it all; Constantine's victory was god-given, though which god had given it was not as apparent at first as it later became. The authenticity or otherwise of Constantine's Christian vision before the battle will never be proven. The tales are too deeply embedded in Christian iconography to be uprooted now by modern speculation, and such a pastime is doomed to failure because the various versions of what he saw and when he saw it are so inconsistent; they range from a simple cross in the sky some days before the battle, to a complicated Chi Rho symbol, combining the first two Greek letters X and P of Christ's name, seen or dreamed on the night before the battle. Allegedly he was informed that in this sign he would conquer, and allegedly he ordered the soldiers to put this Christian device on their shields, which conjures up the scenario of lots of soldiers milling about looking for some paint when they could have been getting a good night's sleep. Veracity is not the important point; it is the legend and the use that Constantine made of it that count, because he re-shaped the Roman Empire and by extension, the western world.

The Elimination of Maximinus & Licinius

Shortly after the battle, when he was established in Rome, having conciliated as many groups as possible with promises that he was just as Roman as other emperors, Constantine wrote to Maximinus to try to persuade him to end the persecution of the Christians in his territories. His letters were probably ineffective. Maximinus was steadily marginalized as Constantine and Licinius drew closer together. Early in 313 the two met at Milan, where Constantine's half sister was married to Licinius, and an edict was issued declaring toleration of all religions. Licinius's part in this undertaking is overshadowed by the glory of Constantine's later reign, and because towards the end of his life Licinius resorted to persecution of the

Christians again, but in 313 he deserved as much credit as his brother-in-law.

Equality was never in Constantine's personal vocabulary for long; in his own territories, inscriptions made it clear that he was the senior emperor, and he began to describe himself as Maximus Augustus, or at least he made no move to prevent others from addressing him as such. Licinius acquiesced, perhaps because he thought that he could eliminate Maximinus and build up a power base in the east that would secure him against anything that Constantine could put into effect against him. He picked a fight with Maximinus because the latter had invaded Thrace; Licinius won the victory and took over Maximinus's provinces. He also made sure that few of Maximinus's family or adherents survived; no risk of any resurgence in his name was to be countenanced, and while he was about this grisly business Licinius seems to have decided to remove any possibility that Diocletian's or Galerius's families might make a bid for power. Whatever his reasons, in 313 or perhaps in 314, Diocletian's daughter Valeria, the widow of Galerius, and Prisca, Diocletian's widow, were killed. Maximinus fled to Tarsus and committed suicide. Constantine now had only one main rival.

Relations remained stable enough through the following years. In 315 Constantine celebrated his ten-year rule. The festivities of the *decennalia* were crowned by the dedication of the arch of Constantine, still visible in Rome near to the Colosseum. It was magnificent but somewhat second hand, in that some of the sculptures were borrowed from other monuments. The text outlines Constantine's achievements, in phrases not unlike the beginning of the *Res Gestae* of the first Augustus, who advertised the fact that at the age of nineteen he had raised his own army to save the republic from faction; Constantine attributes his success to inspiration of the divinity and his own noble mindedness, by which he was enabled to save the republic from the tyrant and his faction. This refers to Maxentius, but could just as well be taken as indicative of any other dissenting elements. Consolidation of his power was achieved in the west. There remained the east, and Licinius. Constantine waited upon events until 316, when he appointed his brother-in-law Bassianus as his Caesar. This man's brother Senecio was a friend of Licinius, and Constantine probably used this relationship to weave a little intrigue. It was said that there was a plot against him, engineered perhaps by Senecio, perhaps by Bassianus, possibly with the support or encouragement of Licinius. It was all rather mysterious, no doubt by design, to increase the aura of subterfuge. Bassianus was executed, and Constantine asked Licinius to surrender Senecio. This was the test of his loyalty, perhaps; he refused to hand him over. Manoeuvring began. Licinius moved up with his army to the borders with Constantine's territories. He appointed an Augustus of his own called Valens. The inevitable war resulted in defeat for Licinius, and a compromise. He ceded territories to Constantine, the frontier province of Pannonia, part of Moesia, and part of the Balkans. The unfortunate Valens was eliminated, and in his place three young Caesars were appointed. These were the fourteen-year-old Crispus, Constantine's son by his first wife, and two very young children, the infant Constantine, and the son of Licinius, not yet two years old. Hereditary succession was back in fashion. From 317 to 323 there was an unofficial truce while each emperor attended to his own territories Consulships were shared, in 318 by Licinius and Crispus, and in 319 by the young Constantine and the young Licinius. During the same year, Constantine campaigned in the Danube provinces while his son Crispus fought against the Franks on the Rhine. Harmonious relations were brief. Licinius departed from Constantine's plan when he began to persecute the Christians. Constantine's response was to take up the Christian cause. Relations deteriorated, and when Constantine crossed the boundaries of his own territories into Thrace while he was campaigning against the Goths in 323, Licinius suspected that Constantine was about to launch an invasion of his territories. Constantine was reasonable; he said that he had defeated the Goths and thrown them back across the Danube, so the methods by which he had accomplished this were less important than the result.

Despite Constantine's studied innocence, preparations for war escalated. Licinius appointed yet another Augustus, Martianus. His reasons may have been to provide himself with administrative assistance, freeing him to concentrate on the war, but it is notable that Constantine kept any promotions within the family, giving the command of his fleet to his son Crispus. Licinius and Constantine faced each other at last in July 324 at Adrianople. Licinius was defeated and fled to Byzantium, but Constantine's fleet under Crispus forced its way through the Hellespont, threatening him with blockade or capture, so he moved on. Constantine won the final battle at Chrysopolis, opposite Byzantium. Licinius surrendered, persuaded by his wife Constantia that her half brother Constantine would be merciful. He made terms, ceding all his territories to Constantine in return for a life of leisure under house arrest. After only a few months he and his son were killed along with Martianus, the new Augustus. It had taken nearly two decades for Constantine to extend his rule over the whole Empire. His path had not been easy or direct, and there had been many casualties, but he had achieved sole rule, and could now devote his attention to reshaping the Empire.

Map 6. Map of the Empire divided between the four emperors, before Constantine defeated the other three and became sole ruler.

8

New Rome: Constantine
to Theodosius the
Great AD 324–395

Constantine Sole Augustus AD 324–337

As sole ruler Constantine created a new world. He brought
to fruition all the mid-third-century developments, of the
adaptations of Gallienus and of the Diocletianic and Tetrarchic
innovations. Once he had all the Empire under his control,
Constantine could rewrite his origins, and put his policies into
effect. He emphasized his descent from Claudius II Gothicus,
with the result that this emperor's achievements were praised
by the historians His press agents were Christian writers,
notably Lactantius and Eusebius. Constantine's promotion of
the Christian Church is his most enduring achievement, and
the one that has received the most attention from the ancient
authors and many modern scholars. His first allegiance to a
single god, Sol Invictus, never faded entirely, and pagan symbols
rather than Christian ones appeared on his coinage, until later
in his reign. It is a matter of opinion whether he believed in
the Christian message or whether he simply used it for political
ends. To some authors he was a true convert to the Christian
faith, largely because he had no pressing need to promote it
and there was no advantage in doing so. All he needed to do
was issue and uphold an edict of toleration and allow all kinds
of religion to flourish. He was baptized only on his deathbed,

but this was not abnormal at the time, and cannot be used as proof that he was only playing along with the Christians. Some scholars insist that Constantine wished only to establish some kind of unifying force throughout the Empire, and used Christianity to achieve it. Since the early Church was rent by schisms from its infancy, it was not the most effective unifying force that he could have chosen.

Constantine was drawn into the dispute of the Donatists in Africa, when the Bishop of Carthage died. The Carthaginian Christians elected Caecilian as the new bishop, but a rival group opted for another candidate, who also died and was replaced by Donatus, who gave his name to the sect. In 312 or 313 the Donatists appealed to Constantine for arbitration as to who was the true Bishop of Carthage. At a hearing in 313 and again at the council of Arles in 314, the claims of Donatus were rejected. In 316 Constantine declared firmly for Caecilian, but by this time the Donatist church had gained many supporters in Africa. The significance of the episode is that the appeal was not directed to the Bishop of Rome as head of the Church, but went straight to Constantine, who was not yet sole emperor.

Constantine took an active part in the councils and synods of the Church, the most famous being the Council of Nicaea in 325, which at first seemed to produce all the answers to thorny questions of doctrine and to quell the factions within the Church, bringing about the hoped for unity. It did not prove wholly successful on this score, though the Nicene Creed still forms the basis of Christian belief. The Church was favoured by Constantine, but it never emerged from a position of subordination to him, losing its erstwhile independence. The clergy were allowed considerable freedom, enjoying the benefits of tax exemptions and being excused municipal obligations, but Constantine remained the master while calling himself the servant. If he had changed his mind about the Church, he still had the power to outlaw Christianity, and would probably have succeeded. The fact that he did not do so indicates that the Church gave him what he wanted. In return he encouraged the foundation of Christian churches, which were not mere copies of pagan temples, but a new form was chosen for them derived from the basilicas, civil buildings with administrative and legal functions. The basilica of St Peter had been founded before 319, and was completed during Constantine's sole reign, in 329. Prudently, most new church foundations were on Imperial lands, or in the case of Rome, they were built either on lands that Constantine owned, or placed outside the city.

Constantine's social policies were bound up with his attitude towards the Christians. He insisted that the men who were eligible to serve as decurions on their town councils should do so, despite the fact that growing impoverishment made it more and more difficult for such individuals to meet the expenses involved. The large number of laws that were passed to try to force eligible councillors to undertake municipal obligations merely highlights the fact that the legislation was not working. Since the clergy were exempted from their municipal obligations, it was hardly surprising that resentment built up against the privileges of the Christians, but at the same time more and more men sought a way out of their municipal burdens by entering the Church, reducing still further the number of people who could serve their communities in the practical sense rather than in the spiritual realm. Eventually the wealthiest men were forbidden to enter the clergy, to try to retain men of means within the sphere of local government of the towns and cities.

There was a distinct advantage in belonging to the Christian fraternity. The officially sanctioned state religion was Christianity, which meant that personal alliances and networks could be built up within Christian circles in the Imperial administration. While promoting Christianity, Constantine tried to retain religious freedom. Although he was less tolerant of paganism after he became sole emperor, it was not stamped out, and those who refused to join the Church still had a part to play. As a means of conciliating the pagan aristocracy of the Empire, Constantine created new senators, bestowing senatorial rank without the obligation to live in Rome or to attend meetings of the Senate. These senators were appointed prefects of Rome, or as governors of the consular provinces, and as *correctores* in Italy.

Constantine did not much alter the arrangements that Diocletian had made with regard to the government of the provinces. He did not attempt a full scale removal of the equestrians as governors and did not radically alter provincial boundaries. The large numbers of experienced personnel necessary for the government of the provinces and command of the armies made it unlikely that he could turn his back on equestrians as a source of supply, so he promoted them and adlected some of them to the Senate.

In view of the potential shortage of manpower, he did nothing to halt or reform the crystallization of professions that Diocletian had instituted. Constantine's policies did not include liberating the inhabitants of the Empire from their hereditary obligations. The *coloni* continued their descent from free men to virtual slaves, while the power of the great landowners, whose nominal tenants they were, increased to the point where they were eventually able to challenge the state itself and defy the attempts of the emperors to control them.

The army was a different matter. There Constantine did make some changes, though controversy still reigns over who created the mobile field armies. The balance of probability is that Constantine remoulded Diocletian's armies and developed something new. The pagan author Zosimus accused Constantine of destroying Diocletian's system, because the latter had secured the frontiers by putting the troops back into their forts, while Constantine took the troops away again and put them into the cities, where they were not needed in the first place. That was perhaps how it seemed to contemporary observers as the mobile cavalry armies (*comitatenses*) and the more static frontier armies (*limitanei*) were developed. The old system whereby the legions and auxiliary troops were stationed on the frontiers made it more difficult to assemble a campaign army and march it to the threatened areas, and in any case, denuding one area of its troops, in order to come to the assistance of another region, invited further trouble at the lightly-garrisoned points. On the Rhine and particularly on the Danube, the tribesmen were fully aware of what was happening on the frontiers, and ready to seize their chance for raiding, or sometimes to force their way into the Empire and settle down because life seemed better on the Roman side.

From the middle of the third century the importance of cavalry units had increased, and Constantine responded to the need for greater mobility by developing the mounted units. The new deployment of the armed forces was reflected in the new military commands, the *magister equitum* in command of the cavalry and the *magister peditum* in command of the infantry. Constantine's contribution to the protection of the Empire was not radically altered by his successors.

The Praetorian Prefects had already been given tremendous responsibilities in the administration of the Empire, and under Constantine they lost all their military functions. One of their tasks was to administer the *annona*, the all important supply system. The Praetorian Guard was abolished after the battle of the Milvian Bridge, and replaced with a new bodyguard called the *scholae*, first established by Diocletian. This bodyguard was commanded by the chief of the civil administration, the *magister officiorum*, who was in charge of all the departments of the administration.

Apart from introducing Christianity as the official religion Constantine's next most famous or notorious innovation was to reinvent Rome in the east, at Byzantium. It was not a complete surprise since the emperors had not lived in Rome for many decades, and some of the short-lived emperors never even saw the capital city. New capitals had been established at different cities nearer to the frontiers at Trier, Milan, Sirmium and Nicomedia; Constantine had chosen Serdica (Sofia) as his residence, and now his choice was Byzantium. Strategically this city offered tremendous advantages. It was eminently defensible; Septimius Severus had reduced it only after very a long siege. Supplies could be brought in directly by sea, unlike Rome which had to be supplied from the port of Ostia. And it was close to the eastern provinces, where the greatest threat to security derived from the Persians, and to the Danube, continually harassed by the tribes from the north. Prime requirements for defence of the Empire were that the emperor and the armies should be close to the potential trouble spots, and Byzantium fulfilled those requirements.

Byzantium officially became the city of Constantine, Constantinople, in 330, but there is evidence that it was already labelled *altera Roma*, another Rome, at least four years before the official foundation date. Probably as soon as he became sole emperor, Constantine decided to create another capital city. In itself the establishment of yet another Imperial headquarters was not a revolutionary move; it only imitated what had happened in other provinces. What was revolutionary was that Constantine transported to his new city the whole of the government administrative machinery. The city had seven hills and fourteen administrative districts, just like Rome, and Constantine gave his new capital a Senate, a Forum, and a circus, and instituted a free corn dole, everything that mirrored Rome itself.

In Rome there remained a shadow of what had gone before. Constantine repaired some of the major buildings and completed the huge basilica that Maxentius had begun, but otherwise he paid the city little attention, except for celebrating his twentieth anniversary as emperor in 326. Without the Imperial presence, commercial and social life went on much as before. Senators still lived out their lives in the city, debates were still held in the Senate House, and some senators took up provincial posts. But the government of the Empire was no longer centred on Rome. For many years the administrative machinery had not been located in the city, but lumbered after the emperor wherever he was; as Herodian recognized at the beginning of the third century, Rome was where the emperor was. But in the end, Rome did not lie down quietly and die. It remained a symbolic centre, part of the ideology of the western Empire, and a focus for the kingdoms that emerged when the Empire lost its cohesion.

After the experiment of the Tetrarchy, the hereditary principle in the Imperial house reasserted itself. Constantine prepared for the succession by proclaiming as Caesars his sons by his wife Fausta. The first born son Constantine was made Caesar as an infant in 317, and his siblings Constantius and Constans were given the same rank in 324 and 333. Crispus, Constantine's son by his first wife, had been given army commands, but was not otherwise promoted, and for reasons unknown he was executed in 326. There may have been palace conspiracies which have not come to light, or Constantine simply grew suspicious. He accused Crispus of having an affair with his wife Fausta, and had her killed as well.

In 328, Constantine the younger was sent to Trier, while Constantine senior campaigned on the Rhine. There were further campaigns against the Goths in 332, when Constantine made a treaty with them, and then against the Sarmatians in 334. The frontiers were secured for the rest of Constantine's reign. The three sons of Constantine had to be content with the rank of Caesars, since the Emperor did not share power with any of them, and did not elevate any of them to the status of Augustus. He raised another of his relatives, Dalmatius, to the rank of Caesar in 335. Echoes of the Tetrarchy were revealed when Constantine divided the Empire into four regions, with one of his Caesars in control of each. His intentions are puzzling to modern scholars. The Diocletianic system had patently not worked, and no one knew its weaknesses better than Constantine. Equality among four rulers would be short-lived, even among the most well balanced individuals, but on the other hand, if Constantine had designated a sole successor, it would have simply promoted rivalry among the other Caesars and led by a different route to civil war. This is exactly what happened after Constantine died in May 337, but it took three years for the fighting to start.

214

Constantine II AD 337–340, Constans AD 337–350 & Constantius II AD 337–361

For about six months after Constantine's death, the Roman world held its breath. The four Caesars made no move until the army made it clear that no one except the sons of Constantine should rule. Dalmatius was quickly assassinated by the soldiers, along with other peripheral members of Constantine's family. Only two boys were spared, Gallus aged twelve and Julian aged six, who were to play a part in the Empire nearly two decades later. The Empire was divided into three parts under each of Constantine's sons, who awarded themselves the title of Augustus. The partition was not an amicable agreement. Constantine II ruled the west, Constantius the east, and Constans controlled Italy with Illyricum and Africa. As the youngest of the brothers he was supervised by Constantine II, the senior Augustus, but the arrangement did not last long. Constans challenged his brother, who responded in 340 by bringing his army to Italy. At Aquileia, Constantine II was defeated and killed, and Constans quickly took over his territories. In the east Constantius was preoccupied with the resurgence to power of the Persian King Shapur II and approved the extension of Constans's Empire.

Constans devoted attention to the defence of the Rhine frontier and the provinces of Britain. He was far from popular with either the troops, because he had restored discipline with a rather heavy hand, or the people who faced increasing impoverishment, so it was easy for conspirators from the army and civil government to form a conspiracy against him. Less than a year after taking over the west, Constans was dead, having been defeated by a Germanic army officer favoured by the troops, called Magnentius. He was acclaimed by the army and accepted by the people, except for the inhabitants of Illyricum, where Constantius's sister had encouraged another so-called usurper, Vetranio, to seize power, because he was preferable to Magnentius. Constantius temporarily patched up the problems in the east and set off to eradicate Magnentius. Vetranio was content to step down, having preserved Illyricum, and his soldiers joined Constantius, who defeated Magnentius at Mursa, leaving Constantius sole ruler in 351. Magnentius was still a free agent, having escaped from Mursa, but he did not represent a serious threat. Two years later at another battle in the French Alps, Magnentius was killed.

The relative peace of Constantine's reign was ended in the 350s, only a few years after his death. Constantius was faced with invasions across the northern frontiers and mounting trouble in the east, and the multiple problems of internal security and frontier defence proved too much for one man alone, so in 351 he turned to his surviving relatives for assistance. He summoned the twenty-eight-year-old Gallus, made him Caesar, married him to his sister Constantia, and sent him to guard the eastern frontier. By 353 it was apparent that he had made the wrong choice, so in 354 he brought Gallus back to Rome and executed him.

For the next few months there was almost continuous fighting. There was a revolt in Gaul, when a Frankish officer called Silvanus was accused of treason, and raised rebellion, then the tribes of the Franks and Alamanni crossed the Rhine. More than ever, Constantius needed an assistant whom he could trust, and his next choice was Gallus's half brother Julian, who was studying at Athens. In 355 he was made Caesar, married to Constantius's daughter Helena, and sent to Gaul where he was appointed military commander in 357, despite having no experience or training in military matters.

Julian's lack of experience was no problem. In a famous battle near Strasbourg he brought the Alamanni to battle and trounced them. The survivors fled back to the Rhine with Julian in pursuit. For the next two campaigning seasons in 358 and 359 he led further expeditions across the Rhine, and repaired the frontier installations. Constantius then asked him to send troops to the east, where he was preparing a campaign against Shapur II, because the Persians had invaded

Roman Mesopotamia and destroyed the city of Amida. This period of Roman history is fully documented by the historian Ammianus, who was a contemporary commentator and had personal experience of what he described.

Julian did not trust Constantius because he suspected that it was he who ordered the army to massacre all his relatives in 337, to remove any opposition after the death of Constantine. Likewise Constantius did not trust Julian because he was not in the habit of trusting anyone, and Julian had been successful and made himself popular with the army, so it was probably no surprise to Constantius to hear, while he was preparing the eastern campaign, that in 360 the troops in Gaul had proclaimed Julian emperor, and that Julian had not refused the offer. The trouble was supposed to have started when Julian was about to obey orders and send his troops to the east. Some of his German soldiers had been enrolled on the basis that they would not be asked to serve anywhere beyond the Alps, and Julian's instructions contravened that agreement. They protested, and the eventual result was the proclamation of Julian.

Constantius refused to recognize Julian as emperor, so war was now inevitable. Rather than wait in Gaul for the onslaught, Julian set off for Constantinople. Constantius also set off from the east, but before the two rivals could meet, he died in Cilicia in 361. It was said that he had named Julian as his successor, which avoided further wars. As sole emperor, Julian inherited the Persian war that Constantius had prepared for. For the few months before he mounted his own Persian campaign, Julian tackled the financial problems of the Empire. He tried to reduce state expenditure, revoked tax exemptions to increase revenue, and stopped civilians from using the Imperial postal service, the *cursus publicus*. The Christians suddenly found themselves out of favour after their prosperous development under Constantine, because as a young man Julian had devoted himself to classical studies while he was divorced from public life, and had been converted from Christianity to the old religion. He did not persecute the Christians at first, but he harassed them, removing support for the clergy, demanding that temples converted to Christian use should be restored, and encouraging various writers to produce pamphlets attacking Christian beliefs and doctrine. Since his rule was very short and his successor was a Christian, this glitch in the progress of Christianity was soon repaired.

Preparations for the Persian campaign began in May 362, when Julian marched to Antioch. In spring 363 Julian took a large army down the banks of the River Euphrates, marched to the Tigris, and finally reached the Persian capital at Ctesiphon, where he won a battle. Several times in the past a Roman army had reached this Persian capital and won a battle, but none of these battles had ever resulted in permanent occupation of Persia, nor had they helped to solve the problem of enmity between the two Empires. Julian's expedition was no exception to the rule. Shapur II arrived with the main Persian force, and Julian marched homewards up the Tigris, dogged all the way by the Persians, who made small attacks but did not join in a main battle. During one of these skirmishes Julian was wounded, possibly by a Persian spear, but some said that one of the Christians in his army had attacked him. He died that same evening. The army immediately chose a successor, the commander of Julian's bodyguard, called Jovian.

Jovian AD 363–364

The new Emperor was in a highly unenviable position, similar to that of Philip the Arab a century earlier, who also took over after the death of the emperor, and had a choice of fighting and losing, or negotiating his way out of Persia. Jovian chose to make peace. It was costly, but the army was extricated, to fight another day. Jovian gave up territory, never a popular move for the Romans. The eastern parts of Mesopotamia were relinquished, along with the important site of Nisibis, where Diocletian had signed a treaty in 299, favourable to the

Romans. Jovian also agreed to renounce control of Armenia, and to pay subsidies to the Persians.

Jovian had no opportunity to reveal any plans or policies, save for allowing freedom of religious worship all over the Empire, and repealing Julian's enactments against the Christians. His reign lasted only eight months. He died of natural causes rather than assassination. He was one of the very few emperors to die a natural death. The military high command, assisted by civil administrators, chose Flavius Valentinianus, an army officer from Pannonia, to succeed Jovian, but the army was not content, because the soldiers had concluded that there was a need for two emperors to take charge of the east and the west. They approved Valentinian's choice of his own brother Valens, and both took the title Augustus.

Valentinian AD 365–375 & Valens AD 365–378

Valens went to the east, while Valentinian took control of the western half of the Empire, and devoted himself to clearing the Rhine provinces of the tribesmen who endangered them. By a combination of warfare, diplomatic efforts and strengthening the frontiers, he brought peace to Gaul and the Rhineland. He fought the Alamanni, the Franks and the Germanic tribes, made lasting treaties with some tribal chiefs, recruited large numbers of tribesmen for the Roman army to keep it up to strength, and rebuilt the chain of forts and bridgeheads from the Upper Danube area, along the Rhine all the way to the western coast. He sealed the gap between the Upper Danube and the Rhine with a chain of forts running along the southern edge of Lake Constance to Basel, and joining the frontier along the west bank of the Rhine to Strasbourg. He was a prolific builder, with the result that it is difficult to discern the work of other emperors who came after him, and he was so thorough that it is tempting to label everything from the fourth century as Valentinianic. His work secured Gaul for some considerable time.

While Valentinian attended to the Rhine and Danube, his trusted general, Count Flavius Theodosius was in Britain.

His proper Latin title was *comes*, plural *comites*, originally meaning companions, but the term was given official status by Constantine and granted to high officers of the civil and military administration. Theodosius repelled the tribes of Picts and Scotti and Saxons, who had invaded all at the same time in 367, giving rise to the theory current in ancient times that there had been a barbarian conspiracy. Theodosius strengthened the British frontier, and also the forts and towns of the interior. He may have been responsible for the addition of towers to some town walls, which would support artillery to keep attackers from coming too close. Theodosius went on to put down a rebellion in the provinces of North Africa, which had begun probably in 373. A chieftain of the Mauri called Firmus was supported by the populace, but he was defeated by Theodosius in 374. Intrigues at the Imperial court led to the execution of Theodosius in the following year, possibly because he had gained knowledge of some serious corruption among senior officers and court officials, who struck him down before he could reveal names.

The first challenge in 365 for Valens was the attempted usurpation of Procopius, one of Julian's extended family and a close associate who had perhaps expected to be named as his successor. He established his base at Constantinople, and controlled Thrace and Bithynia. He stressed his relationship to Julian and Constantius, which engendered considerable support for him. The dynastic principle, and loyalty to the house of Constantine was not dead. However, he had insufficient military strength to sustain a rebellion, let alone make a bid for the whole Empire. More detrimental still, he had not been able to sway the officers of the army to support him. They deserted him after about a year, and went over to Valens in May 366.

War broke out in Thrace, where the Goths continually invaded and devastated the country. Valens defeated a group of them in 369 and made a treaty with the leaders of the tribe. This entailed a levy of tribesmen (*foederati*) for service in the army, and a solemn promise to cease hostilities, but the oath was sworn by a tribal individual to a Roman individual, not to the tribe or state, so the tribesmen in particular considered the treaty invalid once either of the individuals died.

In 367 Valentinian fell dangerously ill, and designated his nine-year-old son Gratian as Augustus, to try to ensure the succession. He recovered, and in the early 370s he went to Pannonia. Tribesmen were again proving troublesome and threatening the security of the Danube provinces, so Valentinian mounted several expeditions against them. After returning from one of these expeditions in 375, he allowed an embassy from the Quadi to see him. They complained that they were not responsible for the raids on Roman territory, which had been carried out by other tribes turned brigands, who had settled near the Danube. Then they complained about the frontier installations that had been built opposite their lands, at which point Valentinian, angered beyond endurance, fell dead of an apoplectic seizure.

Valentinian's son Gratian, now aged about sixteen, succeeded his father, but to make sure of the dynasty, the military leaders persuaded Valentinian's widow to make their four-year-old son Augustus, as Valentinian II. Gratian remained in Gaul and Valentinian II was to govern Illyricum with the help of the military commander Merobaudes, probably of Frankish origin, but a competent general. In 371 Valens went to the eastern frontier to wrest control of Armenia from Shapur II, and bring the country back into the Roman sphere of influence. Between then and 377 he guarded against further encroachments of the Persians, and drove them out of Mesopotamia, but then news came of a serious incursion of the Goths into the Danube provinces.

This time the tribesmen were not simply making raids. The fierce Huns had come sweeping out of Mongolia and entered Gothic territory, massacring the population as they advanced. The Goths were obviously terrified of them, and wanted to settle in Moesia and Thrace, where life seemed much sweeter. A group of Goths known as the Tervingi, under their leader

Fritigern, was allowed to settle, but then another group, the Greuthungi, crossed the Danube without official permission and joined them. The Romans treated them badly, denying them food supplies unless high prices could be extracted. Unable to go back home, and prevented from moving further into the Empire, the Goths took to raiding. The military force sent to assassinate the Gothic leaders failed, and war broke out in 377.

Valens hurried to Constantinople, and then to Adrianople where the Goths who had been drafted into the Roman army had rebelled in support of their fellow tribesmen. The major battle was fought there, where so many other battles had already been fought. Gratian had sent troops from the west, but before they arrived, Valens committed his forces in an attempt to stem the tide. His defeat was total, and he lost his life. His body was never found. The Goths spread out over Thrace and Illyricum, and the problem of how to deal with them was bequeathed to Gratian. He decided to ask for help. He chose Theodosius, son of Count Theodosius who had restored order in Britain after the disasters of 367. When his father was denounced and executed, Theodosius had shared the disgrace and had been dismissed from his post as *Dux* of Moesia Superior and/or Illyricum in 374. Traditionally, Gratian called him from his retirement in Spain, but some scholars now think that Theodosius was already reinstated and held a command on the Danube. Wherever he came from, Theodosius was made *magister militum* under Gratian in 378. In January 379 he was elevated to Augustus, and given command of the eastern Empire.

Theodosius the Great AD 379–395

The Empire was ruled by three emperors: Gratian in the west, Valentinian II, who had been made Augustus at the age of four, in Italy and Illyricum, and Theodosius in the east, specifically Moesia, eastern Illyricum, and the new Dacia, carved out of Moesian territory. The Goths had taken over Thrace and Moesia Inferior, and eventually spilled out into Macedonia and Thessaly. Theodosius took advantage of the endemic disunity among the Goths, and for a while he was able to play rival factions off against each other, to occupy them in internecine struggles instead of attacking Roman territory. He then concentrated on building the garrisons up to strength in Macedonia, and in 380 he arrived in Constantinople.

The policy of letting the Goths fight each other paid off when one of the Gothic leaders, Athanaric, was expelled by his own people, and asked for asylum in Constantinople, where he died soon afterwards. In 381 Theodosius was reinforced by troops from the west under Arbogast and Bauto, Frankish generals. Theodosius had held military commands, but he was not an outstanding military leader, and was content to let these generals drive the Goths out of Macedonia, Thessaly and Illyricum. The tribesmen marched back to Thrace.

Theodosius made a treaty with them in 382, an arrangement for which he was censured by contemporaries and later historians. The terms were that the Goths could settle on the lands they had overrun in Thrace, and were to be ruled by their own leaders. This treaty did not reflect the same conquering spirit as previous ones. Normally the Romans remained in the ascendancy, monitoring the tribes settled on Roman territory, and the treaty stipulated that they should provide soldiers for the Roman army. Theodosius had concluded the sort of treaty that might have been made with tribes outside the Empire. He promised subsidies of food, one of the most important factors in the Gothic eruption that led to the battle of Adrianople, because the Romans short-sightedly withheld food from them.

The contribution of troops was probably one of the most important parts of the treaty of 382, but it is not known on what basis this was carried out, and it is possible that the Goths levied in this way were commanded by their own officers and not by Romans. This would distinguish them from the Goths who were already serving in units of the Roman army, and make them more like the auxiliaries of the Republic, who were not a permanent part of the Roman army, being raised from tribesmen who were commanded by their nobles, returning home after the campaigns ended. Unfortunately, with regard to Theodosius's treaty, none of this is known for certain.

The arrangement with the Goths polarized the Roman world. Romans who hated the so-called barbarians thought that the tribes would simply imagine that the Empire and Theodosius were weak, and would not keep their word. Others advocated Romanizing the Goths, and making them into good Christians. The orator Themistius said that it was better to fill Thrace with farmers and potential soldiers than with corpses.

In truth the Empire *was* weak, if only for lack of recruits for the army. The battle of Adrianople had decimated the eastern army, and there was now a growing reluctance to serve in the ranks. Theodosius recruited wherever and whenever he could, in an attempt to keep up the numbers, and he employed thousands of Goths, who fought well for Rome. Most of them would probably not consider that their military service for Rome was at odds with their Gothic nationality. Tribal organization and cohesion was flexible. Tribesmen were able to join other tribal groups without incurring the charge of betrayal, and provided that the men were accepted by the others and obeyed the leaders, groups were formed and dissolved quite quickly. Nationality was an embryonic concept in tribal organization. A gravestone of a tribesman, admittedly a Frank and not a Goth, epitomizes the easy acceptance of dual identity. His epitaph reads *Francus ego cives, Romanus miles in armis*, meaning I am a Frankish citizen and a Roman soldier.

In 383, a rebellion broke out in the west. A commander in Britain, Magnus Maximus, was hailed as emperor by his troops. He was accepted in Gaul and Spain, where discontent with the rule of Gratian was increasing. Maximus gathered troops, perhaps reducing the garrison of Hadrian's Wall to the danger point, and crossed into Gaul. Gratian took flight, but was captured and handed over by his own soldiers, and executed. Theodosius was not strong enough to challenge

Maximus, so he recognized him as emperor, and Maximus remained in command of most of the west for a few years. In 387 he appointed his son Victor as Caesar, and invaded Italy, part of the realm of Valentinian II, who fled to Thessalonika with his mother and his half-sister, Galla. Theodosius could not allow this action to go unpunished. He had stopped a group of Goths, labelled the Ostrogoths, from crossing the Danube, and he had arranged a peace treaty with Shapur II, whereby he agreed to partition Armenia and share it with the Persians. There was a lull in hostilities in the east, leaving Theodosius free to attend to affairs in the west. He had elevated his elder son Arcadius as Augustus in 383, so he left him in Constantinople, and marched against Maximus. His fleet ensured that Maximus could not leave Italy except over the Alps, and he brought the usurper to battle at Siscia and then at Pola, defeating him in both encounters. At Aquileia, Maximus's troops surrendered him. He had become very unpopular, financing his expedition by seizing the property of the rich and not so rich. He was executed in 388, but he is immortalized in the Welsh heroic tale of the Mabinogion, as Macsen Wledig.

Valentinian II was restored to power, and Theodosius married Galla, Valentinian's half-sister. Valentinian was sent to Gaul, where Victor, Maximus's son, was killed. The Frankish *magister militum* Arbogast accompanied Valentinian, to watch over the young man. Theodosius went to Milan, remaining in the west for some time. At this point, St Ambrose, or Ambrosius, began to exert an influence over the Emperor. He interfered when a Christian mob, incited by local monks, burnt down a Jewish synagogue in Mesopotamia. Theodosius wanted the Christians to rebuild the synagogue, but Ambrose persuaded him against the idea. Two years later, in Thessalonika, a popular charioteer was imprisoned and the general who refused to release him was killed in a riot. Theodosius gave orders for the soldiers to round up and kill the rioters, and in the end it was said that the casualties amounted to 3,000 civilian dead. St Ambrose demanded that the Emperor should perform a public penance, or face exclusion from the Church. After a delay of eight months Theodosius complied. His dilemma was that as an ardent Christian who persecuted heretics, he ought to display unity with the Church. But the episode illustrated how easily the Church and state could be involved in a power struggle.

Theodosius returned to Constantinople in 391, to deal with various troubles. His son Arcadius had quarrelled with Galla, and the Goths had taken to raiding again, but the tribesmen were pacified without a war. The Praetorian Prefect Rufinus, and the general Stilicho, stopped the raiding and exploited the mutual antipathy of some of the Gothic groups. These men were Theodosius's trusted assistants. Stilicho was the son of a Vandal tribesman, a good general and loyal to the house of Theodosius. He married the Emperor's niece and was made *magister militum* in 392. Two years later, Stilicho accompanied Theodosius to the west, to eliminate the usurper Eugenius.

Arbogast had exceeded his brief as protector of Valentinian II, and had gained so much power that he was able to ignore an attempt by the Emperor to dismiss him. In May 392 Valentinian was found dead, the verdict being suicide, but suspicion attached to Arbogast. Since he was a Frankish soldier, Arbogast did not try to make himself emperor, but instead he raised Eugenius, an official at Valentinian's court, as Augustus. Theodosius refused to recognize him. For the best part of two years, Eugenius tried to mollify Theodosius. He asked St Ambrose to mediate, and issued coins depicting Theodosius and Arcadius, much as Zenobia in the 260s had issued coins depicting the Emperor Aurelian. Theodosius responded by appointing his younger son Honorius as Augustus in the west in 393, and gathering an army to face Eugenius in 394.

At the battle of the Frigidus, Arbogast and Eugenius with an army composed mostly of Franks were defeated by Theodosius and Stilicho with their army of Goths. Eugenius was captured and killed, and Arbogast committed suicide. Once again three emperors ruled the Roman world: Arcadius in Constantinople, Honorius based initially at Milan and their father Theodosius on his way to Rome to celebrate the victory. But soon the emperors were reduced to only two, because Theodosius died in January 395 in Milan. Stilicho assumed responsibility for Arcadius and Honorius, and for a while he was the most important man in the Roman world.

From the end of Constantine's reign the problems that he had faced began to increase. The perennial dilemma of the later Roman Empire was that it was threatened or attacked on more than one front, and was too large to be ruled by one man. Various methods of sharing power had been tried since the second century, not always successfully. Even when Imperial rule was kept within the family, with a senior partner as Augustus and a junior Caesar, or with two or more Augusti, the emperors had not always been able to keep the frontiers safe or prevent usurpers from claiming power. The Tetrarchy, theoretically a better system, had shown that non-dynastic power sharing did not always work either. Quartering the Roman world between four rulers ought to have provided better government and protection, but only if all the personnel co-operated with each other and kept to the tasks that were given them. The Empire needed a strong hand to co-ordinate it, and trusted subordinates in different regions to govern and protect it. After the reign of Valens, the emperors no longer led their troops on campaigns as they had done throughout the third century and most of the fourth. By Theodosius's reign, the military leaders, the *magistri militum*, or masters of the soldiers in different parts of the Empire had risen to prominence, sometimes acting on their own initiative, and even influencing policy. These men were often of barbarian origin, good generals, resourceful and capable. They knew their own power and did not hesitate to use it, but without them the Empire would probably have collapsed or been overwhelmed in the fourth century.

Similarly large numbers of barbarians served in the Roman army, particularly the Goths. Among the Romans, service in the army had become very unattractive, to the point where recruitment was well nigh impossible. A series of laws issued by Valentinian I and Valens demonstrates the difficulties of finding enough men to fill the ranks. In 365 the Emperors adopted stern measures to round up deserters, and to punish anyone who sheltered them. Then they tried to identify the men who were eligible to serve but had somehow escaped the recruitment process. Some men preferred to become camp followers or even servants rather than join the ranks, so they were rooted out and turned into soldiers. Casting the net wider, Valentinian reduced the height qualification for soldiers. In 367 he passed laws to force men who had chopped off their fingers, or otherwise mutilated themselves, to join up and serve in some capacity or other. This presumably did not produce the desired result, since he lost patience altogether and passed another law in the following year, where the penalty for self-mutilation to avoid army service was to be burnt to death, and the masters of these evaders were also to be punished for not preventing them from chopping their thumbs off. The lack of willing recruits was countered by drafting large numbers of barbarian soldiers, who either volunteered, or were provided by the terms of a treaty. Viewed in this light, Theodosius's use of Gothic soldiers is the only reasonable alternative that he could have adopted at the time.

The civilian sphere was not much better off. Large scale impoverishment affected many parts of the Empire, cities declined, local councillors were as reluctant to serve their communities as eligible soldiers were to serve in the army, because they too were impoverished and taking a place on the town council was a very expensive business. There were some rich and influential men in civil administration, but they were in the top echelons, close to the emperors. In the first century administrative posts had been filled by freedmen, then as time went on by equestrians, and now by higher class men, who used their proximity to the emperors to advance their own careers. If the civil administrators combined with the military chiefs, they could control the emperors, or even rid themselves of unfavourable ones and set up new emperors in their place. Corruption and self-seeking was rife, and it was a brave man who would try to put an end to it.

Everyone in the Roman world had always been subordinate to the wealthiest men, and in the fourth century the great landowners became more and more powerful. Farmers were forced off their lands through war or impoverishment, and looked to the landowners for protection, becoming tied to them more closely for their livelihoods, while the landowners headed growing communities of men and became powerful enough to protect their estates and their people. Eventually they were strong enough to defy tax collectors and emperors alike. Even Constantine had not been able to prevail against them.

The late fourth century was a time of great upheaval among the tribesmen across the frontiers. It was not a new phenomenon in itself, but the scale of the movements was too vast for the Romans to stem the tide in all parts of the Empire. When Theodosius died in 395, the seeds of fragmentation, both internally and externally, had already taken root.

9

Lost World: The Transformation of the Western Empire & the Survival in the East AD 395–476

Arcadius AD 395–408 & Honorius AD 395–423

After the death of Theodosius the Empire was shared between his two sons, Arcadius, aged about eighteen or nineteen, based in Constantinople, and Honorius aged ten, based at Milan. AD 395 is traditionally the date when the eastern and western Roman Empires parted company, but the people who lived through the end of the fourth century and the beginning of the fifth would not interpret the recent events as the start of a new era. Emperors had shared power and territory on several occasions in the past. Gallienus and Valerian took charge respectively of the west and the east in the third century, Constantine created a new capital while business carried on at Rome, and more recently Valentinian and Valens had shared Imperial power in the two halves of the same Empire, without giving rise to any suggestion that the Empire had split into two separate entities. The date AD 395 only becomes significant when viewed retrospectively, because from then onwards there were two emperors, several of whom were too young to rule alone, and despite efforts to reunite the Empire, which continued sporadically until the middle of the sixth century when Justinian launched expeditions to win back territory, the Empire that had once stretched from Britain to Syria and from Africa to the Danube, was never reconstituted.

The fourth century had seen the rise of a class of military men who directed events and assisted, or in some cases dominated, the emperors. The extreme youth of succeeding emperors in both west and east ensured that this state of affairs was not reversed. The last emperor to lead his armies into battles was Valens, and the last to accompany his armies for some time thereafter was Theodosius I, who relied on his generals to win his battles. After his death, the two young Emperors Arcadius and Honorius remained in their capitals while their armies and commanders fought battle on their behalf. Increasingly, the safety of the Empire depended on the skill of the generals who led the troops. The various *magistri militum* became military dictators, and began sometimes to squabble with each other in their ambitious scramble for power. They could be assisted or opposed by the chief officials in the civil administration, who sometimes ousted the generals from their positions, or even had them executed, and then assumed control of the Empire. Neither the military commanders nor the civilian administrators held onto their power for any significant length of time. At certain periods history descends into a list of who killed whom, like who begat whom in the Bible. Alarmingly, the internal struggles often occupied the attention of commanders and administrators to the detriment of the protection of the Empire and its inhabitants.

The military commanders were mostly of barbarian origin, as were the armies that they led. The *magistri militum* were usually highly Romanized, literate and capable. Stilicho was the son of a Vandal cavalry officer in the Roman army, and a Roman mother. He had served under Theodosius, leading troops at the battle of the Frigidus. At Theodosius's death, Stilicho was the most powerful commander in the western half of the Empire. There was no proof that Theodosius, on his deathbed, had entrusted to Stilicho the care of both his sons, and therefore responsibility for the whole Empire, but Stilicho insisted that this was the case and pursued his aim diligently, opposed by officials at Constantinople, in particular Rufinus, Praetorian Prefect at the court of Arcadius. A war of words was carried on for some time as Stilicho utilized the poet Claudian to extol the exploits of the deceased Theodosius, and to revile the men of the eastern court. It was always useful to have the ear of the local press, and if newspapers and television had existed in his day, Stilicho would have appeared in the columns and on the news programmes.

When the east was threatened by the Goths, Stilicho set off with his army to check them, but Rufinus persuaded Arcadius to refuse the help but demand the return of the troops from the east which had taken part in the battle of the Frigidus. Stilicho complied, but Rufinus did not profit from his machinations, since the leader of these troops, a Goth called Gainas, murdered him. He was replaced by the eunuch Eutropius, an official in the civil administration, who made himself *magister officiorum*, the chief of the administration, and more or less ruled the eastern half of the Empire for four years. Eutropius was definitely not in favour of the Goths, or any of the other barbarians who proliferated in the army.

The so-called barbarization of the Roman army, once considered detrimental, is actually the trend that enabled the battered Roman Empire to survive as long as it did. The Roman field armies still had a part to play, and are sometimes glimpsed in action in the sources, but the rank and file were increasingly drawn from the tribesmen who clustered around the periphery of the Empire or were settled inside it. The various tribes represented a source of manpower that the Romans had always exploited, and during the later Empire the tribesmen were virtually the only source of recruits. They fought well, but as time went on and the tribes realized their power, their usefulness was partially offset by their growing demands. The Goths, for instance, had helped Theodosius to win the battle of the Frigidus against the rebels Arbogast and Eugenius, but they considered that their rewards were not commensurate with their services. At Theodosius's death, a leader had emerged among a group of Goths, called Alaric. He approached Constantinople with demands for food, money and lands, hoping for an official appointment for himself as commander of troops. It was rumoured that he had come to some arrangement with Rufinus, Praetorian Prefect under Arcadius. Whether or not there had been an agreement, it could not be honoured before Eutropius took power after the murder of Rufinus.

Achieving nothing in Constantinople, Alaric moved into Greece at the end of 395 or the beginning of 396, and sacked Athens. Stilicho arrived, brought the Goths to a standstill, and allowed them to settle in Epirus, approximating to modern Albania. Alaric was to feature largely in the history of both halves of the Empire for the next few years. He commanded a large force, and lengthy debate centres on the nature of Alaric's Gothic army. It has been argued that he led a collection of family groups, encumbered with wagons full of women and children, so only part of his group would be fighting men. Other scholars prefer to interpret Alaric's group as a military force, continually seeking employment by the Romans, sometimes successfully when it suited either the east or western governments to use him, and sometimes unsuccessfully, in which case Alaric resorted to pillage, to try to force the Romans to give him a military command. The group was occasionally settled on the land, but the men were unable to sustain themselves on a permanent basis, and if employed by the Romans the men and their commander would be supplied from official sources.

Alaric was not in command of the entire Gothic nation. There were Goths employed or settled over a large part of the Empire, with a foot in both east and west. In Thrace, and around the Black Sea and the Crimea, Gothic tribes were settled on the land. When the Goths arrived at the Danube in 376, seeking asylum, there were two groups called the Tervingi and Greuthungi. At a later time, another two groups began to be distinguished, possibly derived from the Tervingi and Greuthungi, the western groups called the Visigoths, and the eastern groups labelled the Ostrogoths. Then there were the Amal Goths, whose leader Theoderic has received the best press notices of his day. None of these labels denote homogeneous ethnic tribes or nations, or even names that the tribesmen themselves would have recognized.

The Romans did not always bother to distinguish different tribes, lumping them all together under the general heading of Scythians, whatever their original tribes had been. Eutropius disliked all of them, but he was perfectly willing to despatch the Goths on military expeditions, which backfired on him in 399. There was a rebellion in Asia Minor, and the Gothic leader Tribigild was sent to restore order, but joined the rebels instead. Eutropius then sent Gainas to deal with the rebels. Instead, Gainas and Tribigild joined forces, and then persuaded Arcadius to demote and execute Eutropius. The Goths gained nothing from the elimination of Eutropius. Encouraged by the Empress Eudoxia, the civilians of Constantinople rose up against the Goths, and killed thousands of them in the city and surrounding area. It was not wholly a racial hatred that spurred on the populace of the city, but also the fact that the Goths were Arian Christians, and the orthodox church of Constantinople did not approve. Arcadius appointed a new military leader, Fravitta, another Goth who was on friendly terms with him. Fravitta forced Gainas to flee to the Danube, where he was killed by the Huns, but Fravitta himself lasted only until 401, when he too was killed. From then on, the Goths in the east never recovered their superior position. The western tribesmen were denied access to military commands, and recruitment of Armenians and local eastern tribesmen filled the ranks of the eastern Roman army instead of Goths. This was partly necessity at first, in order to replace the Gothic troops who had been killed in the rising at Constantinople, but it became eastern policy to keep recruitment local, employing eastern tribes who would have a vested interest in protecting their territory.

In 401–402 Alaric descended on Italy. It is possible that he had been given a command by the eastern government, and then his supplies or payment had been cut off. If the eastern high command never actually deflected tribal movements towards the west, then the various emperors certainly derived some benefit from such events, and did little or nothing to stop the movements. There was no interference from the east when the Goths marched into Italy. Fortunately, Stilicho was able to stop Alaric after two battles at Pollentia and Verona in northern Italy, but he did not eradicate them. He had other uses for the Goths. The province of Illyricum was partitioned between the east and the west, and Stilicho was determined to win back the eastern section to join it to Honorius's half of the Empire. Alaric and his Goths would be able to help him to do so, so he gave a military command to Alaric in anticipation of battling with the eastern Empire.

Before he embarked on the project, another group of Goths under Radagaisus invaded in 406, so Stilicho turned aside to deal with the threat. In Liguria he defeated the Goths, recruited about 12,000 men for the army and enslaved the rest, flooding the slave market in Italy. There was great rejoicing in Rome, statues were commissioned for the hero Stilicho, and then the news arrived that a commander in Britain had been acclaimed as emperor by the troops. He was called Constantine, labelled the third of that name. He soon crossed the Channel into Gaul, which was attacked from across the Rhine by hordes of Vandals and the Germanic Suebi in 406–407. The usurper Constantine was able to hold everything together in Gaul for the next few years.

Having waited in vain for the launch of Stilicho's project to reclaim Illyricum, Alaric re-entered the scene, demanding the payment that Stilicho had promised him. Honorius and the Roman Senate were inclined to refuse, but Stilicho insisted. His credibility would have been destroyed if it was clear that he could be overruled, so Alaric received 4,000 pounds of gold, raised by the senators and people, somehow.

In 408 Stilicho's ascendancy started to wane. Arcadius died, and Honorius and Stilicho fell out over who should travel to the east to preside over the installation of the next emperor. It was decided that Honorius should attend to the west to try to root out the usurper Constantine, and Stilicho would approach the eastern court, but in the meantime, the *magister officiorum* Olympius, whose influence over Honorius prevailed, spread rumours that Stilicho intended to raise his own son to Augustus in the east. The rumours caught the imagination, and in the end Stilicho virtually gave himself up rather than start a civil war to retain power. He went back to the court of Ravenna, and was executed. Honorius had just rid himself of the one man who could perhaps have protected his Empire.

Olympius decided to take a hard line with the Goths, refusing to meet any of Alaric's demands for cash, food and confirmation of his military command. Legions were summoned from Dalmatia to fight against Alaric, but were defeated. The Praetorian Prefect Jovius was sent to negotiate with Alaric. The Goths were probably hungry by now and their demands were scaled down, this time for food supplies and permission to settle in Noricum, near the Danube frontier. Jovius refused even these terms, so Alaric seized Ostia and cut Rome's food supply, which meant he could scale up his requests to a higher level than before, and Jovius and the Senate capitulated. This time, Alaric appointed his own emperor, Priscus Attalus, who gave him the military command that he wanted. The Goths then went off to besiege Honorius in Ravenna. Attalus was supposed to have gone to Africa to win back control of the provinces, and the food supply, but he did not fulfil his part of the bargain so Alaric removed him, and marched on Rome in 410. The Goths held the city for three days, looting private houses and public buildings, but this famous sack of Rome is now played down. Its moral effects were tremendous, but there was no great destruction of buildings and no wholesale massacre of the population. The Goths were Christians, and spared all the people who took refuge in the churches of St

Peter and St Paul. Alaric captured Galla Placidia, the daughter of Theodosius, and sister of Honorius. The Goths took her with them when they moved off. The seizure of Rome provided lots of portable wealth, but did not solve the problem of feeding the Gothic army, so Alaric moved south towards the coast, intending to cross over to Sicily, but a storm wrecked his ships, and on returning to the mainland, Alaric died, in 411.

Tradition holds that in the same year that Alaric captured Rome, the province of Britain was abandoned. There is little mention of it in the ancient sources after the usurper Constantine crossed into Gaul, but Britain was probably not relinquished entirely. If Honorius did withdraw the troops as tradition states, there may not have been very many of them in the province after Constantine took units of the army to Gaul, and of those that were left, it is to be supposed that many of the soldiers remained where they were, with their families. The end of Roman Britain was not a single, sudden event. A lingering *Romanitas* survived as communities carried on as best they could, but the corporate security and supply systems disappeared, so communities shrank to self-sufficient groups. Some people sought sanctuary in Gaul, perhaps once they had realized that the Romans were not coming back to reclaim the island. How long that hope survived is not known, but the Celtic resurgence began quite rapidly, once Britain was divorced from the crumbling western Empire.

Alaric was succeeded by Athaulf, his brother-in-law, who led the Goths into Gaul in 412. For a while he joined the usurper Jovinus, who made a bid for Imperial rule on the Rhine, supported by tribesmen of the Burgundians and Visigoths. But Athaulf abandoned him in favour of the Romans. By this time, the western Empire had begun to pick up the pieces, as Flavius Constantius took command of the army and enabled the Empire to strike back. The assistance of Athaulf's Goths turned the tables and led to the surrender of Jovinus. This success ought to have raised Athaulf's chances of an alliance with the Romans, and a military command such as Alaric had held, but he overdid things. In 414 he married Galla Placidia, kidnapped from Rome by Alaric. In due course they had a son whom they called Theodosius. As the nephew of Honorius, who had no heirs and had not named a successor, the child was a highly important figure who could be used to persuade the Romans to agree to whatever Athaulf asked for. But the Goths were to be thwarted by Constantius.

Flavius Constantius was a native of the Balkans, whose early career was with the army of the eastern Empire. He may have arrived in the west as part of the force that was sent from the east to help Theodosius in the war that ended at the battle of the Frigidus. It is presumed that he was a supporter of Stilicho, who survived the fall of the general, and became *magister militum* in 410. By the simple policy of keeping the Goths away from supplies, he eventually forced Athaulf out of Gaul and into Spain in 415. Lack of food, combined with the dismal prospect of a continuous trek to find it, led the Goths to assassinate Athaulf, but his murderers survived for only a short time, then a leader called Wallia took over.

In return for supplies from the Romans, Placidia was now released and sent to Ravenna. Her son Theodosius had died as an infant, so there was no bargaining tool for the Goths. Constantius authorized Wallia to attack the tribes who had taken over much of Spain, the Vandals and Suebi, and this Wallia did with considerable success, but he had not completed the task when Constantius recalled him and his tribesmen to Gaul, and settled them in Aquitania. It was said that Wallia had been a little too efficient for Constantius's taste. The new Gothic settlements may have been on Imperial lands, or abandoned farms, since there seems to have been no outcry from displaced Gallic landowners and farmers. The Gothic kingdom in Aquitania survived until the early sixth century.

The power of Constantius at Honorius's court steadily increased. He made sure that he was surrounded by loyal supporters and found posts for them. In 417 he married Galla Placidia, who bore him a daughter, Honoria, and a son,

Valentinian. In 421, Constantius was made Augustus, to share power with Honorius. It seemed as though the western Empire might be reconstituted. Then in the same year, Constantius died. Two years later, Honorius also expired, after a thirty-year reign.

There was now the threat of civil war. Honorius had never produced children and had not appointed another successor after the demise of Constantius. To make matters even worse, he had fallen out with Placidia in the year before his death, and sent her packing to Constantinople with her son. The vacuum was soon filled, as one of the palace officials called John took over the western Empire, supported by a general called Castinus, but opposed by Bonifacius in Africa, who refused to declare for John. For about eighteen months John was able to cling onto power, but in the end he was overthrown by forces sent from the eastern Empire. Placidia and her son, the young Valentinian, were brought to Thessalonika, where Valentinian was declared Caesar, and then in the autumn of 425, mother and son arrived in Italy and Valentinian III was declared emperor in Rome. Placidia was the pre-eminent personality at the western court, but she had to work hard to remain in that position. Her main adversary was to be the general Aetius, called 'the last of the Romans'. He was the general who almost welded the western Empire back together, but was catastrophically interrupted by a seemingly unstoppable force that first threatened the Empire of the east: the Huns under their leader Attila, who first appeared in the east during the reign of Theodosius II.

If the Romans themselves thought of the Empire as a unified whole, modern historians usually treat the east and the west as separate entities from the early fifth century. The chronological approach to the history of both halves of the Empire becomes more difficult as the reigns of the emperors do not coincide, and there are only rare instances of mutual co-operation between the two Empires. It is significant that during the period from 408 to 491, there were only five emperors in the east, two of them sharing power for a year, while in the west there were sixteen, some of them reigning for only a few weeks. The east was not immune from attempted usurpations, but the emperors managed to overcome the usurpers and cling onto power. Their armies were recruited from the tribes within the eastern Empire or on its immediate periphery, and attacks from the northern barbarians were fewer than those in the western Empire. The cohesion of the eastern Empire, where no territory was ceded or taken over permanently except by agreement, meant that the eastern emperors did not lose the revenues and taxes that paid their armies. From the early fifth century, history takes a different course in the east and west.

The Eastern Empire from Theodosius to Zeno AD 408–491

Theodosius II, Emperor of the East, AD 408–450

When Arcadius died in 408, he was succeeded without opposition by his eight-year-old son Theodosius. Fortunately there were good advisers for the new child emperor, one of the most important being the Praetorian Prefect Anthemius, who started by building new walls around the city of Constantinople, making it virtually impregnable. It is significant that during Theodosius's long reign, while the western Empire was more often than not fighting for its life, the officials of the eastern Empire could devote their energies to wall building and to the compilation of the laws known as the Theodosian Code, which was published in the 430s, the exact date being uncertain. The Code contains over 2,000 laws from the western and eastern halves of the Empire, dating from the reign of Constantine. The laws were collated under subject headings, and divested of unnecessary verbiage with the object of making the main points clear and unequivocal. The Theodosian Code is an invaluable source for modern historians, and formed the basis of the laws of the later barbarian kingdoms that arose in the western Empire after Roman rule declined and disappeared.

The expulsion of the Goths from Constantinople in the reign

of Arcadius, and the subsequent recruitment of home-grown soldiers gave the eastern Empire an advantage that was not available to the west, since there was no internal source of troops for the western leaders to exploit, and the west was more highly pressured by the barbarians than the east. It is suggested that one of the reasons why Stilicho was determined to win back the eastern portion of Illyricum was to exploit its manpower for the army.

Compared to the troubles of the west, there was little warfare on the eastern frontiers. The eastern rulers profited from a determined policy of diplomacy with the potential enemies on their frontiers, especially with their most powerful opponents, the Persians. The eastern armies fought wars only occasionally, since the regime preferred to buy off attacks and only went to war if the schemes failed. This was made possible by another advantage that the east enjoyed, which was the preservation of its revenues. Taxes were collected, wealth accrued at Constantinople, territories were not ceded to the barbarians. In the west it was a different story, lands were lost and with them the revenues that ought to have been collected by the government, and taxes were further reduced because the farmers on devastated lands were unable to pay, and had to be given a few year's grace to recover. Although the Empire was still considered a single entity, the cracks were already visible, leading remorselessly to the transformation of the west and the survival of the east.

Two short wars with the Persians were fought, the first in 421–422, and the second after an invasion of the Roman Empire in 441–442. In each case the Romans were victorious. They were less successful against the Huns, a nomadic tribe from Mongolia. The effects of the first movements of the Huns had resulted in the displacement of the Goths *c*.370, which resulted in the great influx into the Roman Empire, and the disaster of Adrianople in 378. The Huns were brilliant horsemen, and many of them had been employed as cavalry in the Roman armies of the west. But the power of the Huns was turned against the Roman Empire when their dynamic new leader Attila emerged and succeeding in welding the tribesmen into a cohesive and destructive force, which was used to threaten the eastern Empire.

By means of annual subsidies, the court at Constantinople managed to buy off attacks, but Attila and his brother Bleda continually demanded increases. In 434 the amount was doubled to 700 pounds of gold. An agreement had been reached that, among other things, restricted the places where the Huns and the Romans could trade. This was standard procedure that had been adopted from at least the second century, but on one market day at Margus, in Moesia, the Huns disguised themselves as traders, then suddenly threw off the pretence and killed the guards and many of the Romans. They took over the city of Margus because the terrified Bishop handed it over to them, but they also managed to take the old legionary fortress of Viminacium on the Danube, and the city of Naissus (modern Nis), which they besieged and sacked. It was the city where Constantine the Great had been born, and held some symbolic significance for the Romans. This was a frightening development. Barbarians were not usually capable of besieging and taking cities. For one thing they could not remain in one place long enough before they ran out of food or started to succumb to disease, or both. For another they did not usually possess the technological skills to build and utilize siege equipment. Modern scholars have expressed extreme doubt that Attila and Bleda had been able to organize a siege train, but perhaps the technicalities do not matter. Naissus fell to them, and the fortress of Viminacium. This was a more formidable force than the Goths or the Vandals, and they had been dangerous enough. The Huns had demonstrated their potential strength and were now able to blackmail the government at Constantinople for higher payments. The agreed amount of 700 pounds of gold was tripled, reaching an annual payment of 2,100 pounds.

Probably in 445, Attila and Bleda quarrelled, for reasons unknown, and Bleda was killed. It was said that Attila had ordered his brother's murder. Still receiving subsidies from Constantinople, Attila moved into Thrace and Greece. Then in 450, two things happened: Theodosius II died, succeeded by Marcian, and Attila began to think of heading west.

Marcian AD 450–457

Theodosius's formidable sister Pulcheria chose, and married, the new Emperor Marcian. He was an experienced military officer. She claimed that he had been Theodosius's choice. Marcian took a firm stance against the Huns, taking steps to recover the Balkans, and he also stopped the annual subsidy payments. There was no retribution, since Attila veered off to find what the west had to offer. Marcian's reign brought peace and prosperity to the eastern Empire, largely due to the absence of the threat from the Huns. Finances improved, enabling Marcian to lighten the tax burden for many of his subjects.

There was some localized trouble with the Blemmyes in Egypt, and the Arabs raided Syria, but these problems were more or less endemic and were dealt with by the Imperial troops. Marcian formed a peaceful relationship with the Vandals in Africa, and he settled various tribes within the eastern Empire. A group of Ostrogoths were settled in Pannonia under the terms of an agreement whereby they contributed troops for the army.

As his successor, Marcian favoured his son-in-law Procopius Anthemius, but at his death in 457 he was succeeded by Leo I, and Anthemius had to wait for another decade before being chosen by Leo as Emperor of the west.

Leo I AD 457–474 & Leo II AD 473–474

Leo was made emperor though the machinations of the *magister militum* Aspar, an Alan, who had fought against the Vandals, the Persians and the Huns under Attila. Aspar may have hoped to achieve the predominance of the western generals who were able to control their emperors, who represented Imperial power, while in reality it was the generals who ran the show. Leo was a Dacian, and too shrewd to become the mere tool of an ambitious general. About 460, Leo recruited a bodyguard from the Isaurian tribesmen, as a counterweight to Aspar, and he married his eldest daughter to one of the foremost Isaurians, Zeno. In 467 Leo nominated Anthemius, Marcian's son-in-law, as emperor in the west, when there was an interregnum after the death of the Emperor Libius Severus in 465.

Although Marcian had come to some arrangement with the Vandals, their sea-borne raids on Italy and Greece did not cease, proving detrimental to both halves of the Empire. Leo decided to mount a naval expedition against them in 468, but it ended in complete disaster, with the Vandals as dangerous as ever. The eastern Empire unable to put together another expedition. The west was equally powerless to deal with the Vandal menace, but by a diplomatic arrangement, the western general Ricimer appointed as emperor a candidate who was related by marriage to the Vandal King Gaiseric, and therefore acceptable to them.

In the penultimate year of his reign, Leo raised his grandson, Leo II, to Augustus, and shared power with him. Leo II was the son of the Isaurian Zeno, but there was an upsurge of antipathy towards the Isaurians at Constantinople, so Leo deemed it prudent to avoid further trouble by raising his son-in-law to Augustus. In the same year, Leo tried to dominate the western Empire by sending Julius Nepos as his chosen candidate as emperor in place of the short-lived Glycerius, who was deposed. Unfortunately for Nepos, Leo died in February 474, and his chosen co-emperor, Leo II, also died in November. Nepos left Italy and returned to Constantinople.

Zeno AD 474–491

When Leo I died, Leo II made his father Zeno his partner as emperor, sharing power with him for only a few months before his own death in November 474. Zeno's reign was challenged by Gothic tribesmen and by more than one usurper. As soon as he succeeded Leo II, the Goths in Thrace, under Theoderic Strabo rebelled, and as soon as the revolt was put down, the brother-in-law of Leo I, Basiliscus, was proclaimed at Constantinople in 475. The ex-Empress Verina, the widow of Leo I and sister of Basiliscus was one of the driving forces behind the usurpation, which was at first successful. Zeno was exiled. Basiliscus and his son Marcus enjoyed a brief joint reign, but soon lost support because of their heretical religious beliefs, which enabled Zeno to re-enter Constantinople and resume power.

His next problem concerned two rival Gothic factions under Theoderic Strabo and Theoderic the Amal. Zeno was not partial to Theoderic Strabo, who had already tried to rebel, so he employed Theoderic the Amal to crush him. Tribal loyalties proved stronger, however, and the two Gothic leaders joined forces to strike against Zeno, who managed to come to an agreement with Strabo in 479. He failed to bring the Amal to heel, probably because he was distracted by the plotting of the *magister militum* Illus and Verina to raise Leontius, an Isaurian general, as Augustus. The struggle went on for the best part of four years, until Zeno's forces captured the usurpers, and executed them in 488.

Zeno's last years were more peaceful. The western Empire had already been carved up into tribal kingdoms, and Rome and Italy had been ruled since 476 by the barbarian Odoacer. Theoderic the Amal had ambitions to replace him, and it was in Zeno's interests to encourage him to descend on Italy rather than linger in the east as a potential threat to stability. Theoderic was still engaged in warfare with Odoacer when Zeno died in 491. He was succeeded by Anastasius, who rid himself of all Isaurian officials and military men, and ruled until 518. By then the eastern Roman Empire had become the Empire of the Byzantines, taking it into a different era and bridging the gap between Rome and the middle ages.

The Fragmentation of the Western Empire
AD 423–476
Valentinian III, Emperor of the West, AD 423–455

When the child-Emperor Valentinian, was proclaimed in Rome, the general Flavius Aetius was on his way to Italy at the head of 60,000 Huns in support of John, the chief of the palace staff, who was for a short time the ruler of the west. Aetius arrived too late for the final showdown, and was therefore on the wrong side with thousands of menacing troops at his back. He escaped punishment, however and gained much credit for sending the Hun army back home, and Placidia, acting as Regent for her son, helped by paying them off. From then onwards she and Aetius were rivals at the western court.

Flavius Aetius was the son of Gaudentius, who had been *magister militum per Gallias*, in command of the armies in Gaul. As a young man Aetius had been sent as a hostage to the Goths and then to the Huns, so he had gained considerable knowledge of tribal customs. His standing among the Huns is demonstrated by the fact that he could raise a large army to fight for John in the west, and then dismiss them when their services were not needed. It took Aetius ten years to ascend to the supreme position of virtual ruler of the west, but even when he had achieved this, he never tried to proclaim himself emperor. During the decade from the accession of Valentinian III until 433, he tried to restore order in the west. The provinces were much reduced and fragmented when he embarked on this task. The short-lived Emperor Constantius had begun to make some progress, but by the time Aetius picked up where he had left off, the Visigoths who had been settled in Aquitania were beginning to agitate for home rule, and to be recognized as an independent unit. The Franks, the Almanni and Burgundians were on the Rhine and in the Alps, or beyond the frontiers with a foothold in Roman territory. In Spain, Wallia the Gothic leader had suppressed but not eradicated the tribes who had settled there, and the Suebi were still in possession of part of the country. The Vandals held the two Mauretanian provinces and part of Numidia, but in Africa, the commander Bonifacius was holding the province. Unfortunately Bonifacius was no friend of Aetius, being a firm adherent of Placidia.

Aetius was a capable and energetic commander, fighting many battles and travelling long distances all over the west, but the sources are not complete and the chronology of his exploits is confused. Some of his battles may be duplicated in the accounts of his first years as commander, for instance he is said to have driven the Goths, by now better described as the Visigoths, from Arles on two occasions, which may be a repetition of the same story. He fought the Franks on the Rhine, probably in 427–428, and the Juthungi north of the Alps, then dealt with the rebels in Noricum, preserving the western Empire from further encroachments by the tribes.

In 432 Placidia and Bonifacius decided that it was time to dispense with Aetius's services. Bonifacius sailed to Italy, and defeated Aetius in battle, but died later of his wounds. For some months Aetius had to lie low and retired to his estates, but he re-emerged stronger than ever in 433 or 434, backed by an army of Huns. He restored the situation in Africa, but had to confirm the Vandal possession of Mauretania and part of Numidia. On the Rhine, Aetius attacked the Burgundians and may have restored the frontier, and he cleared Gaul of the troublesome Bagaudae. The problem is that no one knows precisely who the Bagaudae were. The common rendition of the term is bandits, but this perhaps only applies to hard-pressed Gallic peasants of the late third century, when the Bagaudae are first noted. By Aetius's day the Bagaudae may have gathered together and formed a tribe of sorts, or the term may have been applied to any disruptive group, perhaps disguising a mixed group of tribesmen. Whatever they were, Aetius seems to have stopped them in their tracks in 439, earning the gratitude of the Gauls, especially the landowners.

The year of triumph was marred by bad news from the African provinces. The Visigoths under their vigorous leader Gaiseric seized Carthage, and acquired a fleet. The history of the Republic was about to be repeated, since any people who controlled Carthage and the sea could cripple Rome. This time, though, the Romans were not in the same state of military and political health as they were when they went to war with the Carthaginians. Nonetheless, Africa had to be recovered and the Vandals had to be stopped, so Aetius made a treaty with the Visigoths in order to turn aside to deal with the Vandals. The treaty may have re-affirmed the terms arranged with Constantius in 418, but it gave the Visigoths what they wanted, independence and recognition as a separate state in part of Gaul, which was now lost to the Romans. It was a necessary expedient to enable Valentinian III and Aetius to begin a recruitment campaign to assemble an army to take to Africa. Troops were also sent from the eastern Empire, and the combined army began to move into Sicily, ready for jumping off into Africa.

The campaign to restore Africa never took place, most likely because the Huns under Attila had started to put pressure on the eastern Empire. The Persians had invaded and been repulsed, but now the eastern troops destined for Africa were needed at home. With only the army of the west, Aetius could not conduct a campaign in Africa and defend the northern frontiers at the same time. The African project fell through and a treaty was made with the Vandals, recognizing them in possession of Africa, including Carthage. Like the Carthaginians centuries before, the Vandals also controlled Lilybaeum in Sicily. The Romans took back the two Mauretanias and part, but not all, of Numidia. Gaiseric was recognized as a friendly king and ally of Rome (*Rex socius et amicus*), and his son Huneric was betrothed to Eudocia, one of the daughters of Valentinian III. Now both the Visigoths in Gaul and the Vandals in Africa were independent of Rome, free to conduct their own affairs, form their own policies and alliances, and collect their own revenues, which were henceforth denied to the western Roman Empire.

For the next few years it is not known where Aetius operated. Opinion differs as to the date of the treaty with Gaiseric and the

Vandals, some authors placing it in 442 and others two years later. Aetius reappears in 450–451, when Attila and the Huns moved into Gaul, probably reinforced by contingents from the peoples they had conquered and absorbed on their expeditions. The Visigoths of Gaul, under their King Theoderic, fought for the Romans, with a vested interest in protecting their own territory from the Huns. Aetius had assembled several other allies in his large army, and in June 451 he drove Attila away from Orleans. He then caught them near Troyes, in a battle variously labelled the Catalaunian Plains or the Mauriac fields. The site is not precisely known. It was a resounding victory for Aetius, but the Visigothic leader Theoderic was killed.

Attila was not accustomed to defeats, and it is said that he even contemplated suicide, but he pulled himself together and went on to attack Italy. Aetius was unable to stop him. One by one the cities of northern Italy fell and suffered accordingly, but for some reason Attila did not march on Rome. The legend grew up that the Pope Leo had an interview with him and dissuaded him from doing so, which tale should be taken with more than a pinch of salt. Fortunately for Rome and the western Empire, in 453 Attila married a new wife, had an energetic nuptial celebration and died in the night from a massive nose bleed. The story goes that he was buried in the bed of a river which was diverted while he was interred and then allowed to flow back over him. Thus Attila, the Scourge of God, came to an end, and his vast Hunnic Empire quickly began to fall apart. Modern scholars have pointed out the incredible qualities of the man, his skill in battle, his genius in leadership, his cunning, his knowledge of the psychology of his own men and his enemies. All this may be true, but these sterling qualities may not have been the first things that struck the minds of the inhabitants of the cities that he took and destroyed. With sublime indifference Attila and his Huns destroyed lives and livelihoods, carried off portable wealth from all sources that he could terrify into submission, and produced nothing permanent from it, except a trail of destruction and a lasting fame or infamy.

Aetius did not long survive Attila. Valentinian III executed him in 454. Aetius had been trying to arrange a marriage for his son, to connect his family with that of Valentinian, and so secure his own position in the western Empire. If the Huns had still been at large, threatening Italy or the northern frontiers, Aetius might have survived a little longer, but there was no pressing need for his services now. He had done his job too well, and he had enemies at court, who persuaded Valentinian that he could now take full control of the western Empire without the general. In September 454 the Emperor himself, assisted by the head of his household staff, attended a meeting with Aetius to discuss the finances, and killed him. Then many of Aetius's supporters were killed, but Valentinian had reckoned without the soldiers of the Guard, who resented the death of the general. Two of them set upon the Emperor in March 455 when he went off on horseback to practise archery on the Campus Martius in Rome.

Petronius Maximus AD 455

The man behind the assassination was probably Petronius Maximus, who wanted to be emperor. He got his wish the next day, was proclaimed emperor, and set about shoring up his regime. He made a good start by marrying Valentinian's widow Eudoxia, and sent an ambassador, a Gallic nobleman called Eparchius Avitus, to the Visigoths in Gaul to solicit their support, or at least their non-aggression. Maximus made the mistake of arranging the marriage of his own son Palladius to Eudocia, the daughter of Valentinian and Eudoxia. This would break the arrangement made with the Vandals, since she had been betrothed to Huneric, the son of Gaiseric. Using this as a reasonable excuse, Gaiseric invaded Italy and headed for Rome. Maximus did not stand and fight, but found a horse and tried to leave the city, but was killed before he could do so. Rome was given up to Gaiseric and the Vandals, and unlike Alaric, they made a proper job of sacking the city. When they left, they took Eudoxia and her two daughters back to Carthage, with several other prisoners.

Avitus AD 455–456

The western Empire was now leaderless for a short time, until Avitus, who had been sent to the Visigoths on behalf of Maximus, made a bid for the throne, and immediately negotiated with the eastern Empire. The army accepted Avitus, conscious of the fact that he could call upon Theoderic II, King of the Visigoths, for assistance if he was challenged. Avitus was declared emperor at Arles. Waiting in the wings was an army officer called Ricimer, and his comrade in arms Majorian, who both kept a low profile as long as Avitus could count on the support of the Visigoths. In 456, operating under Avitus, Ricimer won a victory over the Vandals at Agrigentum and destroyed their fleet. He was now on his way to power. He and Majorian plotted to overthrow Avitus, and finally confronted him and his troops at Placentia, where they won a decisive victory. They spared Avitus's life and made him a bishop, but he died soon afterwards. While Ricimer held power in the west, several men died at tremendously opportune moments, giving rise to the suspicion that the deaths were not always from natural causes.

Majorian AD 457–461

The Emperor of the east, Leo I, seems to have recognized and condoned Ricimer's command, or at least no protests have been recorded from the eastern court. Nor did Leo insist on raising an Augustus of his choice, so Ricimer was free to appoint his comrade Majorian, perhaps because he thought that he would be able to control him. As a barbarian, Ricimer preferred not to claim the throne for himself. He was the grandson of Wallia, leader of the Goths after Athaulf and Alaric.

It was said that Eudoxia would have chosen Majorian, but before she could do so Petronius Maximus pre-empted her. If she endorsed the choice, it may have encouraged acceptance of Majorian, who was the first emperor who bore no relation to the Theodosian family. He was also the first emperor since Theodosius I to take the field with an army. He operated against the Visigoths in Gaul and the Vandals in Africa, reversing for a short time the usual pattern where the emperor remained in the palace and the barbarian general directed the expeditions. This time, Ricimer remained in Italy while Majorian fought the battles. It showed that the new Emperor was not willing to be the malleable tool of Ricimer, and so when he returned from his campaigns in August 461, Ricimer met him and suggested very strongly that he should abdicate. Majorian complied, dying soon afterwards, of dysentery, or so Ricimer claimed.

Libius Severus AD 461–465

Some three months passed without an Augustus in the west, with Ricimer in undoubted command. Then in an attempt to reconcile the Senate and the Italian aristocracy, Libius Severus was made emperor, elected by the senators in 461. For four years the partnership worked, though it was clear that it was Ricimer who was directing affairs. During this period, Ricimer tried to negotiate with Gaiseric and the Vandals in Africa, hoping to put an end to the raids on Sicily, but the negotiations came to nothing. The eastern emperor, Leo I, was more successful in 462. Gaiseric had arranged the marriage between his son Huneric and Eudocia, but had kept Valentinian's widow Eudoxia and their younger daughter Placidia in Carthage. Now he agreed to release them both and return them to Constantinople. Placidia was married to Anicius Olybrius, who was to play a small part in the crumbling government of the western Empire a few years later.

Anthemius AD 467–472

When Libius Severus died in 465, no emperor was appointed for two years until Leo I chose Anthemius, the son of the Praetorian Prefect under Theodosius II who had refortified Constantinople. Anthemius was also the son-in-law of the eastern Emperor Marcian. His credentials were good, his reputation was sound, and he was a capable general, which made him acceptable to most of the inhabitants in the west except Ricimer, who had no desire to operate as a subordinate of a capable Roman general turned emperor. But he had little choice, since he could not control the Vandals without help, so acceptance of Leo's candidate was inevitable. To seal the bargain, Ricimer married Anthemius's daughter Alypia.

Ricimer was hemmed in and his independence curbed, exactly as Leo had planned. To make matters worse, Anthemius brought with him his own general, Marcellinus, who had been a supporter of Aetius, and Ricimer's enemy. Fortunately for Ricimer, Marcellinus was murdered in 468, by officers of the army scheduled to fight the Vandals. It was very timely for Ricimer, but Anthemius was steadily divesting him of his barbarian supporters and replacing them with Roman appointees to various posts. Ricimer was facing annihilation. Then the Vandals started to raid Sicily and the coasts of Italy, and Ricimer developed a plan that would perhaps enable him to kill two birds with one stone. He needed to come to an understanding with the Vandals, and he needed to be rid of Anthemius. He raised a new emperor in opposition to Anthemius, who would bridge the gap between the house of Theodosius and the Vandals. This was Anicius Olybrius, married to Placidia, and therefore the son-in-law of the deceased Valentinian III, but also the brother-in-law of the Vandal Prince Huneric, who was married to Placidia's sister Eudocia. Although Olybrius was by no means clamouring for the role, Gaiseric had been agitating for the appointment for some time, and now it suited Ricimer's purpose as well.

Anthemius started to lose support in Italy, save for the few who remained in Rome with him when Ricimer besieged the city in 472. The turning point came when the relief army sent to rescue Anthemius was defeated and the survivors joined Ricimer. Anthemius tried to escape disguised as a beggar, but was discovered and killed, in July 472. Ricimer and Olybrius were now unchallenged – that is, for another month. In August, Ricimer died of a haemorrhage, and two or three months later, Olybrius expired.

Glycerius AD 473–474, Nepos AD 474–475 & Romulus Augustulus AD 475–476

There was another interregnum after the death of Olybrius until March 473. In his few weeks as ruler, Olybrius had replaced Ricimer with Gundobad, the son of the chief of the Burgundians in Gaul, with whom Ricimer had always been on very good terms. Gundobad was also the nephew of Ricimer, so the appointment would appease Ricimer's supporters. Gundobad's only contribution was to raise as Augustus his candidate Glycerius, and then he returned to the Burgundians as their king, shedding all his Roman titles. The eastern court was not prepared to recognize Glycerius. Leo I despatched Julius Nepos to take over in the west. Glycerius was deposed and sent to Salona as bishop. Presumably he was allowed to survive because he represented no threat and had no supporters who would raise rebellion on his behalf.

Julius Nepos may have survived if he had been able to reconcile the barbarian troops to his rule, but he more or less ignored them. In 475 he chose as his military commander Orestes, who was a Roman, but who had experience of the barbarians, having worked for some time with Attila as his secretary. It was not a good choice, since Orestes quickly raised revolt and expelled Nepos, who fled, but lingered in the vain hope that the new eastern Emperor Zeno would reinstate him. Orestes elevated his young son Romulus to the rank of Augustus, soon rendered as Augustulus, little Augustus, by the people.

Orestes arranged a treaty with Gaiseric and the Vandals to ensure peace and quiet from that quarter, but at home he faced the age old problem of troops demanding settlement on the land. In this case it was the Germanic soldiers who wanted to settle in Italy, to which Orestes and the Senate were opposed. Their policy was short-sighted. Barbarians had been settled on Roman territory almost everywhere else, and the western government was not in any position to argue, especially when the troops suddenly found a leader who had been in Anthemius's bodyguard and then gone over to Ricimer. This was Odoacer, a Roman citizen of barbarian origin, who was declared king of the tribal troops that he led, not a homogeneous group, but a collection of different tribesmen united by a common cause. Odoacer defeated Orestes and killed him, and then deposed the young Romulus, who was packed off to a villa and allowed to live out his life in Italy.

Odoacer AD 476–493

The year 476 as an end date for the western Roman Empire is as artificial as the dates of many other turning points in the history of Rome, but it does mark the transition from Roman Imperial rule to rule by the kings of various tribes. Long before Odoacer took control of Italy, other parts of the Empire had been ceded to tribal rulers. Much of Gaul was already divorced from Roman control by the early fifth century. Constantius settled Wallia and the Visigoths in Aquitania, which was not an unusual procedure in the Roman Empire, but soon after Theoderic II was recognized as an independent ruler, with jurisdiction over the Romans as well as his own people. After he was murdered by his brother Euric in 466 or 467, the Visigoths began to extend their control. By 475 Euric controlled the Auvergne and was eventually recognized as ruler of Gaul between the Atlantic seaboard, the Rhone, the Loire and the Pyrenees. Shortly afterwards the Visigoths took over part of Spain. Under Ricimer, the Burgundians were settled in Gaul.

In 476, the same year that Odoacer took over control of Rome and Italy, the eastern Emperor Zeno was forced to acknowledge the Vandal kingdom of Africa, and their possession of Corsica, Sardinia and the Balearic Islands. Africa had been lost to the Romans since the treaty that Aetius made with the Vandals in the 440s, but there had always been the slight possibility that the provinces could be regained. After 476 the western Empire was too fragmented to mount a corporate campaign against the Vandals, and even the well-organized cohesive eastern Empire could not hope to extend control over Africa.

In the sixth century the Byzantine Emperor Justinian made the attempt to recover the lost territories of the west, but failed. Spain was lost to the Romans when the Vandals and the Suebi established themselves there, but the Vandals were defeated by the Visigoths under Wallia, and turned to Africa. By the sixth century the Visigoths had established complete control over the former Hispanic provinces.

Odoacer maintained control of Italy for nearly twenty years. He respected the senators of Rome, appointing a consul each year from among the Romans, and reserving civilian offices for them. He was sensitive enough to refuse to call himself king on his coinage. Military appointments were given to the barbarian soldiers, but this was by now quite customary. The eastern Emperor Zeno did not formally recognize him, and was deliberately vague in dealing with him, waiting for an opportunity to attempt to oust him. It came in 487–488 when he encouraged the Germanic Rugii to invade Italy. Odoacer campaigned against them, but realized that he did not have the military capacity to hold the Danube frontier, and abandoned Noricum, bringing the population to Italy to resettle them. The following year, Zeno tried again, using the Amal Goths, or Ostrogoths, under their King Theoderic to mount another invasion. The war dragged on, until Odoacer died in 493. Zeno had promised Theoderic that he could take Odoacer's place, but refused to recognize him as independent ruler of Italy. Theoderic called himself king without waiting for approval from Constantinople, but he received recognition of a sort from Anastasius, who succeeded Zeno in 491. There was no clear definition of Theoderic's status, and no acknowledgement that he was subordinate to the eastern emperor. It was really just an acceptance of the status quo, while in denial about the split between the two Empires.

The Roman Empire of the east survived and evolved for many more centuries. Its geographical cohesion was not fragmented as was that of the west, enabling the eastern emperors to maintain control of their revenues and taxes, so in the fifth century the east was much wealthier than the west. The barbarian assaults that brought the west to its knees were not experienced to the same degree in the east, and whenever there were threats, more often than not the assailants veered, or were turned, towards the west, where the eastern emperors did not always send military aid. The policy of recruiting soldiers from local tribes enabled the government of Constantinople to create an army that had a vested interest in defending its own territory, whereas the western rulers and military commanders were forced to take whatever they could get, from warriors who were affiliated to the tribes who threatened the Empire. The wonder is that these tribesmen fought so well for the Romans.

In reality, although they caused massive devastation, the various tribes such as the Franks, the Alamanni, the Goths and the Burgundians, who established their kingdoms in the provinces of the western Empire, were not sworn enemies of Rome, but wanted to be part of the Empire and be like the Romans. Their influx did not always entail displacement of the existing population, and thousands of them were officially settled on Roman territory. When they took over lands by force, it may have been a different matter. When Gaiseric and his Vandals took over Africa, he redistributed the land to his own followers, and Roman refugees found their way to Italy, but in Gaul there seems to have been plenty of land to go around. At least one barbarian who had taken over an estate in Gaul went to find the owner so that he could pay for it. Many of the Gallic landowners came to terms with the barbarians in their midst. There was little else they could do, since the army could not always help them, so fighting the tribesmen was no longer an option. When Sidonius Apollinaris, Bishop of Clermont-Ferrand, encouraged the populace to defend their city and homes, the result was a disaster, but Sidonius's letters show how Roman life continued in fifth-century Gaul, with races in the circus, games and shows. When their kingdom was established, the Visigoths used the laws of Rome to formulate their own codes, and in Italy under the Ostrogoths, Latin and

Greek literature was preserved, administration continued as it had under the Romans, coins were issued, trading continued, and peace and prosperity reigned until the sixth century.

Looking back over the centuries, it can be seen that Rome and the western Empire never really fell, but were transformed slowly into the kingdoms of medieval Europe, underpinned by Roman law, administrative systems and language. It is, however, undeniable that there were many casualties during the upheavals of the fourth and fifth centuries, and it is questionable whether the survivors of the various cataclysms were able to take the long-term view, comforted by the fact that what was happening to them was simply a transformation.

Glossary

Aedile: city magistrate originally responsible for supervision of the *aedes*, or the temples of the plebs. During the Republic there were two aediles subordinate to the tribunes of the plebs, and later two more were elected from the patricians (*aediles curules*). In the Empire the main duties of the aediles were care of the city, including keeping the streets clean, keeping public order, attending to the water supply and markets. They were also in charge of the public games (*ludi*) until Augustus transferred this duty to the praetors. All the municipalities of the Empire employed elected aediles fulfilling the same purposes as they did in Rome.

Aerarium militar: military treasury set up by Augustus in AD 6 to provide pensions for veterans.

Ala milliaria: auxiliary cavalry unit of *c.*1,000 men.

Ala quingenaria: auxiliary cavalry unit of *c.*500 men.

Annona militaris: provisions for the army; in the later Empire the Praetorian Prefects were placed in charge of the supplies for the troops.

As: lowest denomination Roman coin, made of bronze.

Atrium: the central reception area of a Roman house, with a square or oblong opening in the roof to let in light. Rain water was caught in a sunken area in the floor, called the *impluvium*, corresponding to the roof opening.

Auctoritas: a measure of the reputation and social and political standing of Roman senators and politicians. The literal translation 'authority' does not convey its true meaning. *Auctoritas* could be earned and increased by political or military achievements and lost after disgraceful conduct.

Aureus: Roman gold coin, worth twenty-five *denarii*.

Auxilia: literally 'help troops', the term used by the Romans to describe the units recruited from non-Romans, organized as *alae* and *cohortes* during the Empire.

Caldarium: the hot room of a bath house.

Canabae: the civilian settlement outside a legionary fortress; see also *vicus*.

Capitatio: a poll-tax, paid in cash.

Capitum: fodder; in the later Empire payments to the soldiers were made partly in kind. *Capitum* and *annona* were the terms used for food for the horses and the men.

Cataphractarii: heavy-armoured cavalry, perhaps armed with lance and shield.

Centuria: a century, or a division of a cohort, nominally of 100 men, but in practice of 80 men, from the late Republic and throughout the Empire; also a voting unit of the people of Rome.

Centurion: commander of a century, or *centuria*.

Clibanarii: slang term for heavy-armoured cavalry, derived from *clibanus*, meaning oven. It is not certain whether these troops were the same as *cataphractarii* or whether they were armed and fought in a different way.

Cohors: a cohort, denoting two types of unit, the first a division of a legion containing six centuries, and the second denoting an auxiliary infantry unit, either 500 or 1,000 strong.

Cohors equitatae: part-mounted auxiliary unit.

Colonus: tenant of a landowner.

Comitatenses: collective name for the units of the late Roman mobile field army, comprising cavalry and infantry.

Comes: the entourage of an emperor consisted of his friends (*comites*) on an unofficial basis at first, but Constantine gave the title *Comes*, usually translated as Count, to his military commanders and provincial governors. There was originally no connotation of rank in the title, but with the passage of time three grades were established, called *ordinis primi, secundi,* and *terti.*

Comitatus: derived from *comes*, initially describing the entourage of the emperor; by the fourth century *comitatus* denoted the field army.

Consul: senior magistrates of the Republic, elected annually in pairs, responsible for civil duties and command of the armies. During the Empire the consuls were still elected annually, but with reduced military responsibilities and subordinate to the emperor.

Consul ordinarius: during the Empire there were often more than two consuls in the year. The *ordinarii* were the officially elected consuls, who might hold office for a month or two, giving way to the *consules suffecti*. The *ordinarii* were the eponymous consuls, giving their name to the year.

Consul suffectus: the suffect consuls were those who held office after the *ordinarii*, gaining experience and rank before going on to other appointments.

Constitutio Antoniniana: act passed by Caracalla in AD 212, making all freeborn inhabitants of the Empire Roman citizens.

Contubernium: tent party or the soldiers sharing one barrack block, normally eight men.

Corrector: (plural *correctores*) Roman officials with the title *corrector* were appointed from the reign of Trajan, originally for the purpose of attending to the financial affairs of free cities which did not come under the jurisdiction of the provincial governors. *Correctores* held military and civil powers and their responsibilities, which eventually extended to any of the cities in a province if the emperor wished to investigate their affairs.

Curiales:members of the city councils.

Denarius: Roman silver coin worth four *sestertii.*

Diocese: administrative grouping of several provinces, instituted by Diocletian.

Dromedarius: camel rider.

Dux: (plural *duces*) literally, leader; the term used for equestrian military officers in command of troops in the frontier regions, usually with the title *dux limitis,* accompanied by an explanation of where they operated, such as *dux limitis per Africam*. Their commands sometimes covered more than one province. *Duces* were raised to senatorial status by Valentinian I.

Equites legionis: cavalry of a legion, initially thought to number 120 men, but increased by the Emperor Gallienus to over 700 men.

Foederati: literally those who are allied in war, derived from *foedus*, a treaty, and denoting troops raised according to the terms of a treaty. To be distinguished from the sixth century *foederati*, which were regular troops.

Imperium: the early kings of Rome were holders of *imperium*, comprising command of the armies and exercise of legal power. During the Republic, this power passed to the higher magistrates, the annually elected consuls and the praetors, and the dictators for their six month term of office. It was extended to the proconsuls and propraetors as commanders and later governors of the provinces. In Imperial times, only the emperors held *imperium*, which was delegated to his appointed commanders and governors.

Iugum: a unit of land for tax purposes, not always a standard measure since the type of land and the crops grown were taken into consideration by the assessors.

legion: the term *legio* originally meant the choosing, or the levy, and was eventually applied to the main unit of the Roman army. Around 5,000 strong, the legion was an infantry unit, but also contained some cavalry. Legions of the late Empire were smaller, newly raised units being only about 1,000 strong.

Limes: (plural *limites*) frontier(s).

Magister equitum: master of horse; in the Republic this title was given to the second in command of a dictator; in the late

Roman army it was an important military post in command of the cavalry units.

Magister militum: master of the soldiers; like the *Dux/Duces* the various *magistri militum* could be in command of the troops of a province or a region, but the title sometimes denotes a supreme commander, otherwise expressed as *magister utruisque militiae*.

Magister officiorum: late Roman head of the secretarial offices.

Magister peditum: master of the infantry of the late Roman army.

Maniple: literally 'a handful', a term denoting a unit of the Republican army consisting of two centuries.

Peristyle: the courtyard of Roman house, usually planted as a garden, surrounded by a colonnade.

Pilum: missile weapon used by legionaries, consisting of a long thin metal shank with a pyramidal tip, attached to a wooden shaft. There were various different sizes and types of *pila*.

Praefectus: prefect, a title given to several different civilian officials and military officers. The summit of an equestrian career was to be appointed to one of the four great prefectures, *Praefectus Annonae* (the Prefect of the *annona*, in charge of military supplies), *Praefectus Vigilum* (the Prefect of the *Vigiles*, the fire brigade in Rome), the Praetorian Prefect, or the Prefect of Egypt.

Praeses: (plural *praesides*) provincial governor of equestrian rank, common from Severan times onwards.

Praetor: the praetorship had a long history. Originally the praetors were the chief magistrates in early Republican Rome, but were superceded by the consuls. When the consuls were absent the praetor was in charge of the courts, acted as president of the Senate, and had the right to command armies.

Proconsul: as the Romans extended their power over wider territories, more magistrates were required to govern the provinces or command armies in wars, so the powers of the consuls could be bestowed upon men who had held a magistracy, or in emergencies upon private individuals for an appointed time.

Protectores: a title used by Gallienus for his military entourage, not simply a bodyguard, but perhaps the foundation of a staff college formed from officers loyal to the emperor.

Quaestor: originally the lowest ranking magistrates of the Republic appointed to assist the consuls in financial matters. The office was held by young men at the start of their career, before they had entered the Senate. As the Empire expanded more quaestors were created to deal with provincial administration. Quaestors acted as deputies to consular governors, and could hold commands in the army. Sometimes in modern versions of ancient works, quaestor is translated in the military context as quartermaster, which is not strictly accurate.

Schola: late Roman cavalry guard unit; *scholae palatinae* were the emperor's guard.

Sestertius: Roman silver coin; four *sestertii* equalled one *denarius*.

Stipendium: military pay, also applied to a period of service.

Triclinium: dining room in a Roman house, with three couches arranged around the central space where the food would be served.

Triumph: during the Republic, a triumph was granted by the Senate to victorious generals, who valued this opportunity to show off their captives and the spoils of war by processing along the Via Sacra in Rome, to the Temple of Jupiter. The *triumphator* rode in a chariot with his face painted red, and was supposed to approach the temple on his knees to dedicate the spoils, with a slave at his side constantly reminding him that he was mortal. Augustus recognized the inflammatory nature of the triumph and took steps to limit it to members of the Imperial family. Other generals were denied the procession, and were granted *ornamenta triumphalia*, triumphal insignia, instead of the procession through the streets of Rome.

Vicarius: governor of a diocese, answerable to the Praetorian Prefects.

Vicus: a term that could mean an area within a town, or a rural village, but in the military context it refers to the civilian settlement outside a Roman auxiliary fort; see also *canabae*.

Vigiles: the fire brigade of the city of Rome, organized in military fashion by Augustus to cover the fourteen regions, or districts, of the city of Rome.

Select Bibliography for Further Reading

Books about the Romans are, as it were, legion, with new books appearing all the time. With the new publications and all the past to catch up on, reading about the Romans could become a full-time occupation. The following list represents only a small percentage of what is available, but the reading lists in each book will cover much of the rest.

Ancient Sources

The surviving sources for the history of the Roman Empire are vast, but fragmentary and uneven. For certain periods such as the foundation of Rome, the rule of the kings and the development of the Republic, and the later Roman Empire of the third century, the sources are frustratingly inadequate. The full panoply of sources from ancient times includes not only literature, but art and architecture, Greek and Latin inscriptions and archaeological evidence. Books on these topics are listed below, while this section includes some of the more accessible translations of ancient works.

A good place to start is with the *Loeb Classical Library*, published by Harvard University Press, with the Latin or Greek text on one page and the English translation on the opposite page, complete with explanatory notes and indexes. This is a brief selection of the more important works for Roman history:

Ammianus Marcellinus: (no title given except the author's name) 3 volumes. Ammianus was a military commander during the second half of the fourth century AD, and wrote a history of his own turbulent times, using other historical sources and his accounts of events, including the expeditions under the Emperor Julian, which he had witnessed for himself.

Appian: *Roman History*. 4 volumes, covering the Civil Wars between Marius and Sulla, Caesar and Pompey, Octavian and Antony.

Caesar: *The Gallic War, the Civil Wars,* and *The Alexandrian, African and Spanish Wars*. 3 volumes, covering most of Caesar's career, as presented by Caesar himself.

Cicero: *Letters to Atticus* and *Letters to his Friends*. 8 volumes, written during the lives of Pompey the Great, Julius Caesar, Octavian and Mark Antony, and providing a detailed and very human account of the political machinations of all the leading men of the times.

Dio Cassius: *Roman History*. 9 volumes. Written at the beginning of the third century, Dio's work covers the period from the earliest years until AD 229, but some of the original books are lost and only some of the gaps can be filled from references in later works.

Livy: (Titus Livius) *History of Rome*. 14 volumes. Livy worked in the reign of Augustus and wrote a history of Rome from its foundation to 9 BC, in142 books, of which only 35 are extant.

Polybius: *Histories*. 6 volumes. Covers the rise of Rome to the later second century BC and is of particular importance for the organization of the Republican army.

Scriptores Historiae Augustae: supposedly written by different authors, but now referred to more commonly as the *Historia Augusta* since it has been shown that there was only one author, picking up where Suetonius (see next entry) left off with biographies of the emperors of the second and third centuries. A good sensationalist read, but use with caution.

Suetonius: *The Lives of the Caesars.* 2 volumes. Suetonius worked in the reign of Hadrian, and wrote biographies of the emperors from Augustus to Domitian.

Tacitus: *Agricola.* 1 volume. Writing in the later first century AD, Tacitus wrote about the exploits in Roman Britain of his father-in-law, the governor Gnaeus Julius Agricola, during the reigns of Vespasian, Titus and Domitian.

Tacitus: *Histories* and *Annals.* 4 volumes. Covers the period from the death of Augustus in AD 14 to the assassination of Domitian in AD 96.

The works of some of these authors are available in English, with introductions, notes, maps and indexes, published in paperback by Penguin Books, of which this is a small selection:

Ammianus Marcellinus: *The Later Roman Empire*, trans W. Hamilton,   1986.

Cicero: *Selected Letters*, trans. D.R. Shackleton Bailey, 1986

Livy: *The Early History of Rome*, trans. Aubrey de Selincourt, 1960.

Rome and Italy, trans. Betty Radice, 1982.

The War with Hannibal, trans. Aubrey de Selincourt, 1965.

Rome and the Mediterranean, trans. Henry Bettenson, 1976.

Pliny: *Letters of the Younger Pliny*, trans. Betty Radice, 1974.

Tacitus: *The Annals of Imperial Rome*, trans. Michael Grant, 1956, revised 1996.

Histories, forthcoming, June 2009.

Reference Books

Oxford Classical Dictionary eds. S. Hornblower and A. Spawforth, Oxford: 3rd ed. 1993. An invaluable reference tool, with alphabetical entries on people, places and topics in Greek and Roman history, each entry accompanied by lists for further reading.

Cambridge Ancient History: several volumes covering Roman history from the earliest times to the later Empire, with chapters written by specialist scholars, and brimming with notes explaining where the information comes from. The price tags for each volume indicate the vast amount of work involved.

Routledge History of the Ancient World: an up to date (1990s to *c.*2004) series devoted to the history of Greece and Rome, available in affordable paperback volumes, bristling with notes to explain details and to give the sources for the information. Specifically, in chronological order for Roman history:

T. Cornell, *The Beginnings of Rome; Italy and the Rome from the Bronze Age to the Punic Wars*, 1995.

M. Goodman, *The Roman World 44 BC–AD 180*, 1997.

D.S. Potter, *The Roman Empire at Bay AD 180–395*, 2004.

A. Cameron, *The Mediterranean World in Late Antiquity AD 395–600*, 1993.

Examples of text-book style works for students, with analyses of events and trends, references to ancient literature, and bibliographies, are the following:

M. Boatwright (et al.), *The Romans from Village to Empire*, Oxford, 2004.

M. Leglay (et al.), *A History of Rome*, Blackwell: 3rd ed. 2005.

Atlases

T. Cornell and J. Matthews, *Atlas of the Roman World*, Phaidon, 1982. Coloured maps of the provinces with the main cities, towns and fortresses, but this book is much more than just a series of maps, containing a historical survey from the earliest times to the sixth century AD, and it is fully illustrated throughout.

C. Scarre, *The Penguin Historical Atlas of Ancient Rome*, Viking Press and Penguin, 1995. This book follows the development of Rome from the beginning to the sixth century, well illustrated, with sections highlighting certain topics, all supported by the coloured maps.

Studies of Specific Periods & Rulers

This list is potentially endless, so here are just a few titles, in chronological order from Republic to Late Empire.

P. Matyszak, *Chronicle of the Roman Republic: the rulers of ancient Rome from Romulus to Augustus*, Thames and Hudson, 1993. A good read as well as a popular reference tool. It concentrates on the various personalities as the title suggests, with timelines, background history and potted biographies of each personality, well illustrated.

R. Syme, *The Roman Revolution*, Oxford University Press, 1936. Very scholarly, still the revered text book for the transformation of the Republic into the Empire under Augustus, written in an unforgettable idiosyncratic style at a time when tyrants were gaining individual power in Europe. Essential for serious students.

E.S. Gruen, *The Last Generation of the Roman Republic*, University of California Press, 1974. Covers the same period as Syme, awesomely detailed and scholarly but readable, not revised since 1974, but for the paperback edition a new introduction contains an annotated bibliography to document the major new work since it was first published.

A series of books on the lives and reigns of various emperors has been published by Batsford, and continued by Routledge:

P. Southern, *Augustus*, 1998.

B. Levick, *Tiberius the Politician*, 1999.

A.A. Barrett, *Caligula: corruption of power*, 1990.

B. Levick, *Claudius*, 1990.

M. Griffin, *Nero: End of a Dynasty*, 1987.

K. Wellesley, *The Year of Four Emperors*, 3rd ed. 2000.

B. Levick, *Vespasian*, 2005.

P. Southern, *Domitian: Tragic Tyrant*, 1997.

J. Bennett, *Trajan: Optimus Princeps*, 1997.

A.R. Birley, *Hadrian: the Restless Emperor*, 1997.

A.R. Birley, *Marcus Aurelius a Biography*, rev. ed. 1996.

A.R. Birley, *Septimius Severus: the African Emperor*, rev. ed. 1988.

A. Watson, *Aurelian and the Third Century*, 1999.

S. Williams, *Diocletian and the Roman Recovery*, 1997.

C.M. Odahl, *Constantine and the Christian Empire*, 2004.

P. Southern, *The Roman Empire from Severus to Constantine*, Routledge, 2001. Chronological history from the accession of Severus to the sole rule of Constantine, with chapters on the contemporary histories of the northern barbarians and the Persians, and how the various threats on the Roman frontiers engendered usurpations and rebellions within the Empire. Lucidly written, it says on the cover.

A.H.M. Jones, *The Later Roman Empire 284–602*, Blackwell, 1964. 2 vols. Once the bible for the study of the later Roman Empire, some points have been revised by succeeding scholars, but it is still invaluable for the amount of references and notes.

S. Mitchell, *A History of the Later Roman Empire AD 284–641*, Blackwell, 2007. Scholarly book, covering chronological history from the reign of Diocletian to the sixth century, then covers topics such as the Roman state, the barbarians, religion, economy, society, with a chronological list of emperors, usurpers and the kings of Persia.

P. Heather, *The Fall of the Roman Empire: a New History*, Macmillan, 2005. Extremely readable on a very complicated period, the first two chapters covering the Romans and the barbarians, followed by the various wars against the tribes. Attila gets a chapter to himself. There is an appendix containing short biographies of the major Romans and leading tribesmen.

Social History

D. Cherry (ed.), *The Roman World: a Sourcebook*, Blackwell, 2001. Latin and Greek source material in translation, derived from literary works, inscriptions, papyri, grouped under chapter headings, such as women, marriage and family, politics and government, economy etc. Accessible and readable history, with an introduction to each section and notes

J.A. Shelton, *As the Romans Did: a Sourcebook in Roman Social history*, Oxford University Press, 2nd ed. 1998. More source material in translation, scholarly but easy to read, and well organized, easy to find relevant sections from the contents list and index, all entries well annotated.

P. Grimal, *The Civilization of Rome*, Allen and Unwin, 1963. Getting on a bit now, but still a good read, packed with black and white photos, and a historical and biographical dictionary.

U.E. Paoli, *Rome, Its People Life and Customs*, Bristol Classical Press 1990. Classic work available in several editions, first published in the 1940s, containing lots of photos and notes on sources.

Government & Administration

Apart from the source books listed above:

A. Lintott, *The Constitution of the Roman Republic*, Oxford University Press, 1999. The Roman Republic did not have a formal written constitution, but this book brings together all the customs and procedures of the popular assemblies and the Senate, and describes how the magistrates functioned.

F. Millar, *The Emperor in the Roman World*, Duckworth, 1977. Although over thirty years old, this is still a valuable work explaining how the emperors governed, their relationship with the senators and equites, the provinces and cities, and latterly the Church. Readable and full of sources and references.

The Roman Army

B. Campbell, *The Roman Army 31 BC to AD 337: a sourcebook*, Routledge, 1994. Various sources from literature, inscriptions and papyri, all translated into English dealing with aspects of the Roman army, readable and well organized.

L. Keppie, *The Making of the Roman Army*, Routledge, 1998. Covers the army of the kings of Rome and its transition into the early Republican army.

A. Goldsworthy, *The Complete Roman Army*, Thames and Hudson, 2003. Covers the whole period from early Republic to later Empire, concentrating on the Imperial army of the second and third centuries, very well illustrated and a good read.

P. Southern and K.R. Dixon, *The Late Roman Army*, Batsford, 1996. Brings together the sporadic evidence for the organization of the late Roman army, arranged in sections including the history of the army from Constantine to Justinian, recruitment, conditions of service, fortifications, and what happened in the end. Criticised for not pushing back the frontiers of knowledge, but then, it was never meant to; it collects what there is.

The Barbarians

P.S. Wells, *The Barbarians Speak: How the Conquered Peoples Shaped Roman Europe*, Princeton University Press, 1999. Covers Rome's relationship with various tribes from the earliest times, including the way in which the barbarians and the Romans interacted beyond the frontiers, and how the blend of cultures affected both.

M. Todd, *Migrants and Invaders: the Movements of Peoples in the Ancient World*, Tempus, 2001. Looks at the relationship between Romans and barbarians from the earliest times to the sixth century AD, in a series of chapters originally designed as lectures. It examines the attractions that the Roman world offered, and concentrates on the transformation of the western Empire.

T.S. Burns, *Barbarians Within the Gates of Rome: a Study of*

Roman Military Policy and the Barbarians ca. 375–425 AD, Indiana University Press, 1994. A study of the relationship between the Romans and the tribesmen in the later Empire, how and why the Romans employed some tribesmen in their armies, the different ways in which they employed them, and the policy of settling whole tribes or groups of barbarians on Roman land.

Illustration Credits

All illustrations are from the author's collection unless otherwise stated. All maps are drawn by Graeme Stobbs.

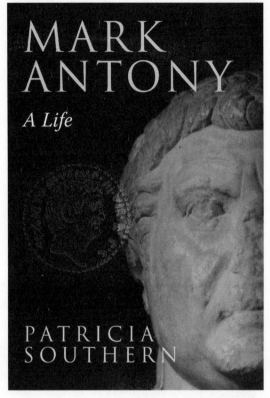

Available from August 2011 from Amberley Publishing

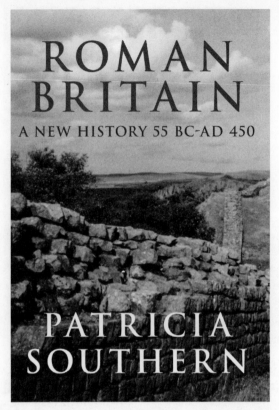

The perfect comprehensive and illustrated introduction to the history of Roman Britain

For nearly four centuries, from AD 43 to 410, Britain was a small province on the north western edge of the vast Roman Empire. Patricia Southern's masterly new history tells the story from first contact, through invasion and conquest, coexistence to eventual decline incorporating the political, social and cultural history of 'Britannia'. For the first time the wealth of 'voices' from the varied population of Roman Britain are placed centre stage in the narrative. Indirectly via the works of ancient historians, annalists and biographers, and directly from building inscriptions, religious dedications, gravestones, graffiti, leaden curse tablets, artifacts and coins.

£25 Hardback
100 illustrations (70 colour)
448 pages
978-1-4456-0146-5

Available from August 2011 from all good bookshops or to order direct
Please call **01285-760-030**
www.amberleybooks.com

Index

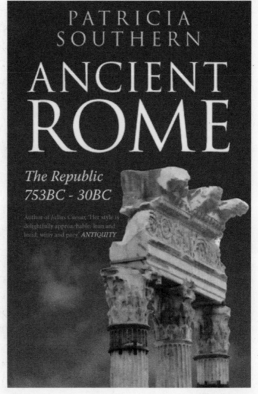